UNRULY
COMPARISON

PERVERSE MODERNITIES

A Series Edited by Jack Halberstam and Lisa Lowe

UNRULY
COMPARISON

QUEERNESS,

HONG KONG,

AND THE

ALVIN K. WONG
SINOPHONE

Duke University Press   *Durham and London*   2025

© 2025 DUKE UNIVERSITY PRESS. All rights reserved
Project Editor: Ihsan Taylor
Typeset in Warnock Pro by Copperline Book Services

Library of Congress Cataloging-in-Publication Data Names:
Wong, Alvin K., author.
Title: Unruly comparison : queerness, Hong Kong, and the
Sinophone / Alvin K. Wong.
Other titles: Perverse modernities.
Description: Durham : Duke University Press, 2025. | Series:
Perverse modernities | Includes bibliographical references
and index.
Identifiers: LCCN 2024044737 (print)
LCCN 2024044738 (ebook)
ISBN 9781478031895 (paperback)
ISBN 9781478028673 (hardcover)
ISBN 9781478060888 (ebook)
Subjects: LCSH: Queer theory—China—Hong Kong. | Sexual
minority culture—China—Hong Kong. | Arts and
transnationalism.
Classification: LCC HQ76.3.H85 W66 2025 (print) |
LCC HQ76.3.H85 (ebook) |
DDC 306.76095125—dc23/eng/20250120
LC record available at https://lccn.loc.gov/2024044737
LC ebook record available at https://lccn.loc.gov/2024044738

Cover art: Jes Fan, *Diagram XX*, 2023. Aqua resin, glass, and
pigments. Courtesy of the artist and Empty Gallery.
Photograph by Pierre Le Hors.

For Lisa Lowe

Contents

Acknowledgments

For a book on the necessity of practicing unruly forms of comparison and queer Sinophone scholarship, I have many people to thank. First and foremost, I thank the unconditional love of my parents, Wong Lai Ling and Wong Chau Ngan, who believe in everything that I do. Living together with them in Hong Kong is the best thing that has happened in my life. Love and affection go to my two older brothers, Henry and David, who support me fully despite not speaking the same academic jargon. My close friends in the United States and Hong Kong remind me to take a break now and then, and here thanks go to Iris Pang, Raymond Ho, Alex Yeung, Linwood Lin, Jessie Cheng, Ci Lok, Nelson, Kenneth, Miss Lit, Betsy, Chi Chi, Vicky Wong, Benny Lu, Amber Carini, Yeleng Her, Julie Pham, and Amy Lee.

I was extremely lucky to meet my first mentor and academic diva of my life, Gayatri Gopinath, during my undergraduate years at UC Davis. Her contagious pedagogy, groundbreaking scholarship on queer diaspora, and intellectual commitment convinced me to become a queer feminist intellectual. Gayatri's impact on my own thinking on unruly comparison is obvious in the pages that follow, and I am so blessed to have her in my life. Other wonderful teachers who influenced my thinking early on include Frances E. Dolan, Suad Joseph, and Juana María Rodríguez.

Being a graduate student in the Department of Literature at UC San Diego was a life-transforming experience. It was an immense honor to study under the co-supervision of Yingjin Zhang and Lisa Lowe. Yingjin's professionalism, unparalleled productivity, intellectual impartiality, and unfailing support through different stages of my career have shaped my life more than I can describe in words. His sudden passing in June 2022 is something that I am still trying to reckon with. Though I can never approximate Yingjin's work ethic, I hope my strong commitment to mentoring undergraduate and graduate students can, in some small ways, honor his example. Ari L. Heinrich mentored me with warm collegiality and affective pedagogy during my time in San Diego, and their amazing scholarship on transnational Chinese and queer Sinophone cultures continue to influence my thinking. I am so blessed to count Ari as my dear friend. Other teachers who shaped my thinking at UC San Diego include Patrick Anderson, the late Rosemary Marangoly George, and Lisa Yoneyama.

I was incredibly lucky to have had Shu-mei Shih as my mentor during my two years as the Andrew Mellon postdoctoral fellow in the Department of Comparative Literature at UCLA. Together with Francoise Lionnet, Shu-mei generously trained the next generation of scholars in transnational studies. Their concepts of minor transnationalism and the creolization of theory have greatly influenced my own thinking on queer theory, Sinophone studies, and the politics of comparison. Shu-mei's inauguration of the field of Sinophone studies has forged a new path for scholars whose objects of study and research topics are often considered too marginal and "insignificant" for established fields such as China studies. Without Shu-mei's intervention and groundbreaking theory of the Sinophone, this book would not exist.

Over the years, I also benefited tremendously from a group of wonderful academic friends who support my work in countless ways. Howard Chiang's elegant scholarship on trans historiography and queer Sinophone theory is a constant source of admiration. I am so proud of our several collaborations. Within the circle of queer Sinophone studies, I deeply treasure the friendship of Lily Wong and E. K. Tan. Their generous feedback on my book improved the overall conceptualization. Shelly Chan carefully read the introduction and offered helpful advice. Inhye Han shares my joy and despair at every step of this journey, and I am so happy to count her as my dear friend. I am in awe of Jamie J. Zhao's amazing intellectual energy and productivity, and our mutual care sustains me every day. Angie Chau has been a dear friend since graduate school, and I thank her for commiserating with me during the final stages of writing this book. I am very honored to count her as my academic ally in the broader field of modern Chinese literature and culture. Jennifer Dorothy Lee is my academic homegirl. To my dear comrades Kathy Mak and Carlos Lin: thanks for enduring my daily nonsense in our Signal chat group.

Other academic friends and intellectuals who crossed paths with me and who indulged in my unruly queer scholarship are Aaron Anderson, Anjali Arondekar, Hongwei Bao, Thomas Baudinette, Brian Bernards, Michelle Bloom, Long Bui, Evans Chan, Shi-Yan Chao, Kai Hang Cheang, Fangdai Chen, Jannis Chen, Adam Chen-Dedman, Fan-Ting Cheng, Jih-Fei Cheng, Lo Kwai Cheung, Chi Ta-wei, Michelle Cho, Eileen Chow, Chow Yiu Fai, Kimberly Chung, Jason Coe, Rebecca Ehrenwirth, Harriet Evans, Donald Goellnicht, Elmo Gonzaga, Feng-Mei Heberer, Todd Henry, Ryan Heryford, Tammy Ho, Jeesoon Hong, Yu-ting Huang, Calvin Hui, Celina Hung, Kit

Hung, Clara Iwasaki, Melody Jue, Lucetta Kam, Dredge Kang, Miliann Kang, Ying-Chao Kao, Lucas Klein, Robert Ku, Kedar Kulkarni, Franco Lai, Siufung Law, Klaudia Lee, Helen Hok-Sze Leung, Eva Li, Li Mei Ting, Chien-ting Lin, Wen Liu, Christopher Lupke, Yahia Ma, Joanna Mansbridge, Naveen Minai, Jackie Hoang Tan Nguyen, Laikwan Pang, Christopher Patterson, Martin Joseph Ponce, Chandan Reddy, Andrea Riemenschnitter, Stevie Ruiz, Tze-lan Sang, Leo Shin, Valerie Soe, Erin Suzuki, Tan Jia, Denise Tang, Y-Dang Troeung, Kelly Tse, Keith Wagner, David Der-wei Wang, Yiman Wang, James Welker, Mary Wong, Harry Wu, Helena Wu, Hangping Xu, Renren Yang, Esther Yau, Audrey Yue, Min-xu Zhan, Charlie Zhang, and Emma Zhang. A special shoutout to Cheng-Chai Chiang, who generously organized a virtual book manuscript workshop where I received smart feedback from graduate students at UC Berkeley who are affiliated with the journal *Critical Times*.

My first tenure-track job took me to the Underwood International College at Yonsei University, South Korea. I thank my former colleagues there, including Bradford Bow, Henry Em, Clara Hong, Astrid Lac, Helen Lee, Tomoko Seto, and Jesse Sloane. My dear colleague and friend Robert Beachy made living in Seoul a great joy. I am so blessed to be surrounded by amazingly supportive colleagues in the Department of Comparative Literature at the University of Hong Kong (HKU) since arriving in 2018. Nicole Huang chaired the department for the first four years following my arrival, and her institutional wisdom, material support, and warm collegiality mean a lot to me. Gina Marchetti's institutional savviness, academic feminist network, and generous mentorship are phenomenal. I collaborate with Daniel Elam on many projects, including the Entanglements book series at HKU Press and our co-directorship of the Center for the Study of Globalization and Cultures (CSGC). His deep intellectual engagement and commitment to social justice inspire me daily. Georgina Challen, our research assistant at CSGC, is the person who actually runs the show! For several years, I co-taught the large Common Core course on globalization and Hong Kong culture with Fiona Law, and I continue to learn from her passionate pedagogy. Winnie Yee is a dear colleague and wonderful lunch buddy, and I learn a great deal from her work on ecocriticism and Hong Kong studies. Dan Vukovich, Chair of Comparative Literature, offers helpful advice on teaching and how to thrive as a junior colleague. My new colleague Jean Ma shares overlapping research interests in film studies, visual culture, and gender and sexuality studies. I treasure her savvy advice and adore her genuine presence. I also want to thank the wonderful support of staff in the school office and in the department, including Kitty Mak, Iris Ng, Doreen Chan, Jo Tang, Tilly Wong, and Francisca Kwok.

Outside of my department at HKU, I treasure the academic wisdom and loving friendship of Pei-yin Lin and Su Yun Kim. Su was already an academic big sister to me during my graduate school years, and since my arrival she has warmly invited me into her collaboration with Pei-yin on various projects. I am energized by our research cluster on Modern East Asian Literature (MEAL). During the final stage of revision, Su, Pei-yin, Edwin Michielsen, and Nicholas Wong offered rigorous feedback that improved the overall quality of this book. Other colleagues at HKU who warmly support my research and teaching include Stephen Chu Yiu Wai, Staci Ford, Song Geng, Petula Ho, Travis Kong, Shuk Man Leung, Li Chong, Eva Ng, Daniel Poch, Vivian Sheng, Vivien Wei Yan, Dingkun Wang, and John Wong. Travis's helpful tips on book writing and his contributions to Hong Kong LGBTQ communities truly amaze me. I am always in awe of Tong King Lee's academic productivity, and he has been a lovely confidant. Alastair McClure and Devika Shankar commiserated with me during the final stage of writing this book, and I treasure their friendship a lot. Marco Wan generously shared his institutional wisdom and offers good cheers along the way. John Carroll welcomed me on my first day at work, and he has been a warm colleague ever since. I am fortunate to have supervised some very smart graduate students, including Jing Peng, Junlin Ma, Lou Rich, and Harmony Yuen. Adam Jaworski and Chris Hutton, the former and current Associate Deans of Research, have offered invaluable advice. Max Deutsch, the Head of the School of Humanities, has firmly supported all my research and teaching endeavors. The Dean of the Faculty of Arts, David Pomfret, has offered meaningful support and generously provided a funding scheme that served as book subvention.

At Duke University Press, Ken Wissoker is the most ideal editor that every first book author would love to work with. He immediately showed enthusiasm for my book project, asked the tough and necessary questions, and guided my manuscript through a rigorous and efficient review process. Ken's steadfast and loving support means a lot to me. I want to thank the three anonymous readers of the book, whose rigorous engagements and endorsements improved the book as a whole. Kate Mullen's superb editorial support brought the book into production smoothly, and Ihsan Taylor's professionalism as the project editor is beyond amazing. And I want to thank the artists, film producers, and community organizers who obtained several high-quality images for me and engaged with relevant parts of the book. They are Marrz Saludez Balaoro, Beatrix Pang, and Mimi Wong.

Since I met her eighteen years ago, Lisa Lowe has totally transformed my life. As a graduate student under her co-supervision, I witnessed her magic of bringing together a radical and intellectually committed group of thinkers, colleagues, and students at UC San Diego. Lisa's feminist materialist approach to Asian American Studies, her concept of the intimacies of four continents, and her critical reckoning with the colonial present have deeply shaped my own intellectual trajectory. Whenever I am at a loss as to what to do, I think of what Lisa might do in a similar situation. But invariably, she has already opened the next door for me. Lisa's unfailing belief in me reaffirms that I am doing something meaningful even when I have self-doubt at times. For her deeply affective pedagogy, intellectual elegance, utterly caring mentorship, and political commitment, I am forever indebted and grateful.

Unless otherwise noted, all translations are my own.

The writing of this book was supported by the GRF grant of the Research Grants Council of Hong Kong under the project code: 17613520.

INTRODUCTION

Queer Hong Kong across
the Transpacific Sinophone

Hong Kong often appears on the global horizon as a city of finance capitalism, rampant real-estate speculation, cosmopolitanism, and East-West cross-cultural encounters. However, these existing imaginaries of Hong Kong actually limit our capacity to theorize the postcolonial region, a special administrative region (SAR) of the People's Republic of China (PRC) since July 1, 1997. These dominant views imply that Hong Kong's global significance derives solely from its intermediary relation to geopolitical superpowers—like the UK (its former colonizer), the United States, and China—and the New Cold War among them. *Unruly Comparison: Queerness, Hong Kong, and the Sinophone* offers a new model for doing transnational and comparative work in queer theory, area studies, and Sinophone studies. It demonstrates how a globally (in)significant region like Hong Kong exemplifies an unruliness that exceeds the political forces and epistemological limits of British colonialism, China-centrism, and global capitalism. If the queerness of Hong Kong exceeds its normative geopolitical referentiality, it follows that a queer decolonial approach to Hong Kong can unbind its ties to the UK, to China, and to late capitalism by linking anti-racist, feminist, and queer political struggles in the city to those happening elsewhere. For instance, when in May 2024 police forces violently removed the barricades of pro-Palestinian and anti-war encampments at UCLA, Columbia University, and college campuses across the United States, it immediately brought to mind state violence against protesters and the Hong Kong government's subsequent branding of protesters as "rioters" since the summer of 2019. By invoking an asymmetrical relationality that reckons with the coloniality of the present, we enter the realm of unruly comparison.

The concept of unruly comparison treats Hong Kong and similarly marginal regions of the world as sites of racial, gender, and sexual incommensurability and differences that refuse the totalizing terms of coloniality, Chinese nationalism, and global capitalism. My understanding of incommensurability expands on women of color feminism and queer of color critique, which offer "an alternative comparative method that, in its deep critique of the racialized, gendered, and sexualized devaluation of human life, gives us a blueprint for coalition around contemporary struggles."[1] Drawing on the insight of queer Sinophone studies that shows how "the Sinophone and the queer promise to denaturalize each other continuously,"[2] I suggest that Hong Kong matters to queer theory (and vice versa) beyond its local particularism, postcolonial "Chinese" differences, and capitalist exceptionality. Alternatively, queer Sinophone studies offers a nontotalizing perspective on Hong Kong itself as a site of racial, gender, sexual, and cultural incommensurability and intersectionality; in turn, this recognition of Hong Kong's queer worldliness binds it to the rest of the world and engenders unruly modes of comparison. First, let me take you, my reader, back to the summer of 2019, an interregnum that demands the wake work of unruly comparison.[3]

During the summer of 2019, Hong Kong was at the center of global attention. The last time people around the world had talked about the city this feverishly was during the summer of 1997, when the transfer of sovereignty over the city from the UK back to the PRC had the world second-guessing Hong Kong's—and probably the world's—future. Would the city remain a place for free-market, laissez-faire capitalism? Would it remain the intermediary for capital that had served its interests well since the mid-nineteenth century? Or would British "positive noninterventionism" and the colonial-modern standard of living see their last glory days before the impending return to China? In short, would Hong Kong remain *the* Hong Kong that we had always known?

Twenty-two years later, more than two million people would take to the streets in Hong Kong to protest the introduction of an extradition law that would send criminal offenders to Mainland China for legal adjudication.

Heavily backed by the conservative political parties of the Hong Kong Legislative Council and swiftly introduced without public consultation by Chief Executive Carrie Lam, the extradition bill ignited deep-seated dissent, demands for democracy and universal suffrage, and the largest-scale civil disobedience experienced in the city's history. For political scientist Ho-fung Hung, the 2019 social movement reveals the fluctuating status of the global city: "Hong Kong is a city constantly on the edge. It is on the edge of great powers, on the edge of being annihilated, and on the edge of breaking free."[4]

While Hung emphasizes that the recent social upheaval constitutes part of the longer geohistory of Hong Kong as caught between multiple colonial and capitalist powers (British colonialism, 1841–1997; Japanese imperialism, during World War II; Communist China, after 1949; and postsocialist Chinese governmentality after 1997), a feminist and queer framing of Hong Kong's colonial past and postcolonial present can open up alternative possibilities. In other words, the Anti-Extradition Law Amendment Bill (Anti-ELAB) movement also witnessed new possibilities for political alliance across race, gender, class, and sexuality. Given the government's tokenist policy toward racial, gender, and sexual diversity and its lack of legal protection for sexual minorities based on gender expression and sexual orientation, this intersectional alliance born from the social movement demanded a new reckoning. For example, South Asian minorities and LGBT celebrities participated at rallies and organized water stations and support groups at iconic landmarks such as Chungking Mansions in Tsim Sha Tsui (figure I.1). While Chungking Mansions has historically been an ethnic enclave for African and South Asian small businesses that sparked racialized fear of criminal activities among Han Chinese Hong Kongers, during the social movement it became a symbol for the possibility of cross-racial solidarity. Most Hong Kong residents, regardless of their racial and ethnic background, expressed anger at the Hong Kong police's use of a water-cannon truck and its "accidental" blue-spraying and defacing of the Kowloon Mosques on October 20, 2019. Feminists, LGBT folks, and NGOs dedicated to queer issues also formed a new alliance when an accusation of gang rape taking place at the police station (made by Sonia Ng, a female student at the Chinese University of Hong Kong) and the later arrest of LGBT singers Anthony Wong and Denise Ho drew attention to the sections of society that most Hong Kongers had simply ignored for far too long. The shifting global preoccupation with the protest and the ongoing US-China trade war coincided with increasingly vocal demands made by gender, racial, and sexual minorities for civil liberties and rights to representation.

FIGURE I.1. South Asians show solidarity with Cantonese Hong Kong protesters at Chungking Mansions during the 2019 protests.

Unruly Comparison intervenes precisely at this moment of crisis, public dissent, and political frustration by conjuring a new social imaginary. It suggests that queering Hong Kong itself could offer an unruly method of comparison that unsettles both the Eurocentrism of queer theory and the China-centrism of area studies. While the academic study of Hong Kong (itself heavily preoccupied with the 1997 postcolonial handover) emerged around the 1990s, the naming of a field called "Hong Kong studies" has happened only in the last ten years or so. But Hong Kong studies as currently institutionalized tends to be heavily skewed toward the fields of history, political science, migration studies, and sociology, and within these iterations of the field, gender and sexuality remain marginal. Situating itself at the critical conjuncture of Hong Kong studies, queer theory, and Sinophone studies, *Unruly Comparison* illuminates new ways of doing queer theory, critiques the heteronormativity of existing studies on Hong Kong and Chineseness, and expands the possibility of a queer imaginary of Hong Kong for global comparison.

The concept of unruly comparison understands Hong Kong as an unruly time-space that troubles historicist, colonial, and China-centric renderings of the city as merely a site of British colonial legacy and a "super special economic/free-trade zone in China."[5] An unruly comparative approach unravels Hong Kong as a site of incommensurability in terms of race, gender, sexuality, and class. This recognition of Hong Kong as a queer region of nontotalizing differences focalizes alternative relationalities such as queer migrations across Hong Kong and Southeast Asia, which would otherwise be occluded by a myopic vision of Hong Kong as existing only between British colonialism, China-centrism, and global capitalism. In other words, the theory of unruly comparison actualizes a perverse relationality that binds Hong Kong with the world through minor transnationalism and South-South comparison across time and space.[6]

Toward Unruly Comparison

One pivotal moment in the intellectual genesis of this book emerged in late January 2021, when the gallery WMA Space in Central, the unmistakable financial district of Hong Kong, held an art exhibition called *Unruly Visions*. I found out about the exhibition through a Facebook post. It was curated by Tse Ka-Man, a queer visual artist and academic based in New York City. The exhibition's title clearly referenced queer theorist Gayatri Gopinath's 2018 book *Unruly Visions*, and Tse opened the exhibition catalog with a quote by Gopinath: "Through a sustained engagement with queer visual aesthetic practices, we can identify alternative ways of seeing and knowing capable of challenging the scopic and sensorial regimes of colonial modernity in their current forms."[7]

Beyond the conceptual indebtedness to Gopinath's theory of queer diaspora and queer regionalism, the exhibition also cited José Esteban Muñoz's idea of queerness as a critique of the political pragmatism of mainstream homonormativity and LGBT politics. In Muñoz's words, "Queerness is that thing that lets us feel that this world is not enough, that indeed something is missing."[8] Here, I am struck by Tse's bold invitation to theorize queer Hong Kong visual culture in dialogue with queer diaspora studies and queer of color critique. In particular, I ask: How are "the scopic and sensorial regimes of colonial modernity" resurfacing in new Sinocentric authoritarian modes in post-2020 Hong Kong with the passing of the National Security Law (NSL)? On June 30, 2020, the National People's Congress (NPC) enacted the National Security Law in Hong Kong, which aimed to ensure the "prosperity and stability" of Hong Kong's postcolonial governance. Its sole aim was to safeguard national security by "preventing, suppressing and imposing punishment for the offences of secession, subversion, organisation and perpetration of terror-

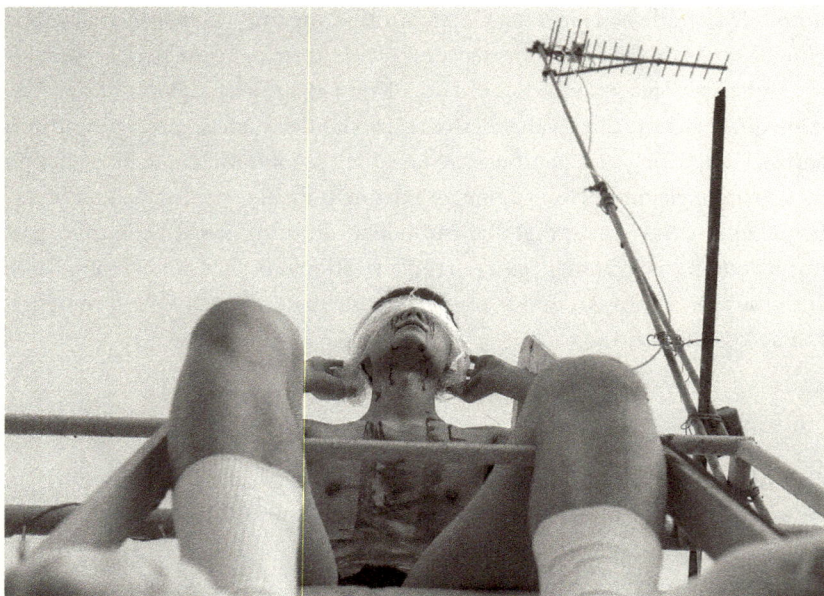

FIGURE I.2. "Reveal" from Rain Chan Wing Ki's *Black* collection.

ist activities, and collusion with a foreign country or with external elements to endanger national security in relation to the Hong Kong Special Administrative Region."[9] What is missing from this new tidal wave to restore "order and prosperity" in post-2020 Hong Kong? How might queer Sinophone visuality offer a critical diagnosis that the present is indeed *not enough*?

I walked through the exhibition with these burning questions in mind and found myself queerly disoriented. In photographer Rain Chan Wing Ki's *Black* collection, a photo called *Reveal* shows a naked young male body from a low-angle, revealing his chest while hiding his cock. The blindfolded male model is wearing a pair of white socks, with splash of red paint resembling human blood dripping from his face (figure I.2). This bloody body may symbolize a young queer protester bleeding, a familiar sight during the frequent physical confrontations between the police and the protesters in the summer of 2019. However, the title of the work without the artist's description simply frames it as *Reveal*.

Another creative queer photograph by the photographer and journalist Nelson Tang Chak-man traffics less in surrealism and symbolism in its rep-

FIGURE I.3. Nelson Tang Chak-man, *Where Are You Going? Where Have You Been?* (2019–20).

resentation of social upheaval, queer sexuality, and historicism. In the photograph, *Where Are You Going? Where Have You Been?* (2019–20), Tang captures a cross-dresser staring back at a young male protester in mask. The transfemme cross-dresser is smiling back at the photographer, turning her gaze back at the camera. She is also dressed in a wedding gown, and the location of the photoshoot indicates that she is bidding farewell to the masked young man in Sheung Wan, one of the popular protest sites in the summer of 2019, where teargas left indelible toxic smell on the street (figure I.3). Tang, a Baptist University student journalist, was arrested by the police on November 5, 2019, for "disorder in a public place" while covering a protest rally inside a mall.[10] During his arrest, he yelled sarcastically to fellow protesters and pedestrians that he is very healthy and has no suicidal intention (alluding to the possible unlawful abuses of protesters at police stations and detention centers). Tang also wrote the following artist's statement: "As an observer, I have seen protestors use umbrellas like police with guns. I have watched a couple celebrating Christmas, while protestors demonstrated right next to them. I witnessed a protestor unknowingly escape a bullet."[11]

Whereas Rain Chan Wing Ki's *Black* collection imagines the queer body as one that bears witness to historical and political violence, Tang's trans photography deviates from local journalism that tends to romanticize young protesters as defiant subjects and heterosexual lovers as torn apart by illegal activities and impending imprisonment. In staring back at us, the trans-femme subject in Tang's photo conjures what Nicholas Mirzoeff calls "the right to look." He writes, "The right to look claims autonomy, not individualism or voyeurism, but the claim to a political subjectivity and collectivity."[12] Tse Ka-Man's *Unruly Visions* thus proffers a queer Sinophone engagement with queer diaspora studies and queer of color critique in its insistence on queer visuality as a mode of disorientation and disidentification. It unsettles the deadening political pessimism in contemporary Hong Kong by thinking displacement, unsettlement, and political exile *within* Hong Kong. It beckons us to see Hong Kong queerly by visualizing the city as an unruly queer parasite that might not assimilate smoothly into the grand narrative of prosperity and restoration of order and capitalism in post-2020 Hong Kong.[13] While the *Unruly Visions* exhibition offers a visual statement on unruly comparison as a queer Sinophone methodology, it is also necessary to trace the conceptual contour of "unruly comparison" and investigate how this concept intervenes into existing debates in area studies, queer theory, and Sinophone studies.

Instead of relying heavily on "area specificity" and the fetishization of Chineseness as conventionally practiced in queer area studies scholarship, the model of unruly comparison intersects queerness, Hong Kong, and the Sinophone through friction, asymmetry, and perverse juxtapositions. As a concept, unruly comparison names three theoretical interventions that have broad implications for queer theory, Sinophone studies, and comparative literature. First, unruly comparison explodes the temporal and spatial limits for cross-cultural comparison by enabling small and marginal regions of the world (like Hong Kong) to be linked, juxtaposed, and studied in unlikely modes of affiliation and relationality. In this way, unruly comparison expands on Wai Chee Dimock's concept of deep time, which she defines as "a set of longitudinal frames, at once projective and recessional, with input going both ways, and binding continents and millennia into many loops of relations, a densely interactive fabric."[14] The deep time approach certainly informs the recent turn to "worlding" by Pheng Cheah. Cheah writes, "As an enactment of the opening of worlds by the coming of time, world literature points to something that will always exceed and disrupt capital."[15] *Unruly Comparison* takes up the long durational capacity of literary and other expressive cultural forms by showing how, once we bracket the premodern, modern, the national, and the regional as standard units of temporal and spatial measurement, more unruly and queer forms of comparison come into view.

The queer worlding force of unruly comparison assembles nonequivalent queer figures from different times and spaces of Hong Kong Sinophone modernity, including a local gay mafia boss and a queer Scottish colonial officer in World War II (chapter 1), gay male cosmopolitan travelers and their neo-colonial complicity in Hong Kong cinema (chapter 2), queer migrant domestic workers who negotiate lesbian desire across Southeast Asia, Hong Kong, and Taiwan (chapter 4), and more. As a conceptual model, it demonstrates how a small but globally significant city and region like Hong Kong can un-know itself through broader and innovative temporal and spatial comparisons, disrupting the dominant legacies of British colonialism and the late capitalism of China-centrism.

Second, unruly comparison reframes the debate of translatability and (in)commensurability in the field of comparative literature by showing how cultural productions in "a small place" like Hong Kong both exemplify immense differences and cultural incommensurability internally while entering into relational tension, collision, and alliances with the rest of the world.[16] Framing translational politics and comparison in a different light, Emily Apter unpacks the double bind of translatability. Apter ironically claims that "nothing is translatable" and "everything is translatable."[17] Hong Kong traffics in the double bind of translatability and untranslatability in the sense that the city often appears on the global horizon as the "freest capitalist city," an "emporium of trade," a "global city," and an exemplar of economic modernization— one of the four Asian tigers in its pre-1997 era. In the post-1997 era, and especially in the doomful post-2019 contemporary moment, these preexisting imaginaries of the city seem insufficient in translating Hong Kong. *Unruly Comparison* takes stock of existing postcolonial terminologies that seek to translate Hong Kong within critical theory. Building on concepts such as "disappearance," "between colonizers," and "lost in transition," I argue that the queerness of Hong Kong exceeds the epistemological limits of British colonialism, China-centrism and governmentality, and late capitalism as this "three masters" analogy hamstrings our creative capacity to theorize a queer Sinophone Hong Kong.[18] Unruly comparison as a concept boldly gestures toward alternative possibilities of comparison that dig into archives of queer subjects lost to history (chapter 1), cinematic modes of queer minor transnationalism (chapter 2), trans visuality that deviates from queer liberalism (chapter 3), and more.

The framework of unruly comparison takes cultural incommensurability as a point of departure from which to theorize queer differences in a small place like Hong Kong. To compare things in unruly ways is to acknowledge what Natalie Melas calls the "incommensurability" of comparative literature and cultural forms. In her book *All the Difference in the World*, Melas argues that postcolonial theory and the comparative literary studies of empire and colonies (both literal and metaphorical) offer "a ground of comparison, but no given basis of equivalence."[19] Bypassing the anxiety of debunking the Eurocentrism of comparative literature and queer theory, a queer Sinophone approach to Hong Kong shows that Hong Kong as a historical colonial city and postcolonial special administrative region under the shadow of China-centrism and global capitalism already evinces infinite possibilities for transnational comparison and worldliness. In other words, Hong Kong already embodies "all the difference in the world," to borrow Melas's provocative phrase again. Treating cultural incommensurability in racial, gender, sexual, and ethnic terms as both limit and possibility, unruly comparison frees cultural production and theorists within a small place in the world (to borrow from Kincaid's again) from the anxiety of measuring up to certain implied norms within academic disciplinarity—it enables us to study the worldliness and immense differences and incommensurability within a given place while expanding that unruly scale of comparison through perverse juxtaposition and asymmetry across different temporalities, spaces, and genres. In this way, unruly comparison is akin to what Kandice Chuh calls illiberal humanisms that "facilitate the articulation and elaboration of epistemes thoroughly incommensurate with the developmental geographies and temporalities of bourgeois liberal humanism."[20]

Third, unruly comparison frames queer Sinophone culture as a site for exemplifying relational comparison and decoloniality that reckons with the asymmetries of nationalism, imperialism, coloniality, settler colonialism, and late capitalism. Naming a model of relational comparison that reads slavery and the plantation arc across American, Caribbean, and Sinophone Malaysian literatures, Shu-mei Shih writes: "Comparison as relation means setting into motion historical relationalities between entities brought together for comparison, and bringing into relation terms that have traditionally been pushed apart from each other.... The excavation of these relationalities is ... the ethical practice of comparison, where the workings of power are not concealed but necessarily revealed."[21] Excavating an analytic of relation in their theorization of comparative global humanities, Lisa Lowe and

Kris Manjapra similarly take Édouard Glissant's poetics of Relation as one source of inspiration among other theorists of decoloniality and comparative racialization. They write, "This analytic of relation recognizes the limits of a more established comparativism that presumes analogous, discretely bounded units, yet explores instead the interdependence, relatedness, and coproduction of communities."[22]

Thinking queerness relationally means that I can read a queer Sinophone film like Scud's *Permanent Residence* (2009) as a cinematic narrative of a gay Mainlander Ivan, who accrues capital and wealth in Hong Kong as an engineer yet exploits Southeast Asian bodies in his sexcape to Bangkok on the way to his next destination for pinkwashing, like Tel Aviv. Queer Sinophone visuality focalizes the unruly comparison of queer bodies and desire across incommensurable geographies rooted in differently layered forms of empire and settler colonialism. Similarly, while queer female migrant domestic workers face different obstacles, immobility, and exploitation in Hong Kong and Taiwan, queer Sinophone documentary films like *Sunday Beauty Queen* (dir. Baby Ruth Villarama, 2016) and *Lesbian Factory* (dir. Susan Chen, 2010) (as I will explore in chapter 4) visualize what Neferti X. M. Tadiar terms the "remaindered life" of queer Sinophone intimacies.[23] These queer migrant workers practice love and intimacy as they navigate queer ways of being in the world mediated by brutal capitalist regimes of work in Sinophone sites.

Framing queer Sinophone studies as a knowledge formation for excavating queer relationality across imperialism, colonialism, and neoliberalism also puts my work into conversation with Laura Doyle's concept of interimperiality, which tracks the formation of literature and other expressive cultural forms amid vying empires and geopolitical forces. In other words, unruly comparison can be a queer method of tracing interimperiality, which is "a long-historical, dialectical theory of relationality and power that integrates feminist-intersectional, economic, materialist, literary, and geopolitical thought."[24] Each chapter of my book turns to a specific concept that has animated the fields of area studies, Hong Kong studies, and queer theory in relational terms, including the archive (chapter 1), transnationalism (chapter 2), transgender (chapter 3), intimacies (chapter 4), and borders (chapter 5). It shows how an unruly entanglement of queerness, Hong Kong, and the Sinophone puts analytical pressure on these concepts, which in turn troubles the disciplinary habits of area studies, China studies, and queer theory.

A queer Sinophone approach that enacts an unruly comparison of Hong Kong necessarily presumes a double theoretical gesture. First, queer Sinophone theory provincializes the Eurocentrism of queer studies by expanding the implications of queer of color critique and queer diaspora studies within the racial and sexual formations of Hong Kong and its global diasporas. Second, it *queers* China studies by using the Sinophone Hong Kong optic to unsettle Chinese nationalism and the disciplinary conventions of East Asian area studies. It would be heuristically useful to trace how queer Sinophone theory has reframed debates in queer studies over the last twenty years. Queer of color critique, queer diaspora studies, and critiques on homonationalism proposed by theorists like David L. Eng, Roderick A. Ferguson, José Esteban Muñoz, Gayatri Gopinath, Martin F. Manalansan, Chandan Reddy, and Jasbir K. Puar, among others, have brought questions of racialization, intersectionality, empires and colonialism, and homonationalism to bear on gender, sexuality, and queerness.[25] This genealogy of transnational queer studies suggests several reorientations of the field of queer studies that have broad implications for queer Chinese studies and queer Sinophone studies. On the one hand, the critique of dominant forms of historical materialism, sociology, and US liberalism in reproducing disciplinary regimes that render nonwhite queer subjects as "deviant" exposes the racial, gender, sexual, and classed contradictions of US liberalism and nationalism, thus underlining the false promise of multiculturalism. Similarly, queer diaspora studies unsettles the queer liberalism that would assume North America as a site of the arrival of modernity for global queer subjects.

The critique of queer liberalism has generated some productive debates within queer Asian studies as well. For Ara Wilson, the queer diaspora model can at times recenter queer diasporic lives and cultural productions rooted in the Global North. Wilson argues, "But more generally, while such analyses create alternative queer narratives within the global north, diasporic queer critiques of Western hegemony still pivot on the first world. Is there a way to make queer life in the complex modernities of the non-West, third-world and global south itself the centre of transnational queer analysis?"[26] While Wilson is perceptive in naming the possible danger of recentering North America as a site for queer diaspora studies, her conflation of queer diaspora studies with the Western academic knowledge production called "queer theory" has the tendency to flatten out queer diasporic studies that do not center the West as such.[27] Furthermore, Wilson's automatic turn to "queer Asia" as a site producing "complex modernities" that can debunk the Eurocentrism of queer studies might problematically assume "queer Asia" as a site of particularism, difference, and alterity. This tendency in the work of queer Asian studies reveals the persistent need and indeed anxiety to speak back to an imaginary and universalist frame of reference called "the West," in which this entity could mean both the spatial location of Euro-America and the theoretical muscle of Eurocentric queer theory itself. We are at a conundrum of area studies versus queer theory: would not a debunking of Western queer theory from locally situated perspectives of area studies and non-Western sources simply reproduce the West as a universal frame of reference?

Rey Chow has framed the problem of area studies and theory somewhat differently, using a formula wherein the very assertion of ethnic, national, and sexual differences called "X" will simply reproduce predictable resistance to "Western theory" and Eurocentrism that in the end fails to change the game. Chow asserts, "When scholars of marginalized groups and non-Western subjects rely on notions of resistance (to Western theory) in their attempts to argue the specificity of X, they are unwittingly replicating the conundrum whereby the specificity of an object of study is conceived of in terms of a differential—a differential, moreover, that has to be incorporated in the chain of signification in order to attain recognition."[28] In the specific case of thinking the relationality among queer theory, area studies, and Asia, we might reframe Chow's provocation in the following ways: How can we do queer theory without assuming its Eurocentrism? How can we disentangle queer theory from Eurocentrism without resorting too easily to a theory of localism and the non-West as markers of stable "difference"? What might a non–area studies framework of queer Hong Kong look like?[29]

One generative discussion on provincializing queer theory from the vantage point of queer Asia has been the debate on queering Chineseness within queer Chinese studies. In his book *Queer Marxism in Two Chinas*, Petrus Liu offers a historical argument that sees the 1949 geopolitical division of the "two Chinas," namely the PRC and the Republic of China (ROC) in Taiwan, as productive in the emergence of queer Marxism in the literatures and intellectual circles in both sites.[30] While Liu makes the disclaimer that his project "is not a Sinophone studies book," his book is most productive in illustrating the divergent approaches in the field to queering Chineseness.[31] For queer Sinophone historian Howard Chiang, Liu's "obsession with a 'Chinese materialist queer theory that sets it apart from its Euro-American counterparts' not only begs the question of whose Chineseness is at stake, but also risks reifying the

East-West binary via . . . 'self- or re-Orientalization.'"[32] Liu's latest book, *The Specter of Materialism*, attempts to "rework the methodologies of queer theory through a decentered perspective on the history of global capitalism."[33] If a queer materialist approach to the two Chinas unsettles the Eurocentric basis of queer theory and its 1990s emergence, queer Sinophone theory disrupts the referentiality of Chineseness in the first place.

In parsing this debate between queer Chinese studies and queer Sinophone studies on the reification of queer Chineseness as a nonliberal critique, I am less interested in adding fuel to the flame. Rather, the model of unruly comparison offers a productive way to reframe the debate in fresh light. A queer Sinophone approach emphasizes the fruitfulness of studying the complexity of queer desire, intimacy, and resistance across the distinctive temporality and spatiality of Sinophone modernities without homogenizing what Chineseness might signify in advance. Tracing this queer Sinophone line of inquiry and building on existing works in queer Chinese studies that deconstruct Chineseness both spatially and temporally, *Unruly Comparison* calls for a queer Hong Kong method that enacts a critique of the presumed hierarchy between an "original" China and its lesser "Sinophone" copies.[34] In other words, the concept of unruly comparison queers the ontology of Chineseness through the politics of unknowing Hong Kong itself. To *unknow* Hong Kong is to appreciate the city-region beyond its position as a pawn between geopolitical rivalries. Specifically, unknowing shatters the myth of Hong Kong as a middleman of global capitalism for China and the West by imagining instead the "perverse modernities" of Hong Kong. Instead of turning to Hong Kong to fetishize the global city and special administrative region through postcolonial anomaly and capitalist exceptionalism, the politic of unknowing Hong Kong frames it as a geopolitical and conceptual domain that troubles any essentialist claim to Chineseness and queerness as such. An unruly queer methodology also rethinks Hong Kong and queer Asias in their multiplicity: it forestalls the desire to turn to non-Western areas and regions to catalog differences and particularity for the sake of countering the Eurocentrism of queerness. In a more disturbing mode, unruly comparison treats Hong Kong (and other similarly marginal and interimperial regions of the world) as an immense site of differences unto itself while expanding an elastic scale of relational comparison to other regions, archives, spaces, and temporalities in the world.

Queer Sinophone studies interrupts queer theory's universalist tendency and queer Asian studies' reassertion of difference as "X" (á la Rey Chow).[35] Shu-mei Shih defines the Sinophone as "a network of places of cultural production outside China and on the margins of China and Chineseness, where a historical process of heterogenizing and localizing of continental Chinese culture has been taking place for several centuries."[36] Like queer theory's emphasis on discontinuity across sex, gender, and sexuality and its suspicion of essentialism, then, the concept of the Sinophone decenters the ontological and ethnonational equivalence between China as a nation-state, Chinese as language, and Chinese as identity politics. In a subsequent formulation, Shih provides a materialist and historical definition of Sinophone studies through the critique of Chinese empire and continental colonialism within the PRC, whose present-day territory largely inherits the Qing conquest of Tibet, Xinjiang, and Inner Mongolia.

China-centrism operates through this largely ignored imperial history of Chinese empire. Deriving its strength from the myth of the homeland, it problematically ties descendants from the diasporas of Southeast Asia, Taiwan, Hong Kong, and the world at large to "China."[37] Likewise, Ien Ang's invocation of "not speaking Chinese" playfully deconstructs the politics of racial authenticity and long-distance diasporic nationalism.[38] Ang's solution to the perennial problem of looking Chinese but not speaking Chinese (a problem well-known to most Chinese Americans born in the United States, often referred to as "ABCS") is one of strategic and conditional refusal. Ang writes: "If I am inescapably Chinese by *descent*, I am only sometimes Chinese by *consent*."[39]

If postcolonial and postmodern deconstruction of the dominant politics of Chineseness some twenty years ago by theorists like Ien Ang and Rey Chow sought to bracket "Chineseness" and put it productively "under erasure," Sinophone studies retains this deontological and poststructuralist emphasis by giving the critique of Chineseness a global, transnational, and materialist dimension.[40] It gives voices to those deemed "inauthentic" due to historical, racial, and/or gendered circumstances. Sinophone studies thus shares with queer theory two major theoretical investments—a tendency against essentialism and a politics of disidentification.[41] *Unruly Comparison* engages fruitfully with the theory of disidentification that originates from queer of color critique and queer diaspora studies. All these intellectual formations demonstrate the politics of living with and transgressing dominant regimes of knowing, whether those dominant epistemologies and powers go by the name of China-centrism, heterosexism, ethnic nationalism, and/or white homonormativity.

The idea of unruly comparison expands on the theory of minor transnationalism by turning to the queer incommensurability of minor regions like Hong Kong.[42] Structurally, *Unruly Comparison* imagines a queer Hong Kong modernity through archival undoing (chapter 1); it maps South-South transnationalism in Hong Kong cinema (chapter 2); it transnationalizes transgender in Sinophone Hong Kong (chapter 3); it visualizes queer intimacies among migrant domestic workers (chapter 4); and it queers the Sinophone border across the PRC and Hong Kong cinematically (chapter 5). As a whole, it offers a global, transnational, and Sinophone method of comparison. I theorize comparison as a method of putting unlikely entities in relational proximity, of making Hong Kong signify strangeness and negativity unto itself, and of refusing the call of China-centrism even as Hong Kong is already geopolitically incorporated into the PRC.

Unruly Comparison offers a Sinophone and transpacific method of comparison insofar as China-centrism is merely one of its many objects of critique. Many cultural forms examined here, such as Hong Kong films, literature, and visual cultures—including films on queer diasporas, such as *Happy Together*, directed by Wong Kar-wai (1997), and *Permanent Residence*, directed by Scud (2009), and the queer novel *Once Upon a Time in Hong Kong*, by Ma Ka Fai (2016)—all imagine queer desire against the backdrop of global modernity, queer diasporic journeys, and interracial colonial intimacy. By linking seemingly incommensurable visuality and narratives of war, diaspora, feminism, and interracial intimacy within a comparative framework, my book also envisions queer Hong Kong as method—it frees Hong Kong from existing wellworn terminologies such as colony, region, global city, and "cultural desert" through alternative spatial and temporal resignifications. It scales up the regional and spatial specificity of Hong Kong across wider temporal, transnational, and transpacific scales of comparison. In so doing, it advances a model of unruly comparison that disrupts the disciplinary orientations of area studies (China studies, Asian studies, and to a lesser degree Hong Kong studies), comparative literature, and queer theory. *Unruly Comparison* situates Hong Kong itself as an important site of thinking queerness comparatively and works this comparative aim outward into global and transnational terrains.

Theorizing Hong Kong relationally is another way of saying that Hong Kong can be a queer method, for queer theory provides nonbinary and nondualistic modes of thinking. My invocation of "queer Hong Kong as method" as a cognate concept with unruly comparison is obviously inspired by Kuan-Hsing Chen's concept of "Asia as method." Whereas Chen argues that the Cold War and the United States' military and empire-building in Asia have prevented the possibilities of decolonization and de-imperialization, my conjoining of *queer* with *Hong Kong as method* unsettles any masculinist and heteronormative accounts of nationalism and decolonization that often underline the transitional period of Hong Kong's 1997 return to the "motherland" that is the PRC.[43] Conceptually, queering Hong Kong is a multidirectional method that disrupts masculinist narrations of Hong Kong modernity and postcoloniality on the one hand while linking Hong Kong to queer temporalities and regions in the Other Asias through what Chen terms "inter-referencing strategy."[44] Chapter 1 further outlines queer Hong Kong as a Sinophone method by turning to a queer unruly archive of Hong Kong modernity that ruptures masculine narratives of modernization, war, and historicism.

Unruly Comparison turns to transpacific and minor-to-minor forms of queer transnationalism that place Hong Kong within the narratives of global modernity, war, queer diasporas, migration, intimacies, and border-crossing femininity. The transpacific here denotes less the regional economic partnership between Southeast Asian, East Asian, and North American countries and more what Janet Hoskins and Viet Thanh Nguyen call "another vision of the Pacific as a contact zone" mediated by "alternate narratives of translocalism, oppositional localism, and oppositional regionalism."[45] Indeed, transpacific and Sinophone approaches have given rise to a more complex, worldly, and entangled imaginary of Hong Kong, one that rethinks existing methods of comparison.

Chapter Outlines

Unruly Comparison treats Hong Kong as part of the broader story of global modernity, in which queer sexuality and desire transform our existing ways of seeing the city. Beyond the dominant modes of seeing Hong Kong through East-West comparisons, queering Hong Kong is also another way of framing it relationally across incommensurable but linked global histories, spatiality, and temporality. Each chapter in the book sets Hong Kong, the Sinophone, and queerness into motion and situates queer cultural formations across wider temporal, spatial, and transnational scales of comparison.

Chapter 1, "Queer Hong Kong as a Sinophone Method," reads queer Hong Kong literature as a material force of worlding, one that provides a deep reflection on affect, history, and queer archive. In particular, I analyze a novel by the award-winning Hong Kong author Wong Bik-wan, whose novels and short stories narrate issues of migration, the Asia-Pacific War, criminal history, gendered violence, and the law. Specifically, Wong's 1999 feminist novel *Lienü tu* (烈女圖, Portraits of martyred women) imagines the possibility of feminist solidarity and lesbian intimacy, namely affective modes that are often overshadowed by the larger narratives of war and political leftism in 1940–70s Hong Kong.[46] I also place Wong's novel alongside *Zi shu* (自梳, *Intimates*, dir. Jacob Cheung, 1997), a film of lesbian eros and regionalism, and Ma Ka Fai's 2016 queer novel *Long tou feng wei* (龍頭鳳尾, Once upon a time in Hong Kong), which presents a story of colonial complicity in the affair between a Scottish officer and a local mafia boss. Beyond narrating a homoerotic tale often buried in historical accounts of the Japanese occupation of Hong Kong (1941–45), Ma's novel also serves as a self-reflexive theorization of queer archive. Overall, Wong, Cheung, and Ma's works actualize a queer Sinophone worlding of Hong Kong through deep archival illuminations and unruly juxtapositions of lesbian desire and male homoeroticism that ultimately disrupt masculinist narrations of Hong Kong modernity.

Chapter 2, "Postcoloniality beyond China-Centrism," explores Hong Kong cinema in the post-1997 period as a rich site for queer Sinophone theory, positioning Hong Kong as a geographic locale through the visual mapping of global intimacies and connections. It expands on Shu-mei Shih's insight into the Sinophone as a nonrelational approach toward Chineseness and draws upon Lisa Lowe's concept of "the intimacies of four continents." Queerness in Hong Kong cinema precisely points to modes of disorientation and transnational mobility that deviate from the geopolitics of British colonial legacy and China-centrism. I examine queer nonrelationality to Chineseness in independent filmmaker Scud's two films, *Yongjiu juliu* (永久居留, *Permanent Residence*, 2009) and *An fei ta ming* (安非他命, *Amphetamine*, 2010), that link Hong Kong with Guangzhou in China as well as with Thailand and the Israeli occupation of Palestinian lands and that map queer desire across Australia and Hong Kong, respectively. I also examine Sinophone local and regional lesbian cinematic aesthetics in *Hudie* (蝴蝶, *Butterfly*, dir. Mak Yan Yan, 2004). Mak's film narrates the transnational and Sinophone connections of Hong Kong with an "elsewhere" (whether real or imaginary) through lesbian desire. In visualizing a model of postcoloniality beyond dominant Chineseness, queer Sinophone theory foregrounds Hong Kong cinematic transnationalism across worldly geographies and local intimacies.

Chapter 3, "Transnationalizing Transgender," demonstrates that studying queer Hong Kong requires an alternative framework of "queer globalities." Conceptually, queer globalities illustrate the convergent dynamics of global queer rights discourses, local geopolitics, and so-called pink capitalism within the global modernities of queer Asia. The plural emphasis of "queer globalities" points to the unevenness with which the global forces of queer liberalism and LGBT human rights discourses encounter the postcolonial modernity of Hong Kong, where the government, NGOs, activists, and cultural workers redefine queer liberalism to unpredictable ends. This concept thus moves beyond the simplistic binary of the local-global or the postmodern meshing of the *glocal* by coming to terms with the many ways of being queer *and* global. In short, it reclaims globality for queer Hong Kong. The first part of this chapter offers a critical legal analysis of queer and trans rights in Hong Kong. Next, I provide a queer transnational analysis of the film *Cui si* (翠絲, *Tracey*, dir. Jun Li, 2018) by mapping the condition of being trans through multiple queer temporalities and transnational spaces. I then contrast *Tracey* with Maisy Suen's *Nuren jiushi nuren* (女人就是女人, *A Woman Is a Woman*, 2018), which narrates the struggle of a married trans woman named Sung Chi Yu and the life of a feminine high school boy, Chiu Ling Fung. The film maps the double life journeys of Sung and Chiu by visualizing multiple ways of being trans in Sinophone Hong Kong, where the erotic density of embodying transness spatially at school and church, and in familial spaces, challenges any essentialist notion of trans personhood. I also examine a successful series of photo exhibitions of trans subjects and public workshops inspired by the film. Overall, this chapter considers the *trans* of transgender as a prefix that highlights transnational movement, trans mobility, and trans-medial Sinophone creativity.

While migration studies of Hong Kong tend to track the outward flow of people due to political instability and postcolonial transition, they seldom connect the situations of Hong Kong's "flexible citizens" with the migration of domestic workers into Hong Kong. Furthermore, existing sociological studies of migrant domestic workers by scholars like Rhacel Salazar Parreñas reinforce a heteronormative assumption in the model of the international division of reproductive labor.[47] Chapter 4, "Queer Sinophone Intimacies," analyzes documentary films about queer migrants, beauty pageants, and activism such as Susan Chen's *T po gong chang* (T婆工廠, *Lesbian Factory*, 2010), its sequel *Caihong ba le* (彩虹芭樂, *Rainbow Popcorn*, 2012), and Baby Ruth Villarama's *Sunday Beauty Queen* (2016) to show how a Sinophone comparison of queer intimacies in contemporary Taiwan and Hong Kong yields a sorely needed intersectional critique of race, migration, and queerness in Sinophone theory and Hong Kong studies.

Chapter 5, "Trespassing the Sinophone Border," examines Fruit Chan's three Sinophone films on the figure of the sex worker, *Liu lian piao piao* (榴槤飄飄, *Durian Durian*, 2000), *Xianggang you ge he li huo* (香港有個荷里活, *Hollywood Hong Kong*, 2001), and *San fu* (三夫, *Three Husbands*, 2018). In *Durian Durian*, the friendship between a sex worker named Yan and illegal immigrant girl named Fan in Hong Kong takes center stage, but the film's evocation of Yan's more peaceful life back home in Northeast China subverts the stereotypical idea that Hong Kong is a more desirable city of social mobility for young Chinese women. *Hollywood Hong Kong* further queers the border of the PRC and Hong Kong through the global border-crossing travels of Hung Hung, a sex worker. Finally, *Three Husbands* most daringly symbolizes the geopolitical tension within Hong Kong by showing how the female protagonist, Ah Mui, and her erotic attachments to her first, second, and third husbands conjure the symbolism of Hong Kong mediated by the forces of British colonial legacy, Chinese nationalism, and global capitalism. In a deconstructive queer move, the film also undoes this masculinist positioning of Ah Mui by emphasizing her constant mobility across the human and nonhuman divide through the visuality of water, oceanic current, and spatial unbelonging. Overall, Chan's cinematic aesthetic trespasses the Sinophone border of Mainland China and Hong Kong by queering the border of Chineseness on the Sinophone screen.

As evident in this outline of chapters, *Unruly Comparison* very much engages with a messy, unruly, and minor archive of queer visuality in the vein of what Jack Halberstam calls a queer scavenger methodology.[48] In framing queer Sinophone visuality as an optic for relational comparison that reads wildly across incommensurable histories, temporalities, regions, and archives, my book is further indebted to Gopinath, here to her idea of unruly visions as aesthetic practices that "allow us to see, sense, and feel the promiscuous intimacies of multiple times and spaces."[49] In the epilogue, I perform a final act of unruly comparison by juxtaposing a recent film on homelessness and queer intimacies in Hong Kong following the 2019 protests, *Zhuo shui piaoliu* (濁水漂流, *Drifting*, dir. Jun Li, 2021), with Eric Yip's queer poem "Fricatives" (2021). Both texts disorient the dark political mood of contemporary Hong Kong's nihilism by visually conjuring a queer undercommons not based on homogeneity but incommensurability.

In sum, *Unruly Comparison* demonstrates the possibility of thinking queerness, Hong Kong, and the Sinophone relationally and comparatively. It advances a transdisciplinary and intersectional approach for studying race, gender, sexuality, postcolonialism, and queerness in and beyond Hong Kong. By entangling Hong Kong with the broader Sinophone world, it shows how queer cultural productions "made in Hong Kong" can offer a new model of unruly comparison for queer theory, Hong Kong studies, and Sinophone studies.

1

QUEER HONG KONG AS A
SINOPHONE METHOD
An Archival Undoing

In recent years, queer studies has been embroiled in a "method war." Queer social scientists have been keen to integrate empiricism with the deconstructive thrust of queer studies. Specifically, Amin Ghaziani and Matt Brim write, "'Queering methods' functions as a verb, and it inspires a different question: How can we use queer insights to adjust established protocols in the humanities and social sciences?"[1] A provocative voice in this debate comes from Heather Love, who argues for the value of studying the "behavioral components of experience.... Through its exhaustive, fine-grained attention to phenomena, thin description offers a model for close reading after the decline of the linguistic turn."[2] In other words, thin description draws on the strength of empiricism in the social and behavior sciences and champions the value of it for literary and queer studies, which tend to offer "thick descriptions" of texts and contexts. While the recent turn to theorize the concept of the archive in queer theory does not always feature within this broader debate, I suggest that the "archival turn" in queer studies actually provides a productive angle from which to envision queer Hong Kong as a Sinophone method.

Extending Anjali Arondekar's argument that queerness in the colonial archive often operates through logics of absence and plenitude and that we need to interrogate both the archive's "fictive effects" and "truth effects" as co-constitutive, I turn to Hong Kong literary and cinematic "archives" of queerness to do more than merely uncover the hidden queer past.[3] Instead, through a parallel reading of feminism, lesbianism, and male homoeroticism in the representations of the minor, the affective, and the archival in selected queer literature and films, I show how queer desire and history can impress upon each other through embodied and unpredictable ways. My queer archival hermeneutic here echoes what Gayatri Spivak calls the "singular and unverifiable" force of literature.[4] To elaborate these three interventions on the queer archiving of Sinophone Hong Kong, I first sketch out the ways in which Hong Kong modernity is often narrated through the masculine logic of economic determinism, while pointing to minor gestures, affect, and the archive as queer perversions of the dominant historiography of Hong Kong. Through an aesthetic of unruly comparison, I weave together unruly figures such as lesbian factory workers in 1960s Hong Kong, self-combed women who are textile workers and lesbians from Guangdong on the eve of the Asia-Pacific War, and homoerotic desire between a Hong Kong mafia boss and a Scottish officer during World War II. By purposefully crisscrossing these queer figures into one analytical frame, my unruly comparative methodology forestalls masculinist and recuperative queer historicism that would otherwise recenter gay male homoeroticism. By juxtaposing disparate times and places of Hong Kong modernity in an unruly mode, this chapter queers the archive by undoing conventional forms of narrating queer Hong Kong modernity.

Hong Kong often symbolizes the success of Asian modernity in the global cultural imaginary. The late economist Milton Friedman famously proclaimed Hong Kong the freest market in the world and said: "If you want to see capitalism in action, go to Hong Kong."[5] Historically, Hong Kong represents what David R. Meyer has called "the intermediary of capital," the emporium of trade in the Far East since Britain declared sovereignty over the city in 1841 under the terms of the Treaty of Nanking at the end of the First Opium War (1839–42).[6] For cultural theorist Lisa Lowe, Hong Kong serves as a crucial site for the imperial experiment of free trade and the global coolie trade, both of which are pivotal to the emergence of Western liberal thought and the intimacies of four continents.[7]

Despite the rich dynamics of Hong Kong's historical and cultural encounters with global modernity and its Sinophone articulations, the study of Hong Kong in the humanities and social sciences tends to be confined within two intellectual formations, namely, postcolonial theory and area studies. Within area studies, it is further ghettoized as a "subfield" of China studies.[8] Hong Kong studies has only recently emerged as a legitimate field, thanks largely to the effort of various intellectuals in Hong Kong. Building on Yiu-Wai Chu's recent call to see Hong Kong itself as method, my invocation of "queer Hong Kong as a Sinophone method" theorizes queerness as both the geopolitics of desire in Sinophone Hong Kong as well as the modes of unknowability, opacity, and indeterminacy that expand the spatial and temporal horizons of queer Sinophone critique.[9] Taking my cue from José Esteban Muñoz's phrase, "queerness is not yet here,"[10] and Howard Chiang's concept of transtopia as different "*ways of knowing*,"[11] my formulation also draws on Kuan-Hsing Chen's idea that Asia can be a place for theory without assuming that "Theory" operates through the capital T originating from the West, "for theory too must be deimperialized."[12]

Though previous critics have discussed various iterations of "Hong Kong as method," the point of departure and condition of knowledge remain largely tied either to the 1997 handover, on the one hand, or to the China-centrism and dominance of the current moment, on the other.[13] How might we multiply our existing frames of reference and put Hong Kong into relational comparison with other entities, other histories, and other desires? Relational comparison is an inherently Sinophone project insofar as it looks "at the ways in which texts from different parts of the world are related to each other through their partaking and representation of world historical events."[14] In what follows, I argue that the project of queering Hong Kong modernity must theorize queerness *beyond the logic of performativity* as conventionally understood in queer theory, which postulates that gender identification and sexed bodies are only effects of the repetitive citationality of gendered acts over time within existing laws and discursive regimes.[15] Instead, drawing from an alternative genealogy of queerness, I understand *queer* as the perversity, alternative embodiment, and utopian desire that coexist within neoliberalism, late capitalism, migration, and settler colonialism and yet exceed their epistemological grids and disciplinarity through queer of color and queer Sinophone interventions.[16] In other words, by understanding Hong Kong's in-betweenness as not simply a postcolonial predicament, we can better appreciate its liminal position as structured by multiple power relations: historically by late Qing's geographical marginalization, the British opium trade, and the nineteenth-century global discourse of "free trade"; the brief but violent episode of Japanese occupation (1941–45), US-China Cold War political bifurcation and maneuverings; and post-1997 governance by an increasingly authoritarian PRC.[17] Queering Hong Kong provides a method of reading how social subjects are sexed and gendered within the geohistorical formation of multiple alliances, complicity, and asymmetrical power relations that constitute Hong Kong Sinophone modernity. In turn, queer narratives and cultural productions provide alternative methods of reading minor histories, bodies, and affects, which serve as a queer archival hermeneutics.[18]

My invocation of queer Hong Kong as a Sinophone method highlights the conceptual affinity between Hong Kong studies, postcolonial theory, and queer theory. If the 1990s postcolonial theorizing on Hong Kong demonstrates how Hong Kong-ness is not a given but rather a hybrid or even an impure condition (what Chan Koon-chung elsewhere terms "Hong Kong's bastardization as Hong Kong's authenticity"[19]), queer theory likewise emphasizes that there is no givenness of identity. A queer Sinophone method suggests that both Hong Kong studies and queer theory have much to learn from one another. If a major theoretical move in queer studies in recent years has been the provincializing of Eurocentrism and its critique of queer liberal inclusion in the institution of marriage via queer diaspora and queer of color perspectives, Hong Kong as a historical meeting place for global capitalism without substantial queer liberalism exposes the very unevenness of queer modernity. A queer Hong Kong perspective thus challenges the linear narrative that treats queer rights and inclusion as a logical next step in global capitalism, from which liberalism and neoliberal rights might readily follow. In other words, a place like Hong Kong challenges queer theory to *critique* the critique of queer liberalism and instead to see global capitalism as always already internal to Hong Kong modernity, which then creates uneven experiments and encounters between late capitalism and queerness.

This chapter contributes to these debates on Hong Kong modernity and the universalism of queer theory by drawing on the analytical potential of feminism and queer theory for alternative structures of feeling, what Raymond Williams calls "the affective elements of consciousness and relationships: not feeling against thought, but thought as felt and feeling as thought."[20] In my queer Sinophone comparative method, feminist solidarity during the Asia-Pacific War, lesbian intimacy among working-class women in the 1960s, and interracial desire against the backdrop of multiple empires altogether envision thick textures of affective histories. By turning to these queer modes of affective history, queer Hong Kong as a Sinophone method demonstrates how nonnormative desire and queer affect are, in fact, constitutive of Hong Kong modernity itself. Queer Hong Kong as method thus hails into being an archive of unruly comparison that places incommensurable queer figures alongside each other in order to disrupt the dominant historical materialism of Hong Kong modernity.

To concretize queer Hong Kong as a Sinophone method, I turn to three particular examples that focus on minor acts and gestures, affective history, and the queer archive. These three interventions on the minor, the affective, and the archival suggest that the minor act constitutes the major event as much as the queer constitutes the normative in Hong Kong modernity.[21] First, I examine Wong Bik-wan's 1999 feminist novel *Portraits of Martyred Women*, which marks an ambitious narration of Hong Kong women's lives across three generations through the force of the minor. Namely, the novel narrates feminism and lesbian desire within major Hong Kong historical events in a minor key. In my reading of *Portraits of Martyred Women*, I analyze mainly the first and second segments of the novel, which narrate feminist survival during World War II and lesbian intimacy between two women workers during the 1967 Hong Kong Riots. Taken together, Wong's queer literary interventions signal a disidentification from heteronormative Hong Kong historicism.

Next, I turn to Jacob Cheung's 1997 film *Intimates*, which narrates the romance between two women, a "self-combed" woman and a courtesan, in mid-twentieth-century Shunde, Guangdong, from the perspective of a young woman in contemporary Hong Kong. Self-combing refers to "the lives and life-choices of a group of women called *zishu nü* [自梳女] in the Guangdong Delta region of southern China," who vowed never to marry and who "declared their status as permanently unmarried through a rite which involved combing their hair into a bun similar to that of a married woman."[22] Female industrial participation in the textile and silk industries in Shunde and other Canton regions enabled a large group of women to sustain themselves economically and escape unwanted marriage. As a cultural text that rewrites the regional practice of self-combing to resist heterosexual marriage in Guangdong into a subjugated knowledge of lesbian intimacy during the Asia-Pacific War, the film uses wider spatial and temporal comparisons to provide a queer Sinophone approach to Hong Kong.

Finally, this chapter analyzes Ma Ka Fai's 2016 novel *Once Upon a Time in Hong Kong*, which presents a story of colonial complicity between a Scottish officer working for the British colonial government, Morris Davidson, and a local mafia boss called Luk Naam Coi [陸南才], with whom Davidson has a sexual affair. Ma's novel retells Hong Kong's colonial modernity through a queer Sinophone lens that is mediated by the multiple relations of Chinese political forces and the British and Japanese empires. Overall, Ma's novel demonstrates the possibility of queering the violence of the colonial archive by imagining the protagonists of Hong Kong history as queer.

Wong Bik-wan's Feminist and Queer Cartographies of Hong Kong

Wong Bik-wan is one of the most prolific writers to have emerged from the late 1980s Hong Kong literary scene. Her writings often combine a startling attention to violence with an understated sensitivity to Hong Kong history and politics. In addition, many of the stories, which contain transnational aspects, have been gathered and published in collections such as *Ta shi nüzi, wo ye shi nüzi* (她是女子，我也是女子, She is a woman, I am also a woman).[23] Previous studies of Wong have compared her literary style to that of Zhang Ailing or Lu Xun;[24] or they have used her work to illustrate the figurative language of dark violence more generally.[25] Another strand of scholarship connects Wong's literary representation of violence and tragedy in migration narratives to the very fate of postcolonial Hong Kong, in which migration becomes the last option for many Hong Kong citizens who feel that they are at risk of losing their city in the 1997 return to the PRC. Wong's best-known short story, "Shi cheng" (失城, Losing the city), from her 1994 collection, *Wenrou yu baolie* (溫柔與暴烈, Tenderness and violence), is often read as a postcolonial allegory of migration and exile. Literary critic Xu Zidong even characterizes Wong's text as representative of a genre of Hong Kong literature called the "Nineties Lost City Literature."[26] Of course, the feeling of loss and "no future" resounds even more loudly in the post-2019 present, as Hong Kong experiences the largest ever exodus of citizens migrating to London, Vancouver, Los Angeles, Taiwan, and elsewhere.[27]

There are considerably fewer studies on Wong's treatment of queer desire, and those that undertake a lesbian or queer reading often highlight female homoeroticism as a thematic trope of lesbian memory and temporality, a kind of "backward glance" that characterizes many lesbian stories and films across transnational Chinese cultures.[28] Wong's 1999 feminist novel, *Portraits of Martyred Women*, evokes the force of queer desire and minor gestures of feminist solidarity that resist the conventional gendered and masculine historiography of Hong Kong modernity. The word *lie* [烈], the first word in the novel's Chinese title (*Lienü tu*, 烈女圖), usually connotes a quality of heroism, individual sacrifice for the emperor in Chinese dynastic eras, and those who are deemed fit for enshrinement. In Wong's literary cartography, this normative notion of heroism receives a more humbling and "minor" treatment. The martyred women do not come from the intellectual class of Hong Kong, nor are they patriots who fought the Japanese invasion on the eve of the Asia-Pacific War. Rather, Wong identifies *lie* with the lower rung of society. On the back cover of the novel's 2004 edition, the author describes her tough women as follows: "Born as Chinese women, suffering already is the norm of their lives. No matter what era they live in, Chinese women must always be more enduring, hard-working, and forgiving than their men. Those who could not live have already become dust, and those who endure will survive through each succeeding era."[29] Beyond its conventional designation as piety due to modest and filial modes of conduct, *lie* here points to a politics of surviving through historical and social hardship, compounded by the very fact of being a woman.

Portraits of Martyred Women is full of the trials and tribulations of working-class women who endure violence and marginalization. Take, for instance, the main protagonists Sung Heung [宋香] and Lam Hing [林卿], who are the first wife and the second wife/mistress of Little Moon [阿月仔] in the first segment of the novel. Sung sells cigarettes on the street for a living. Little Moon rarely returns home, and when he makes money, he spends it all on gambling. After he marries Lam Hing, Little Moon further denigrates Sung by telling other folks that she is his "second wife." After Lam gives birth to a daughter, Little Moon abandons both wives and starts courting a dancing girl at the Red Diamond Café. Lam, losing all hope for her life, decides to drown herself in the ocean. Inviting the reader in through a second-person narration, the narrator describes Lam as "your grandmother": "Your grandmother Lam Hing jumps into the sea, kicking a little and swallowing a mouthful of salty water. Help! Your grandmother holds onto the mooring and climbs up. She opens her mouth and breathes in deeply. This is not right! I can't be this stupid. Lion doesn't eat me, Japanese soldiers couldn't kill me, I don't want to die."[30] To be a tough Hong Kong woman during the Japanese occupation is to be self-reliant, because men like Little Moon simply cannot be trusted to provide support, financial or otherwise. Sung even gives Lam the post-birth herbal treatment, their so-called husband nowhere to be found. Toughness here evokes a sense of resilience at the edge of hopelessness—these women know that after the loss of hope they still need to survive and come up with a means for living.

While *Portraits of Martyred Women* is often read as a nonlinear narrative of Hong Kong women's lives with a feminist sensibility, it also constitutes a queer Sinophone method insofar as it maps horizontal alliances among marginalized women, brings into focus minor women's histories, and excavates lesbian intimacies as coexisting with the dominant working-class history of Hong Kong's modernization. Wong's queer Sinophone literary aesthetic is akin to what Erin Manning terms the "minor gesture." Manning writes, "The minor gesture, allied to Gilles Deleuze and Félix Guattari's concept of the minor, is the gestural force that opens experience to its potential variation. It does this from within experience itself, activating a shift in tone, a difference in quality."[31] The minor includes that which is forgotten and cast aside but without which the major and the normative could not come into being in the first place. Wong Bik-wan's attention to the minor gesture is evident in the novel's textualization of lesbian intimacy during the 1967 Hong Kong Riots.

Specifically, as the novel progresses toward the 1960s era of political riots, leftism (mediated by the Cultural Revolution in China), and the rise of working-class women's culture, it imagines queer female solidarity. In the second segment of the novel, "My Mother," the narrative centers on two women, Ngan Ji / Yinzhi [銀枝] and Daai Hei / Daixi [帶喜], whose names literally mean "silver bough" and "bring happiness" or "bring fertility," respectively. Working in a textile factory as part of the growing light manufacturing industry that contributes to the modernization of 1950–70s Hong Kong, these two young female workers commiserate during work and carry out a sisterly romance with homoerotic undertones at night.[32] The narrator observes, "One night, as they walk home after watching a Hollywood film, Daai Hei impersonates the male character in the film and tells Ngan Ji: 'I love you, I will love you my whole life.' Your mother Ngan Ji laughs: We will marry men eventually. Daai Hei wholeheartedly promises: even after marriage, I will still love you . . . the two of them hold hands. If there were no men in this world, how wonderful would it be?"[33] Daai Hei later dons masculine attire, holds a workers' strike on the street, and drops fake bombs on the road during the 1967 Hong Kong Riots. Here, female solidarity is politicized into a "revolution plus queer love" story, with lesbian and female-to-female intimacy existing alongside a more recognizable form of Hong Kong history in the form of movements, riots, and class struggle.

By placing the story of two working-class wives abandoned by their husband during World War II alongside a narrative of lesbian intimacy during the turbulent year of the 1967 Hong Kong Riots, Wong's novel, *Portraits of Martyred Women*, evokes an aesthetic of unruly comparison. It questions the heteronormative and temporal linearity of Hong Kong modernity while positing lesbian intimacy and minor gestures as heuristics for relational comparisons across 1940s and 1960s Hong Kong women's lives.

Intimates: A Lesbian Erotohistoriography of Hong Kong

Jacob Cheung's 1997 film *Intimates* offers another intervention of queer Hong Kong as method: a historiography charged with the power of lesbian erotics across the incommensurable Sinophone geographies of Shunde and Hong Kong. Although this film seems obsessed with a nostalgic past of lesbian desire in the Guangdong region of Shunde, I read it as a cinematic narrative of lesbian intimacy that crisscrosses different nodes of temporality within the wider transpacific spaces of imagination. In other words, queer Hong Kong as a Sinophone method demands that we pay attention to an erotic historiography that narrates desire and affect at the crossroads of empire, war, and migration in an unruly mode.

Intimates begins with a panoramic view of the Tsing Ma Bridge in Hong Kong, set to be completed by 1997 when the region is returned to China. An independent female architect, Wai, leads a team of engineers and instructs them confidently, noting all the errors they have made that have resulted in a big mess that must be cleaned up. One of the engineers is none other than her boyfriend, who will soon leave her for a new girl. Meanwhile, Wai's father gives her the important task of taking an old female servant, Auntie Foon, back to Shunde to seek her elderly relative. The servant is also identified as a self-combed woman. But by the end of the film, we learn that the actual self-combed woman is Auntie Foon's lesbian lover, from whom she has been separated for years due to the Asia-Pacific War. Foon's lover is Yee Foon; "Auntie Foon," whose real name is Yu Wan, was a courtesan who long ago married the owner of the silk factory where all the self-combed women in the village, including Yee Foon, worked. Wai, the young and independent architect, who begins by detesting the old servant Auntie Foon/Yu Wan as old-fashioned, non-modern, and an old virgin who cannot understand her, eventually becomes sympathetic to the past lesbian love deeply shared by Yu Wan and Yee Foon.

How do we understand the intersecting temporalities of contemporary Hong Kong with the past lesbian utopian space of Shunde? What is queer about this lesbian film, and how does it offer a queer Hong Kong method? While Helen Hok-Sze Leung perceptively reads the film's exploration of non-normative sexuality as symptomatic of political anxiety in the moment of handover, I am less concerned with what Leung diagnoses as the film's "failure to articulate the significance of this act [nostalgia/lesbian desire] to the present" than with how the film connects the present Hong Kong with a mode of telling history that is affective and charted through lesbian intimacy.[34] Furthermore, this lesbian erotohistoriography places contemporary Hong Kong and the past Shunde within the material history of female labor, the Second Sino-Japanese War (1937–45), and transpacific mobility—a mode of queer relationality that I term unruly comparison. Queer theorist Elizabeth Freeman defines erotohistoriography as "the way queer relations complexly exceed the present.... [It] produce[s] forms of time consciousness—even historical consciousness—that can intervene into the material damage done in the name of development, civilization, and so on."[35] I extend Freeman's concept to suggest that queer temporality in the film powerfully invokes lesbian affect in the past as a form of reparative and pedagogical practice for seemingly nonqueer desire in the present. Namely, taking care of the emotionally vulnerable Wai reminds Auntie Foon of Yee Foon; similarly, learning of the queer desire between Yee Foon and Yu Wan in the past enables Wai to rethink the limit of heterosexuality in the present. Specifically, in one powerful flashback sequence, the younger Yu Wan is taken to a business meeting in Shunde by her husband, Master Chen, the silk factory owner, to meet a powerful Chinese warlord. During the meeting, Yu Wan rests in a quiet guestroom upstairs, only to find out that in fact her husband has abandoned her for the night as a "gift" for the warlord, whose economic power colludes with the Japanese empire. While Yee Foon, the self-combed girl, accompanies Yu Wan to the meeting, Foon is thrown out of the building by a guard. After two nights of abusive sex, Yu Wan is finally "returned" to her husband only to find out that, despite constant heavy rain, Yee Foon has stayed on the ground outside the guest house, awaiting her release.

After returning home, Yu Wan finds out that while she was being sexually violated by the warlord in return for the business deal, her husband was frolicking with a new mistress. Yu Wan lashes out at her husband: "I was sold to the pander at thirteen; I've tolerated numerous men! Tall, short, old, young.... They don't scare me. I thought I could settle down here under the Chen family's roof, but who knew that this house is a poisonous well!" (See figure 1.1.) This flashback sequence is cinematically interwoven with the present when Wai accompanies Yu Wan, as Auntie Foon, to Shunde at the same time as Wai herself is told by her cheating boyfriend that he has fallen in love with a new woman. Auntie Foon/Yu Wan assumes the intimate role of caring for the young woman (Wai) who numbs herself by drinking whiskey, throwing up, and even at one moment contemplating suicide.

The temporally interwoven structure of the film transforms what seems to be a nostalgic film of lesbian past and ethnographic visuality of the self-

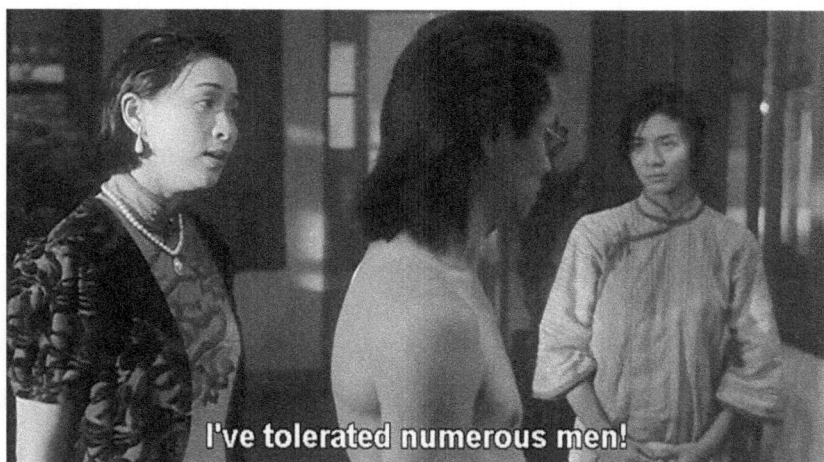

FIGURE 1.1. Yu Wan (*left*) lashes out at Master Chen as Yee Foon (*right*) supports her. Still from Jacob Cheung's *Intimates* (1997).

combing *zishu nu* into a lesson on the possibility and limits of feminism facing women in both the past (in Shunde, China) and the present (in contemporary Hong Kong). About two-thirds of the way into the film, in another flashback, Yu Wan leaves the Chen household and briefly sets up a dumpling stall on the street with Yee Foon. As Japanese forces move south after the Nanjing Massacre, bombs explode in the background. Ironically, it is precisely at this moment of impending war and danger that Yu Wan and Yee Foon share temporary relief from heterosexual domestic violence and betrayal. (Similar to Yu Wan's mistreatment by men, so too has Yee Foon endured hardship. She had once become pregnant after having premarital sex with her first crush, a man named Ah Shing. Ah Shing was too scared to run away with Yee Foon, and soon Yee Foon would attempt suicide, only to be saved at the last moment by Yu Wan.) By the time Yee Foon and Yu Wan relocate to a more urban area of Guangzhou, Master Chen tracks down Yu Wan and persuades her to board, with him, a steamship that will take wealthy Chinese folks to the United States to escape from the war. Yu Wan accepts the ship ticket but swears to Yee Foon that she will board the ship only if Foon comes with her too. At a critical moment in the narrative, Yu Wan is aboard and finds that Yee Foon is still at the dock, held back by police guards. As the ship departs for its destination in America, Yu Wan jumps off the deck, much to Master Chen's surprise, and swims across the ocean to reunite with

Yee Foon. A loud air bomb is heard, and the film narrative shifts back to the present where Auntie Foon is retelling her past life to Wai.

By queering the history of the Second Sino-Japanese War through an aborted transpacific migration to the United States, the filmmaker Cheung visualizes the intimacy of a lesbian utopia precisely at the intersection of war, empire, and diaspora. At once a tale of regional migration, lesbian intimacy, and failed transpacific crossing, the film evokes what Lisa Yoneyama terms "a decolonial genealogy of the transpacific."[36] Yoneyama observes "that 'transpacific' as a critical methodology must mean more than the resignification of movements and interfaces across and within the arena that happens to be called the Pacific."[37] While the film fails to capture how Euro-American interest and participation in "free trade" predates, competes, and collaborates with Japanese occupation during the Asia-Pacific War and the "unredressability" of war crimes after the postwar period, its parallel juxtaposition of lesbian intimacy in both World War II and 1990s Hong Kong seeks to recapture queer female desire from that which was made unknown to "History" with a capital H.

The cinematic enmeshment of Shunde in the past with Hong Kong in the present through a tale of war, migration, and displacement thus focalizes what Shelly Chan terms a "diaspora moment," which "erupts and recurs when diaspora time interacts with other temporalities and produces unexpectedly wide reverberations."[38] In my queer inflection, I am drawn to how these diaspora moments of rupture and discontinuity fracture coherence across bodies, desire, geographies, and Chineseness through queer Sinophone temporality. This is a cinematic temporality of Hong Kong that connects on an intersubjective level; in other words, Yu Wan's past lesbian romance with Yee Foon, the self-combed girl, provides an alternative to the violence of heterosexual marriage in Chen's household, and in turn offers a widening worldview for the contemporary Wai, who is economically independent but powerless in dealing with her boyfriend. Overall, the film narrates the flourishing of lesbianism in the regional space of Shunde, the displacement of the two women and their eventual settlement across Guangdong and Hong Kong due to the Asia-Pacific War, and the subsequent possibility of reunion through the help of a Hong Kong girl. Visually, the frequent uses of flashback sequences and cinematic dissolves disorientingly fuse contemporary Hong Kong femininity (Wai) with queer erotic embodiment in the past Shunde. Thus, the film evinces queer Sinophone temporality as a mode of unruly visuality that both cuts across and unites disparate spatial coordinates, sexual orientation, subjectivity, and temporal scales. It offers queer Hong Kong as a Sinophone method that reads the dense layers and intimacy of human desire across time and space.

Queer Hong Kong as a Sinophone Method: Archive Lost and Found

Ma Ka Fai's novel *Once Upon a Time in Hong Kong* (2016) takes queer Hong Kong as a Sinophone method from the affective register to the archival, demonstrating the extent to which queer desire permeates the very project of narrating Hong Kong history. Furthermore, it shows how literature exemplifies a form of queer literary archive and, in turn, calls into question the very status of a queer archive. Queer Hong Kong as a Sinophone method through Ma's work evinces both the possibility of forming a queer archive and its undoing, what Derrida in *Archive Fever* terms the "institutive and conservative" and "revolutionary and traditional" aspects of archive.[39] It insists that the writing of Hong Kong modernity can be a practice of queer archival hermeneutics.

The novel begins with perhaps the most quotidian form of queer archive: a family story about Ma's grandfather's secret homoerotic past. Throughout, Ma eschews the usual voice of the omniscient third-person narrator and instead infuses his own family history into Hong Kong colonial history. Ma remembers watching his grandfather chewing on a curious, eight-inch-long object while he watches the popular television show *Enjoy Yourself Tonight* [歡樂今宵]. Asked what he is chewing on, the old man replies: "It is cow penis. You are still very young, you don't need it yet."[40] Years later, when Ma is studying in Chicago, his sister reveals that their grandfather had a queer past, confirmed by a photograph of him laying lovingly on the chest of a tall, handsome ship captain during his years of seafaring. Significantly, Ma's grandfather's queer past resurfaces only after his death, when Ma's mother finds the photograph among his remains. Just as *Intimates* fractures the slow and linear temporality of conventional narratives of migration with queer Sinophone temporality, the queer grandfather's diaspora moment of seafaring ruptures the assumed heterosexuality of his life and thus Ma's family history in Hong Kong. Here, Hong Kong history is interwoven with the expansive layers of queer Sinophone temporality globally.

Another kind of queer history appears in an anecdote the grandfather used to tell Ma, about a certain mafia big shot called Whistle Tooth Bing [哨牙炳], who once, during his retirement party, performed a ceremony called "washing the penis in a gold container" [金盆洗撚]. In local Cantonese parlance, "washing one's hands in a gold container" means that one is done with something and ready to retire. It turns out that Whistle Tooth Bing had so many girlfriends and mistresses and that all of them wanted to say farewell to his cock.[41] From this amorous, phallocentric story, we meet Bing's real mafia boss, Luk Naam Coi [陸南才], the protagonist of the novel. As the narrative unfolds, the narrator traces Luk's childhood in Mowming [茂名市], a relatively unknown town in Guangdong, and includes Luk's apparent experience of sexual assault by his older Seventh Uncle; the novel's depiction is ambivalent, and Luk later claims to have enjoyed it. Later, Luk enters an arranged marriage with Ah Gyun [阿娟], who constantly demands sex from him but who doesn't care about Luk's sexual needs at all.

Through twists and turns, Luk leaves for Hong Kong in the 1930s and eventually joins a powerful gang called Hung Mun [洪門], led by Du Yuesheng [杜月笙], a historical figure and KMT general with ties to Triad societies in Shanghai and Hong Kong.[42] Before joining the Triad society and becoming the big boss, Luk works briefly as a rickshaw puller, where he befriends a Scottish police investigator, Morris Davidson, known as Cheung Dik-san [張迪臣] in Cantonese. Davidson works for the British colonial force and will soon become the most important man in Luk's life. Their relationship turns queer one night when, after riding in the rickshaw, Davidson invites Luk home and has sex with him. After that, all the encounters between Davidson and Luk are both erotic and political in nature: Davidson provides information to Luk so that the gang can watch out for police raids, while Luk provides information on suspected Chinese collaborators with imperial Japan.

As this dense and layered narrative demonstrates, Ma's novel embodies several senses of a queer literary archive. The narrative device of using the author's own family history generates a queer archival fever, because the search for the "truth" of his grandfather's sexuality is impossible to resolve. Was his grandfather "gay"? Why did he marry? Does it matter? The depiction of a queer interracial bond between Luk and Davidson then imagines queer affect and sexual encounters at the heart of 1930–40s Hong Kong, a time and place when the city was caught between multiple imperial formations. Like Wong's novel and Cheung's film, Ma's novel invents its own distinctive mode of narrating a queer Hong Kong past. This narrative mode traffics less in the desire to "uncover what really happened" than in the pull to imagine "what could have been"—what feminist historian Tani E. Barlow terms "future anteriority."[43]

Following Ann Laura Stoler's injunction, to "explore the grain with care and read along it first,"[44] reveals how Ma's novel both frames Luk's and Davidson's queer desire as constitutive of the interimperial situation of 1940s Hong Kong and details modes of queer desire that escape normative categorization. First, Ma's novel places queerness at the heart of the interimperial formation that was Hong Kong. Despite its official status—on the eve of the 1941 Japanese invasion—as a neutral zone according to the British defense policy, Hong Kong still functioned, as John M. Carroll relates, as an intermediary and strategic zone where the KMT Nationalists and Communists both built their bases and where pro-Japanese sympathizers built their influence.[45] Hong Kong's situation thus lends itself to a queer method of reading that is attentive to what Laura Doyle terms interimperiality: "a political and historical set of conditions created by the violent histories of plural interacting empires and by interacting persons moving between and against empires."[46]

Reading along the grain suggests that a queer Sinophone method must be attentive to all the complexity, ellipses, ephemeral acts, and affective tensions within interimperiality. In fact, the Chinese title of the novel, 龍頭鳳尾 / *Lung tau fung mei* (in Cantonese), connotes the interpenetrability between queerness and interimperial relations. The narrator describes one moment of queer sexual encounter: "Luk can't refuse but obediently lays down on his bed, giving his whole back to Davidson and willing to be his excited and crying 'bad boy.' Luk Naam Coi is Syun Hing Society's [孫興社] dragon head, but he is also Davidson's phoenix tail" (170). Specifically, while the word *dragon head* [龍頭] is local Cantonese slang for the status of the gang leader, the *phoenix tail* [鳳尾] reference hints at the racialized subject position of Luk as the "bottom boy." The use of the word "boy" here recalls a certain colonial taxonomy, as Black slaves and Native men in North America were often described as boys and considered less masculine within the contexts of slavery and colonialism. If postcolonial theory about Hong Kong hinges on the language of in-betweenness, collaborative colonialism, and hybridity, Ma's novel demonstrates that queerness and the erotics of imperialism in fact take center stage in the interimperial condition. Namely, Luk's own interimperiality—his multiple allegiances to Davidson, to KMT, and to the mafia gang—constitutes him as a particularly useful subject. Furthermore, the novel often evinces queer desire most tellingly when Luk ponders his status as a queer Hong Kong subject against the historical backdrop of the fall of Hong Kong. This queer Sinophone temporality is often narrated with a temporal refraction to his past life in Guangdong in order to show how much he has *become* a queer Hong Kong subject.

If queerness lies at the heart of the interimperiality that is Hong Kong, its place in the archive also escapes normative categorization and traffics in

the realm of what Derrida terms "archival violence."[47] The violence of the archive functions to reduce a queer subject like Luk Naam Coi to the status
of the nonnormative and the perverse, a criminal subject of sexual buggery.
Ma's novel is attentive to this archival violence as well as to the possibility of rupturing the archive to tell something otherwise; and this rupturing
of the archive is crucial to my formulation of "queer Hong Kong as a Sinophone method," which traffics in modes of unknowability, opacity, and indeterminacy. As the Japanese side is about to surrender in 1945, Luk gets hold
of Davidson's whereabouts in the prisoner-of-war camp and tries to use his
influence in the Triad society to help Davidson escape. However, once he is
able to escape and meet Luk in a secret place, it turns out that he has brought
with him another Chinese boy named Aa Ban [阿斌], whom he met and with
whom he shared an intimate relationship while in the prison camp. Enraged
by this betrayal, Luk decides that he will no longer be Davidson's "bad boy."
He promises Davidson to arrange for their escape while informing the Japanese military officers that they can catch both Davidson and Aa Ban at the
Shek Tong Tsui [石塘咀] harbor (315). If what cements the smooth function-
ing of the interimperial logic in the novel is Luk and Davidson's secretive and
queer relation, the rupture of this queer bond also marks the colonized queer
Sinophone subject Luk's desperate attempt to reclaim his masculinity by exposing Davidson's escape plan to another imperial power, the Japanese force.
And while throughout his life Luk seeks to keep his queer relationship with
Davidson under the radar, the final evidentiary revelation of him as queer in
the "official" British national archive turns out to be nothing of importance,
ironically. It marks him as a "perverse" Hong Kong subject who simply happens to share a "perverse" relation with a British officer.

Ma Ka Fai, narrating at the conclusion of the novel in a self-reflexive mode,
tells the reader that he found a document at the British National Archives
that contained the post–World War II legal adjudication of Japanese war
crimes. In the document, one Japanese officer explains why and how he tor-
tures Morris Davidson to death. The justification for Davidson's torture is
that he resists interrogation, and the main reason he resists is that the Japanese officer informs that it was his "Chinese" friend who betrayed him and
notified the Japanese of his escape plan. Davidson reasons that Luk couldn't
possibly have betrayed him because "he is mine." When asked by the British
interrogator whom Davidson claims as "his," the Japanese officer writes down
the name: "Luk Naam Coi." Ma Ka Fai thus concludes the novel: "Dear Boss
Naam, there is god above our heads. No one in the world can live without
leaving a trace. Who really cares? Luk Naam Coi, it is because of me, Ma Ka

Fai, that the old neighbors in Wan Chai will forever remember you, maybe not in the way you want to be remembered" (333). By ending the novel with multiple takes on "the archive," Ma seems to suggest that queer figures like Luk, Davidson, and others are everywhere in the archive of Hong Kong history; but their existence might be seen only as statistics of perversion. Thus, queerness is central to the archive precisely due to its perverse (in)significance.[48] Alternatively, Ma's insistence on telling this story of interracial queer desire at the heart of interimperial Hong Kong also implies that queer desire often emerges through the cracks in the dominant historicism; hence, the act of literary narration begs the critical question of the *what* and the *how* of a queer Hong Kong archive that verges on ethics of unknowability and opacity.

Focusing our attention on queer Hong Kong texts that illuminate the minor gesture, lesbian erotohistoriography, and the queer archive provides some clues about what queer Hong Kong as method can offer to Hong Kong studies, Sinophone theory, and queer studies. A queer Hong Kong method is attentive to the minor gesture of queer desire, which takes the form of feminist solidarity, lesbian intimacy, and interimperial sexuality. It demonstrates how queerness, while often pressed to the fringe of dominant historical narration, also holds critical potential in mapping affective genealogies and clandestine structures of feeling. Queer Hong Kong as a Sinophone method both acknowledges that *queerness is not yet here* (to borrow Muñoz's suggestive phrase again) and insists on the possibility of telling Hong Kong history otherwise, through the expansive horizon of queer temporality. Whereas Wong Bik-wan's novel infuses Hong Kong feminist literary history with the force of the minor, Cheung's film traces the missed connection of queer regionalism across Shunde and Hong Kong through queer erotohistoriography in a transpacific frame. Ma's novel further infuses the official Hong Kong history of Japanese invasion through a queer interimperial framing that ultimately undoes any certainty of archiving a queer Hong Kong. Through the analytic of unruly comparison, other relationalities and imperial asymmetries come into view that question *how* one narrates queer Sinophone Hong Kong.

2

POSTCOLONIALITY BEYOND CHINA-CENTRISM

*South-South Transnationalism and Queer Sinophone
Localism in Hong Kong Cinema*

Hong Kong, as an administrative region of the PRC, a global city in East Asia, and a former British crown colony, always signifies something beyond the existing terminology in postcolonial theory, area studies, and China studies. As I have discussed, within postcolonial theory, Hong Kong often appears as an exception, an anomaly because the once-colonized city is in many respects far more "modern" and developed than its motherland (that is, the PRC) in the post-1997 landscape. The very language of postcolonial hybridity, disappearance, and loss, while bespeaking pessimism in Hong Kong postcolonial theory, might be symptomatic of a broader set of concerns that run deep in any study of post-1997 Hong Kong: the impossibility of approaching Hong Kong without conjuring up that equally illusive entity called "China." Hence, Rey Chow, in a prophetic mode while observing Western media coverage of the climactic event of the handover, astutely called it a "King Kong syndrome." This mode of cross-cultural representation is "aimed at producing 'China' as a spectacular primitive monster whose despotism necessitates the salvation of its people by outsiders."[1]

This chapter draws on two decades of postcolonial theorizing on Hong Kong while suggesting that, rather than indicating an obsessive relation to China-centrism, the queer Sinophone visuality of Hong Kong cinema in the last twenty years expresses a dystopian, rhizomatic, and multidirectional mode of queerness that I term *postcoloniality beyond China-centrism*. In particular, Sinophone studies offers both a relational and a comparative lens on queer Hong Kong cinema vis-à-vis temporal and geographical scales that are often outside the purview of the Britain–China–Hong Kong deadlock. Conceptually, the Sinophone in Shu-mei Shih's framework provides a multidirectional theory that moves beyond binary thinking. As Shih puts it, the Sinophone "can be a site of both a longing for and a rejection of various constructions of Chineseness; it can be a site of both nationalism of the long-distance kind, anti-China politics, or even nonrelation with China, whether real or imaginary."[2]

In other words, while the theoretical idioms of hybridity, in-betweenness, and loss are symptomatic of a Hong Kong culture that finds itself always on the brink of disappearance and political marginalization, the Sinophone can offer alternative ways of dissecting cultural and geopolitical issues facing Hong Kong by invoking a nonrelational approach toward China, with a good dose of queer attitude and playfulness. As a form of postcolonialism beyond China-centrism, queer Hong Kong cinema evinces what Françoise Lionnet and Shih term minor transnationalism, which points to "minor-to-minor networks that circumvent the major altogether."[3] While queer minor transnationalism reckons with the very real force of Chinese capitalism and authoritarian control over Hong Kong, queerness in Hong Kong cinema points precisely to modes of disorientation and transnational and transborder mobility that deviate from the normative geopolitics of British and Chinese influences. In particular, the 1997 queer classic film *Chun guang zha xie* (春光乍洩 / *Happy Together*), directed by Wong Kar-wai, embodies a visuality of minor-to-minor connection that links Hong Kong with Argentina and Taiwan. In so doing, Wong's film unsettles Chineseness through a visuality of nonarrival.

In addition, I examine similar queer nonrelationality to Chineseness as well as possible queer complicity with global capitalism and China-centrism in the rich body of work by Mainland-born Hong Kong queer filmmaker Scud. Scud's films often invite the charge of sexploitation through the camera's obsessive focus on beautiful and muscular male bodies and occasional female nudity. Specifically, the visual focus is often on a young Hong Kong man who is erotically desired by an outsider, whether the outsider is a self-made capitalist from the Mainland or another transnationally mobile and wealthy "Chinese" gay male subject. Given the complexity of Chineseness in Scud's queer oeuvre, both nonrelation to China and complicity with Chinese capitalism are at play, inflecting postcolonialism in the case of queer Hong Kong cinema. It is precisely through this complex configuration of resistance, nonrelationality, and queer complicity that Scud offers a more multidirectional critique for queer Sinophone studies. In what follows, I elaborate on the South-South queer minor transnationalism of *Happy Together*, and I then explore how queer Sinophone desire permeates Scud's 2009 film *Permanent Residence* through both complicity with Chinese capitalism and flexible migration and orientation toward worldly intimacies. The latter part of this chapter unpacks the logics of queer nonrelation to China and Chineseness in Scud's film *Amphetamine* (2010), which maps queer desire and cosmopolitanism across Australia and Hong Kong. In visualizing a model of postcoloniality without dominant Chineseness, an unruly queer approach foregrounds alternative models of Hong Kong transnationalism across worldly geographies and intimacies.

Finally, this chapter considers an emerging body of work by queer lesbian filmmakers in post-1997 Hong Kong that altogether disrupts the gay male cosmopolitanism and neocolonial complicity in Scud's films. In particular, Mak Yan Yan's *Butterfly* (2004) points to a queer regional imaginary across Hong Kong and Taiwan as lesbian desire surfaces from tension between the past and the present and the queer and the heteronormative. Mak's film demonstrates the possibility of queering dominant Chineseness, in this case through a queer regional lesbian aesthetics. By placing the queer diaspora of *Happy Together* alongside the gay male neocolonial complicity of Scud's work and Mak's queer regionalism of lesbian desire, this chapter deploys unruly comparison as a South-South transnational cinematic framework. Namely, it highlights queer desire across incommensurable Sinophone geographies from the late 1990s postcolonial moment to the neoliberal present.

Happy Together and the Queer Sinophone Trajectory of Nonarrival

Wong Kar-wai's 1997 film *Happy Together* tells the love story of Lai Yiu-fai (Tony Leung) and Ho Bo-wing (the late Leslie Cheung), following the gay couple's journey from Hong Kong to Buenos Aires, Argentina. The film is shot mostly in black-and-white, documentary-style close-up shots, with many slow-motion montages. This temporally fragmented style is linked to an almost subliminal emphasis on the power of nature, represented by Iguazu

Falls on the border between Brazil and Argentina, which Lai and Ho desire to witness. The film largely focuses on Lai and Ho's incompatibility: the former is more care-taking, domestic, and faithful, while the latter is sexually perverse, always whiny, and relatively selfish. About two-thirds into the story, the film introduces a young Taiwanese man, Chang (Chang Chen), whom Lai befriends in the Chinese restaurant where they both work. Lai confides his love problems and his eventual breakup with Ho to the young man but never consummates his desire for Chang.

Happy Together is often read through the trope of what Helen Hok-Sze Leung terms the queer undercurrent of postcolonial anxiety, or it is seen as a visual metanarrative of queer postsocialist futurity.[4] Few critics pay attention to the very transnational temporality and geographies that the film traverses. Specifically, the triangular relationship between Ho, Lai, and Chang, queer subjects from Hong Kong and Taiwan, as well as Ho and Lai's occasional sexual encounters with local Argentinian men through cruising, already trouble conventional approaches to the film through the lens of postcolonial anxiety. In the shadow of the looming handover, director Wong Kar-wai expressed anxiety that he wouldn't be permitted to make a film about gay love after Hong Kong's return to China, so "he had to do it now"—meaning before July 1, 1997.[5] However, the film itself arguably bypasses the anxiety of returning to the "motherland" through its expansive focus on the temporality and geography of South-South queer exile and minor transnationalism. Specifically, the film begins with a quick shot in color of Ho and Lai's passports, which indicate their status as "British Nationals Overseas." The visual positioning of Ho and Lai as British Hong Kong colonial subjects and the passport stamps for their entry to Argentina (showing the date of May 12, 1995) mark a certain obsession with time, place, and official history. Specifically, the next scene, one-minute long, is shot in black-and-white and captures a scene of intense sexual intercourse between Ho and Lai in a nondescript motel room that is anywhere and nowhere at once. Here, "realistic" visual details are juxtaposed with nonlinear and an almost nonhistorical emphasis on queer sex. In other words, queer sexuality in the film mediates a form of affect that transcends historical and geographical limits.[6] Following the sex scene, we witness their multiple travel frustrations—such as getting lost and their car breaking down—on the journey to Buenos Aires. But again, immediately after this "realistic" filmic portrayal of their frustrating road trip, which almost causes them to break up, the filmmaker interrupts the narrative through a timeless aerial view of Iguazu Falls with Argentinian music playing in the score.

Given Wong's cinematic juxtaposition of official history (immigration checkpoint), queer sexuality, and the sublime of nature, *Happy Together* thus offers a queer Sinophone worlding of minor transnationalism. In this cinematic worlding, gay men from Hong Kong and more broadly from the geography of Southeast Asia "escape" the city's impending postcolonial handover only to be rejuvenated (or lost) in the sublime power of nature. Jinah Kim and Neda Atanasoski, in analyzing the possibility of postsocialist and decolonizing futurity offered by the film, also argue from the standpoint of South-South transnationalism. They write, "The South-South connection replaces the homonormative couple form; this is one of several moments where the film's queer affect anticipates a queer timespace that is at once haunted by what has been evacuated . . . this is a calling forth of a still-undefined South-South connection through which postcolonial and postsocialist spaces and temporalities are apprehended."[7]

Happy Together's South-South minor transnationalism ends on an even more queer note as Lai, the lone lover who attempts to return to Hong Kong, actually makes a detour to another Southern locale that connotes a different sense of "China." While Lai earns enough money and travels to Taiwan, Ho remains melancholy and alone in the deserted apartment in Argentina. Meanwhile, Chang travels by himself all the way to Tierra del Fuego, disposing of a cassette tape on which Lai has confided (and recorded) his sorrow. The film ends on a slightly optimistic note, with Lai leaving Taipei. En route from Taipei to Hong Kong, Lai boards a subway train, and the film ends on the musical notes of Danny Chung's rendition of "Happy Together." As viewers, we never know whether Lai will arrive in Hong Kong or not.

By weaving together the roots and routes of Ho (forever stuck in Argentina), Lai (detouring through Taipei on the way to Hong Kong), and Chang (seemingly never returning home), *Happy Together* names the sense of traversing the world through a minor transnational mode. This queer minor transnationalism is part of what Karl Schoonover and Rosalind Galt term "queer cinema in the world," namely, "how queer films intersect with shifting ideas of global politics and world cinema aesthetics in order to open out queer cinema's potential to disturb dominant modes of world making."[8] David L. Eng also observes the queer worlding potential of the film beyond normative structures of kinship in anthropological and psychoanalytical theories. Eng writes, "Wong's film thus might be seen as a different type of coming-out narrative: it is a coming out into the world, a 'worlding,' through other forms of psychic displacement."[9]

Building on Eng's psychoanalytical and queer diasporic interventions, I read Wong's film as a queer Sinophone work that evinces unruly deviations from dominant forms of Chineseness. While Ho's pitiable stasis in Argentina disrupts the model minority myth of Asian immigrants in conventional narratives (that of upward social mobility), Lai and Chang's queer diasporic deviations from their respective homelands also posit a queer Sinophone nonrelationality to "the Chinas." In other words, the film models a postcoloniality beyond China-centrism through its traversing of multiple South-South transnational geographies and the juxtaposition of Hong Kong, Argentina, and Taiwan. By retheorizing *Happy Together* beyond postcolonial anxiety and in-betweenness, we can appreciate the ways in which minor transnationalism activates desire in the most unlikely places—on a road trip from Hong Kong to Argentina, across the absent space of Iguazu Falls that never becomes a reality (the couple never get there), and through the melancholy soundscape of Lai's weeping voice on the cassette tape, now disposed of in Tierra del Fuego, an archipelago off the southernmost tip of the South American mainland.

Capitalism, Complicity, and Queer Nonrelationality to China in Scud's Films

An emergent body of queer Hong Kong films also turns inward from queer transnationalism into the actually existing time-space of postcolonial Hong Kong. The city in these post-handover films turns out to be driven by real-estate speculation, financial insecurity, and crisis (the 1997 and 2008 financial crises) as well as by the impossibility of remaining "local" forever (given the influx of new immigrants from the Mainland). In particular, Scud's films explore diverse topics such as adolescent gay love and bisexuality in a Hong Kong baseball team (*City without Baseball* [無野之城], 2008); a queer coming-of-age story of financial success and lamentation on life, death, and queer love (*Permanent Residence* [永久居留], 2009); a fatal romance between an Australian cosmopolitan gay man and a local Hong Kong working-class man that verges on mysticism and postmodernism (*Amphetamine* [安非他命], 2010); and an anti-romance film titled *Love Actually . . . Sucks!* [愛很爛] (2011).

Traveling mostly on the international gay and lesbian film festival circuits, Scud's films have gathered a cult fan base devoted to queer independent and arthouse films. Remarkably, Scud has been able to set up his own production firm, Artwalker, and relies on various independent funding sources. This fiscal independence positions his films outside of the Hong Kong–China coproduction CEPA (Closer Economic Partnership Arrangement) formula and partakes of what Mirana M. Szeto has termed "Hong Kong SAR (Special Administrative Region) New Wave."[10] This cinema "tends to offer a more horizontal, inter-local, quotidian and hybrid set of cultural politics that are decidedly Sinophone. . . . Hong Kong SAR New Wave positions itself against (1) the kinds of hegemonic masculinities that have defined the Hong Kong gangster film, *Kungfu* film and killer film, (2) the kind of masculinity expected of discourses about the rising China and its modern national traumas, and (3) the new hegemonic 'neoliberal masculinity' representative of Hong Kong as a global financial market."[11] However, given that Scud's cinema often includes queer figures who benefit from the tidal wave of capitalism and neoliberalization since Hong Kong's return to China—even as his films thematically disentangle queer love from capital accumulation—his work may offer an even more nuanced diagnosis of queer complicity and Sinophone articulations within the Hong Kong SAR New Wave genre.

Permanent Residence begins with a close-up shot of a page in a diary, indicating that "today" is already June 13, 2047—the year when Hong Kong's promised high degree of economic and political autonomy will come to an end as stipulated in the Sino-British Joint Declaration of 1984. From this futuristic visual beginning, the film jumps back in time to narrate the life of the gay male protagonist Ivan (played by newcomer Sean Li). Beginning with his childhood at the end of the Cultural Revolution and his close relationship with his grandmother in Guangzhou, we see his coming-of-age in Hong Kong and his successful career as an IT software engineer. In fact, Ivan becomes so successful that he is featured in a TV interview with a fellow gay engineer, Josh (Jach Chow), with whom he shares a brief fling. Eventually, Ivan meets "the love of his life," Windson (played by Osman Hung, of the local band EO2). Ivan and Windson's romance borders on bisexuality and revolves around the tragic dilemma of a gay man, Ivan, falling for a straight boy, Windson. Ivan's love for Windson is frustrated by the fact that while Windson is willing to let Ivan anally penetrate him as a bottom, he never agrees to penetrate Ivan, despite Ivan's repeated request. Strangely enough, refusing to assume the role of a top is a way for Windson to keep his heterosexuality intact. The film eventually shows Windson committing suicide in despair over his unconsummated love for Ivan shortly after their reunion later in life. Years later, in 2047, Ivan comes up with a plan to die in a coffin he has designed himself, in a luxurious house in Hong Kong, thus alluding to the film's title of "permanent residence."

Central to the cinematic intersection of queer love and the return of Hong Kong to China is the role of queer complicity with capitalist normativity. Specifically, the color palette in the first fifteen minutes of the film, which portrays Ivan's birth and early life in a village in Guangzhou, is often gloomy. Ivan develops an obsession with keeping a diary, which records monumental and small details that traverse the historical and the personal, including Deng Xiaoping's announcement of the One Country, Two Systems doctrine in Hong Kong in 1984; Mike Tyson becoming the new heavyweight world champion in 1986; and the relatively queer local history of the 1991 decriminalization of sodomy in Hong Kong. At work, Ivan models a workaholic *Homo economicus* lifestyle, turns down invitations for dates from his female coworkers, and indeed outperforms many of his white expat colleagues.

Fifteen minutes into the film, when Ivan finally purchases his own apartment, the scene shifts sharply into fully bright coloration. Ivan is so thrilled with his achievement that he takes off all his clothes, runs around the empty but well-designed apartment, and even flexes his muscles, naked, while facing Victoria Harbor in the middle of the day! While this early narrative segment of queer economic success and entrepreneurial self-making verges on narcissism and normative masculinity, it also reveals Hong Kong-ness itself as a flexible and fungible identity formation for Ivan. In other words, becoming a Hong Konger for him involves a gradual movement away from a Mainland Chinese identity to one that is more worldly and Sinophone. Specifically, Shumei Shih lays out the open-endedness of Sinophone linguistic communities and privileges becoming and plasticity as the conditional possibility of the Sinophone. Shih writes, "Sinophone studies takes as its premise the plasticity of Sinitic languages to no predetermined destinies, even to the extent that the field of Sinophone studies might reach its demise at the limit."[12]

Shih's argument that the Sinophone is a multidirectional nexus of power relations that is at the same time open to its own plasticity critically draws attention to the ever-shifting morphology of linguistic community as it anchors to race, geography, body, and capital. These mutational factors are all central to the formation of local community in and beyond Hong Kong. Similarly, Ivan's childhood memories, narrated in southern-accented Mandarin; his high school life, narrated in Mandarin-accented Cantonese; and the very embeddedness of his life (via the act of diary writing) with political events both in and outside China and Hong Kong reveal the co-constitutive convergence of global identity and multiple local articulations of cosmopolitan Hong Kong-ness. Here, becoming a Hong Konger for Ivan also involves a neoliberal and homonormative life story of successful capital accumulation and masculine self-making in Sinophone Hong Kong. Put differently, the film's multilingual and cross-border queer life trajectory compels viewers to rethink the intellectual condition of "including China" within the gendered geopolitics of China-centrism, in which migration, border-crossing, and flexible citizenship are attached to modes of becoming Hong Kong subjects.[13]

Queer complicity with neoliberal market logics heavily marks the intimate relationship between Ivan and Windson, even as their romance forges a cross-border network of queer kinship and affiliation. Specifically, the first scene that cements the bond of erotic brotherhood between the two young men happens when Ivan is confronted by an Israeli IT engineer, Josh (Ivan's short-term fling and later queer confidant), with the question of whether he is gay or not. The question makes Ivan suspect he may display some kind of "gay" or "sissy" characteristics and leads him to work out his already muscular body even harder. Ivan and Windson's first erotic encounter happens in an elite local athletic facility called South China Athletic Association (SCAA). In the sauna room, Windson, the tan and equally muscular guy, suddenly performs several flying roundhouse kicks and drops his towel, resulting in full frontal nudity for Ivan's (and the viewers') visual pleasure. The two strike up a conversation after the gym and decide to deepen their friendship another night by swimming naked in the Repulse Bay area. While Windson claims to have a girlfriend named Kelly in Mainland China, she never actually appears on screen. Meanwhile, Ivan has become such a close friend of Windson that he offers to pay all medical expenses for Windson's mother, who suffers from lung problems and eventually passes away about two-thirds of the way through the film. Ivan's close bond with Windson's mother begins just after his own grandmother passes away in Guangzhou.

How do we understand the convergence of neoliberal masculinity, horizontal gay friendship, and alternative queer kinship? At what point does Ivan and Windson's relationship cross from the sexual into the familial realm? It is tempting to analyze the two queer men's intimate bonds through the concept of homonormativity, which Lisa Duggan defines as the ways in which "'equality' becomes narrow, formal access to a few conservatizing institutions, 'freedom' becomes impunity for bigotry and vast inequalities in commercial life and civil society, the 'right to privacy' becomes domestic confinement, and democratic politics itself becomes something to be escaped."[14] However, the fact that Hong Kong lacks legal and political inclusion and protection for LGBT subjects across many issues like gay marriage, antidiscrimination laws, and queer immigration rights suggests that *homonormativity* is insufficient for naming the complex dynamics between Ivan and Windson. A queer Sinophone framework can demonstrate how economic life and complicity are compensatory in the absence of formal queer equality. In turn, this neoliberal governmentality of the self is inextricable from queer alternative kinship arrangements like caring for a lover's mother. Within these queer social bonds, intersectional tensions and possibilities emerge at the nexus of queer complicity, capital accumulation, and alternative kinship bonds. And all this happens in a city that is increasingly mediated by cross-border romance, real-estate speculation, and income inequality—social conditions that make queer love and queer life an almost impossible option.[15]

Permanent Residence offers its most powerful visual entanglement of queer complicity and worldly intimacy when it connects disparate locations such as Hong Kong, Thailand, and Israel, all sites that have endured various colonial regimes or that still practice brutal settler colonialism. Right after Ivan's grandmother passes away in Guangzhou, he needs emotional support. But Windson alienates Ivan by talking about the need to marry his girlfriend in Mainland China because he is, after all, a real heterosexual man. After an emotional battle with Windson, Ivan is contemplating suicide when a phone call from Josh, in Tel Aviv, saves his life. Ivan then visits Israel, makes a pilgrimage to Jerusalem, and enjoys a day of meditation floating on the Dead Sea with Josh. Right before his trip to Israel, Ivan also embarks on a brief trip to Bangkok and enjoys a night of random hook-ups at a gay bar. The visual tourist gaze across incommensurable locales implicates the queer capitalist subject, Ivan, within the mobility of queer capital and erotic fulfillment at the expense of the actual sexual exploitation that happens every day in Bangkok and the military occupation of Gaza (figure 2.1). Yet, it is precisely through Ivan's partially colonial gaze that viewers become aware of how he, the queer Hong Kong capitalist originally born in Mainland China, can in fact partake of various forms of queer mobility and cosmopolitanism through necropolitics, that is, the necessary debility and destruction of other subjects already destined for slow death and unending violence.[16] Scud's film thus ironically reminds us that the "permanent residence" of some queers is in fact co-constituted by the unending rootlessness, un-belonging, and the valuelessness of other subjects. *Permanent Residence*, in its aesthetic lamentation on death, Hong Kong, and ongoing violence in other parts of the world, offers a queer visual statement on colonial occupation, pinkwashing, and necropolitics.[17] Indeed, a retheorization of the Sinophone and its relevance to Hong Kong studies through the optic of queer complicity can draw our attention to the possible intersection of Sinophone studies and the emerging body of work on decolonial critique.[18]

If *Permanent Residence* reorients viewers to the absent presence of ongoing colonial violence through the unruly comparison of Hong Kong, Main-

基督教 伊斯兰教 犹太教的圣地
The holy place for Christian,Islam and Jews

FIGURE 2.1. Ivan and Josh overlook the Dome of the Rock in Jerusalem. Stills from Scud's *Permanent Residence* (2009).

land China, Thailand, Israel, and Palestine, *Amphetamine* returns to Hong Kong as a site of internal class segmentation and neocolonial capitalism. The film narrates the stormy relationship between a straight man, Kafka (Bryon Pang), and a Hong Kong–born Australian gay expat Daniel (Thomas Price). Kafka is a swimming instructor who is in a relationship with a Mainland Chinese woman. However, after meeting Daniel he becomes attracted to him. Beyond their difference in class and local versus cosmopolitan upbringings, they both indulge in consuming amphetamines (also known as *speed* or *ice*). While Daniel at various points tries to "save" Kafka from overconsuming the drug, the film ends with Kafka's death while Daniel embarks on a new journey.

The film opens with a slow-motion shot of the protagonist Kafka standing naked on the roof of a building overlooking the iconic Victoria Harbor. The young man wears zombie-like makeup with his hair dyed silver. He is also wearing a pair of angel wings and posing as Michelangelo's *David*. This surreal and corporeally charged opening shot in fact foreshadows the film's ending, in which Kafka's stormy relationship with Daniel, a handsome investment banker, goes wrong and leads to Kafka's suicide. The next shot presents an equally elusive vision of a dark whirlpool of ocean water that gradually calms into ripples. At the end of the ripples, a mystical and ghostly figure in a white medical robe escapes the whirlpool and flies up into the middle of the camera's frame like an angel. The film's third sequence presents another breath-taking night view of Victoria Harbor from inside a taxi, capturing in particular the SCAA building (where Ivan first meets Windson in *Permanent Residence*—perhaps a playful attempt at queer intertextuality by the filmmaker?). The conversation between the taxi driver and Daniel reveals that the action in the film takes place amid the 2008 financial crisis. When asked by the taxi driver what his profession is, the Hong Kong–born Australian expat nonchalantly replies, "I work in finance."

The rest of the film paints the blossoming of the queer romance between the two young men. At the outset, Kafka and Daniel's lives could not be more drastically different in terms of social position and sexual orientation. Kafka works as a swim instructor at the SCAA, earning a salary that hardly sustains him—and from which he must also pay for his mother's medical expenses. Daniel, by contrast, hangs out regularly at upscale cafés and cocktail bars with his coworkers, whose profession as investment bankers "banks on" the very volatility of the stock market and real estate market during the economic crisis. In fact, the first encounter between Daniel and Kafka is filmed through a point-of-view shot from Kafka's perspective in which Daniel's coworkers chat about how cheap cars are now in Hong Kong and suggest that he purchase a sports car before going back to Australia, pointing at a showy yellow Porsche that has just parked on the street. Daniel, however, only half pays attention to this conversation as he has set his sights on a much more alluring object of desire: Kafka. Kafka is waiting for his girlfriend, May, at the bar. When she arrives, they quarrel with each other in Mandarin, establishing May's Mainland cultural identity.

The next scene shows Daniel indeed driving a yellow Porsche. The two men encounter each other again at a local temple, where both draw Chinese fortune sticks [求籤 / *kau cim*]; the very act of fortune telling or speculation is linked symbolically to the uncertainties of both eros and economy. The next morning, Daniel waits for Kafka outside his public housing estate. He tells Kafka that he has a day off work and offers to take him to the swimming pool in Causeway Bay where he works as a swimming coach. During the brief car ride, several important facts emerge. Daniel actually grew up in Shek O, a remote beachside village in Hong Kong and immigrated to Australia when he was fifteen. When Kafka inquires whether Daniel has come back to Hong Kong because he has dated all the boys "over there" already, Daniel is taken aback and asks: "Do I look gay?" Daniel resolves the awkward conversation by assuring Kafka that he doesn't care if Kafka is gay or not. Kafka responds in a sarcastic manner that focalizes queer complicity with global capitalism: "Buying whatever you crave, chasing whoever you fancy. Money really is power." Indeed, the rest of the film depicts an unequal and erotically charged queer romance as Daniel gets more attached to Kafka, finds out that his lover is addicted to amphetamines, tries to "save him" but gets addicted himself, and ultimately returns to Australia because he finds Kafka too difficult to love.

If the previous discussion of the visuality of the absent presence of settler colonialism and worldly intimacies in *Permanent Residence* demonstrates that Scud's cinema is attuned to issues of queer complicity and ongoing colonial violence, here coloniality takes on an economic and erotic dimension. Specifically, Daniel's mixed cultural background, his flexibility in maneuvering the economic downturn of Hong Kong to his own advantage, and his unequal relationship with Kafka are all factors that cement their romance in the first place. Hence, Daniel's Sinophone subjectivity as an inside outsider speaking Cantonese with an Australian accent points to his linguistic and social porosity across the transpacific regionalism of Hong Kong and Australia as well as to his flexible citizenship, what Aihwa Ong characterizes as "the cultural logics of capitalist accumulation, travel, and displacement that induce subjects to respond fluidly and opportunistically to changing political-economic conditions."[19]

But it would be too simplistic to restrict the conceptual rigor of queer Sinophone studies to the task of diagnosing the exploitation of the local Hong Kong gay boy by the inhabitant of global hegemony simply because of Daniel's Australian cultural capital. Another conversation between the two (during another car ride) concerns the very name of our local Hong Kong gay boy. Kafka tells Daniel that he was given the name by his sword-fighting *Kungfu* master, and he believes that it is a Japanese boy's name. Daniel relates his lover's name to *Kafka on the Shore*, the novel by contemporary Japanese writer Haruki Murakami. Of course, the name also suggests a possible homage to the Jewish writer Franz Kafka, whose writings often fuse elements of realism with the fantastic in ways similar to the film's gradual turn toward the blurring of reality and fantasy. Employing a queer Sinophone lens to dissect the film's multiple references and the intersection of queer love, neoliberal capitalism, and queer complicity thus troubles the neat division between Australia and Hong Kong and the global-local dichotomy. It brings to mind Ackbar Abbas's provocation that "the local is *already a translation*."[20]

If economic gap, social difference, and linguistic flexibility both cement and separate the queer bonds between Kafka and Daniel, the film's aesthetic fusion of the real and the fantastic seems to promise alternative modes of intimate futurity. As the two stroll along the river in one scene, the construction of the Stonecutters Bridge is in full view; they can see that a final piece is lacking, exposing a gap in the structure. Daniel remarks tellingly, "Maybe when the bridge meets, there'll be no gap between us." Another scene about forty minutes into the film shows the two men taking a boat ride under the partially finished bridge after getting high. The blurred focus captures cinematically the hallucinatory effect of amphetamines; at this moment, the viewers are seeing through the eyes of Kafka and Daniel. Not only are Kafka and Daniel's close bonds enabled by the drug, but we as viewers are temporally held under the effect of the drug as well. Such a queer and hallucinatory vision aligns closely with what Abbas terms the cultural politics of disappearance. Reversing Abbas's "reverse hallucination [of] *not* seeing what *is* there," Hong Kong New Wave films by directors such as Wong Kar-wai and Stanley Kwan seek to make visible our blindness to the vibrant Hong Kong cultural landscape in the midst of postcolonial transition.[21] Here, Scud's film implies that perhaps Hong Kong, after ten years of governance by China, is increasingly made high by liquid capitalism fed on by the most extreme real-estate land development regime in the world.[22] Precisely because of our habitual addiction to the capitalist way of life, a queer Sinophone vision must counter our myopia by turning to corporeal hallucination, drug addiction, and queer risk as bold chances for cultural survival, namely, learning the difficult task of queer love in a city that is otherwise economically unsustainable.

The closing sequences of *Amphetamine* hinge on queer utopian longing as an alternative Sinophone ontology of being. During the Christmas party Daniel hosts at his luxurious apartment with rooftop access, Kafka is once again under the influence of drugs. Encouraged by the cheers and excitement of the guests, Kafka takes off his clothes and performs some acrobatic moves. The guests paint Kafka's naked torso silver to show off his muscular glory. However, this moment of ecstasy forces Kafka to recall a traumatic moment earlier in his life when his body was abjectified in a gang rape by a local mafia gang. The next morning, Kafka stands on the rooftop with angel wing feathers that must have been decorated by the party guests. At this moment, he is under the false belief that he is an angel himself. He eventually jumps off the roof, but luckily Daniel discovers his body just in time to send him to the emergency room. As Kafka recovers consciousness after his injury, he escapes the hospital to find out whether the gap in the Stonecutters Bridge has been completed; to his relief, the gap is still there. Kafka's obsession with the construction of the bridge shows that he might psychically associate the closing of the gap with his possible submission to Daniel to be anally penetrated,

FIGURE 2.2. Under the effect of amphetamine, Daniel finally caresses Kafka. Stills from Scud's *Amphetamine* (2010).

which also arouses his trauma of having been raped. Such a conflation between the completion of the bridge and anal sex might not be far-fetched, as the local Cantonese phrase *to bridge* [接通 / *zip tung*] also phonetically links to the act of anal sex, at least in this filmic context: 通屎忽 [*tung si fat*] is vulgar Cantonese slang that describes someone fucking someone's ass.

The last moment of the film powerfully heightens the tensions and (im)possibility of love between Kafka and Daniel through the optic of queer complicity and global mobility. As Daniel takes a taxi to the airport for a flight back to Australia, Kafka contemplates a final act of jumping into the ocean through the gap between the incomplete sides of the bridge. He eventually jumps into the dark oceanic water at night; under the hallucinatory effect of amphetamines, Kafka imagines his naked body finally caressing the naked body of Daniel (figure 2.2). However, this is obviously a queer fantasy all in Kafka's own mind as Daniel is embarking on his journey home, where "home" might signify Australia more so than Hong Kong—or it could be whatever destination in Asia next finds itself in financial crisis, with equally desperate gay young men in need of queer salvation. Through this powerful juxtaposition of a fantastical oceanic queer union and the realistic act of separation, the last filmic image of a dark whirlpool is followed by a final caption, which reads "Kafka Tam, 1982–2008." Kafka's queer fantasy results in his own death at the age of twenty-six.

If Scud's films visualize the aesthetics of unruly comparison through the cinematic entanglement of gay male cosmopolitanism with neoliberal capitalism and imperial tourist gazes, Mak Yan Yan's film *Butterfly* offers an alternative queer Sinophone localism mediated by lesbian memory, political activism, and Hong Kong-Taiwan regional connections. It is part of a regional cinematic approach that understands transnationalism through the re-localizing of cultures. While dominant theorists of transnationalism resort to languages of global disjuncture, flexible migration and citizenship across nation-states, and the center-periphery dynamics of the capitalist world system, they tend to focus attention on large-scale phenomena across East-West and North-South divides and overlook the interregional dynamics within Asia.[23] Therefore, other scholars have more recently turned to the possibility of studying Asian regional connections via East-East and South-South cultural flows dating back as early as the sixteenth-century China-centric tributary system in the silver trade.[24] Likewise, Prasenjit Duara calls for the study of contemporary forms of Asian regionalism accelerated by flows in media and technology across Asian global cities because, he argues, "region formation in Asia is a multipath, uneven, and pluralistic development that is significantly different from European regionalism."[25] Certainly, queer culture actively participates in the interregionalization of culture happening through twenty-first-century Asian connections across the borders of the nation-state. This regional route of Asian transnationalism also means that Hong Kong cultural producers may find inspiration for making films from other Sinophone sources, whether on the Mainland or in Taiwan. (One well-known example of this interregional queer cultural production is Stanley Kwan's film *Lan Yu* (2001), based on a 1997 Mainland story published anonymously online.)

While Mak's *Butterfly* is funded mainly by Hong Kong sources, including the Hong Kong Arts Development Council and Filmko Entertainment, its content is based on a 1996 novella by Taiwanese lesbian writer Chen Xue. Mak's film title is adapted from Chen's story, "The Mark of the Butterfly" [*Hudie de jihao*], in the collection of stories titled *Butterfly* [*Hudie*]. The film, like the novella, tells the story of Flavia (also called Xiao Die; *die* means butterfly in Chinese), a young housewife living a mundane, bourgeois life until she happens to see a girl, Yip, eating cookies without paying for them at a local supermarket. Yip has been kicked out of her home by Rosa, her ex-girlfriend. In the film she is a musician based in Wuhan, a city in central China, while in Chen's novella Yip is described simply as an eighteen-year-old girl. Flavia and Yip fall in love, and Flavia must juggle her identities as a young married mother and a lesbian. Yip reminds Flavia of her unrequited high school romance with Jin, a tomboy who is also a political dissident, and the film constantly shuffles between the past, shot in Super-8 film, and the present, shot in 35-mm film. Meanwhile, Flavia's troubles with her husband, Ming, run parallel to the long-term marital problems of her own parents. When Flavia was young, during the time when she dated Jin, her father was having an affair; now, years later, her mother is asking for a divorce. At the end of the film, Flavia decides to leave her family and pursue happiness with Yip. The film concludes on a hopeful note, with both women sitting on the balcony under a bright afternoon sun.

While adaptation from literature to film always runs the risk of being "unfaithful" to the original text, Mak creatively balances the task of sticking to Chen's Taiwanese story, on the one hand, and inserting the local Hong Kong flavor of lesbian historiography, on the other. One example of the complex decisions Mak makes concerns the parental parallel subplot and queer desire. Mak's adaptation fails to include one aspect of the mother's story: in Chen's novella, Flavia's mother also has a lesbian relationship later in life. In one scene, Flavia and Yip meet with Flavia's mother, who brings along an older woman. Chen narrates, "A very interesting scene. Mother brings a woman who looks like forty something years old. . . . Yip is staying with me, and all of us seem to have known each other for a long time, even though this is our first meeting. I suddenly realize; my mother is facing the same situation as me."[26] The scene in the film that comes closest to challenging the patriarchal meaning of home, although it leaves the gender of Flavia's mother's lover unspecified, still points to the hypocrisies of patriarchal entitlement. Specifically, Flavia's mother asks for a divorce in front of her children. She confesses: "Yes, I am with somebody else. I want to get out of here." Flavia's father as patriarch challenges her: "Aren't you ashamed talking like that in front of your children?" The mother logically responds: "Aren't you ashamed of fooling around with women in front of Flavia in the past?"

In Mak's rendition, the viewers never learn that the mother's lover is a lesbian. In fact, the lesbian mother quite literally disappears from the film altogether in what might be a "safe" choice in marketing the film to transnational audiences. One possible interpretation is that portraying a lesbian mother with a lesbian daughter might provoke discomfort among older generations of Chinese viewers, who might be sympathetic to a lesbian coming-out story but less so to a lesbian-mother coming-out story. And if my reading about the pitfalls of adaptation makes any sense, the film indeed reconciles Flavia with the father figure because she never severs ties with her father. Indeed, one scene lovingly shows Flavia and her father sharing afternoon tea, a local Hong Kong tradition. The father offers her the pineapple bun, a favorite local sweet, which Flavia enjoys—just as she did as a child.

While the politics of re-localizing the film and catering to Sinophone audiences may compromise the more radical potential of queering the patriarchal core of the family, Mak's creative Sinophone localization of Chen's novella offers some critical possibilities for narrating a Hong Kong lesbian past and a utopian future as alternatives to the confines of heterosexuality. As both Helen Hok-Sze Leung and Fran Martin point out in their readings of the film, while the Super-8 stock depicting nostalgic scenes predominates in the beginning of the film, emphasizing Flavia's past traumatic romance with Jin, the film eventually shifts to portray her past memories in 35-mm stock and the present love affair with Yip in Super-8.[27] This cinematic technique of entangling the present with the past blurs the very temporal distinction between a lesbian adolescence and the present. Leung's convincing analysis emphasizes that what Mak's film and Chen's novella invite us to think about is not so much a lesbian coming-out story but the story of a lesbian coming back to herself.[28]

However, it would be a mistake to reduce Mak's film to a native, purely local Hong Kong version of Chen's Taiwanese story because part of Flavia's memory also connects her personal lesbian past to the larger collectivity of Hong Kong citizens protesting against the Mainland's suppression of the student movement. Her vivid memories of her former lover Jin recur again and again, detailing Jin's frequent participation in Hong Kong activism against the Mainland Communist government after the bloody crackdown in Tiananmen Square on June 4, 1989. This part of the film is Mak's own insertion of a local Sinophone narrative; it is not part of Chen's original story. By inventing Jin as a lesbian activist figure and through Flavia's recurring memories of Jin's political identity, Mak's film infuses politics with lesbian identity and suggests that there are still more stories to be told beyond a conventional political historiography that places masculinist leadership (e.g., Mao Zedong in Communist China) at the heart of a political movement. Mak's invention of a political lesbian past suggests that it is precisely by remembering a critical lesbian "history" that Flavia can claim her own present and future identity as a lesbian subject. The fact that a lesbian reinterpretation of Mainland politics becomes a central narrative thread in Mak's film also renders impossible a merely localist Hong Kong reading of the film. Consequently, the film can be read as containing Taiwanese "roots," exhibiting Hong Kong flavor, and offering a Sinophone critique of authoritarian forms of Chinese nationalism all at once.

Indeed, the locational politics of the film seems to shift from site to site, from its literary origin in Taiwan, to its filming of streets in Hong Kong, and finally to a more imaginary and utopian elsewhere in the end. In a passionate scene with Yip, Flavia lies on the bed with her and picks up a black marker. She uses the marker to draw the shape of a butterfly on her lover's chest, indicating that her love is forever marked on Yip's body. The next scene is the last, in which both of them sit at the edge of the balcony, toss their slippers, and let them fall to the ground below. In the original text by Chen, Yip tells Flavia about the quintessential meaning of Flavia's Chinese name, *hudie*, or "butterfly": "Butterfly cannot be butterfly if it doesn't fly."[29] The film does not end with this revelation; however, in its Sinophone localization of two women enjoying each other's presence amid the crowded Hong Kong landscape, it seems that both have already flown away from the confines of heterosexuality to a utopian lesbian "home" elsewhere.

Hong Kong, Queer Sinophone Studies, and Worldly Intimacies

Through the representations of separation and togetherness, realism and fantasy, and global mobility and local poverty, *Amphetamine* injects queer Sinophone visuality with the analytical acumen of neoliberal capitalism and queer complicity. By contrast, Mak Yan Yan's *Butterfly* evinces a particular queer Sinophone localism and regionalism that points to how queer lesbian subjects in postcolonial Hong Kong negotiate the politics of late capitalist heteronormative space, neo-Confucianist kinship, China-centric politics, and historical violence. At the present moment, Hong Kong finds itself increasingly under the influence of late capitalist processes of regionalization and incorporation into the geopolitics of the PRC through what Wai Kit Choi terms the "postcolonial state of exception," as "a city colonized by multinational corporations and transnational governing bodies dominated by the core capitalist states."[30] While Hong Kong is indeed a Sinophone region of both inclusion in the PRC and exception (in terms of freedom of expression, relative judicial autonomy and rule of law, and free market economy), a simplistic application of the state of exception theory confined to the tri-formula of China–Hong Kong–global capital may overlook the kind of minor-to-minor, South-South, and transnational scales through which queer desire, bodies, and complicity become entangled with one another.

By invoking the monikers of "postcoloniality beyond China-centrism" and queer Sinophone "localism," this chapter attempts to map a way out of the cultural logics and perpetual obsession of arguing whether Hong Kong is included or excluded by China, or whether Sinophone studies in the case of Hong Kong should include or exclude China.[31] A more productive way to parse the possible linkage between the Sinophone, queer theory, and Hong Kong is to engage in broader frames of reference and comparison through the concept of minor transnationalism. A queer Sinophone studies informed by minor transnationalism makes visible the inextricability of mobility, queer cosmopolitanism, and the ongoingness of neoliberalism and settler colonialism both symbolically and materially, both in and out of Hong Kong. Furthermore, it overcomes the consigning of Hong Kong to the rubric of smaller regions under area studies and engages the queer and the Sinophone through worldly geographies and intimacies.

A queer minor transnational framing of Hong Kong cinema since the 1990s thus offers a critical methodology of unruly comparison. It links Hong Kong, queerness, and the Sinophone to the expansive web of colonial histories, displacement, and intimate crossings of bodies and desire. To account for queer movements of body, sexuality, coloniality, and capital in our study of Hong Kong is to engage in the intellectual labor of unruly comparison that entangles Hong Kong with the world through alternative methods of reading and queer genealogies. A queer Sinophone intervention demands nothing short of this task. The next chapter performs another theoretical exercise of unruly comparison by transnationalizing the category of *transgender* across the Sinophone cultural domains of legality, cinema, photography, and activism in contemporary Hong Kong.

3

TRANSNATIONALIZING
TRANSGENDER

Tracey, *Queer Globalities,*
and Sinophone Regionalism

The Anti-Extradition Law Amendment Bill (Anti-ELAB) movement that began in June 2019 has proved to be a lasting fight for democracy in Hong
Kong.[1] While the extradition law amendment introduced by the chief executive of Hong Kong, Carrie Lam, sparked the protests that summer by raising fears that political dissidents in Hong Kong could face judgments in the
PRC without legal due process, the roots of this protest go farther back to
the social democratization inspired by the 2014 Umbrella Movement. The
Umbrella Movement refers to a seventy-nine-day occupation of the city by
protesters comprised of student-led activist groups, including Scholarism,
the Hong Kong Federation of Students, and Occupy Central with Love and
Peace. These groups and many local Hong Kongers protested the decision
of the Standing Committee of the National People's Congress of the PRC
(NPCSC) on August 31, 2014, that preselected candidates for the 2017 elec-
tion of the Chief Executive of Hong Kong. In the recent Anti-ELAB movement, occasionally LGBT groups such as Pink Alliance, BigLove Alliance, and
highly visible queer celebrities like Anthony Wong and Denise Ho are present
at the protest rallies. Ho even criticized China at the 2019 UN Human Rights

Council meeting in Geneva, stating that "the Vienna Declaration guarantees democracy and human rights. Yet in Hong Kong, these are under serious attack."[2] Ho's public persona as both an openly queer Cantopop star and a fearless fighter for democracy means that gender diversity, gay marriage, and LGBT rights are increasingly linked to the broader issue of social democratization.

But while issues such as sexual diversity, antidiscrimination laws based on gender expression and sexual orientation, gay marriage, and migrant domestic workers' rights could have intersected with the social democratization, the escalating chaos of the protests has hidden them from public view. Some conservative camps have even labeled the protests "violent" and "subversive" to the national security of the PRC. While one can carry on endless debates about whether the police and pro-establishment camp or the protester side is responsible for the most "violence," gender and sexuality take center stage in reports of increasing police aggression toward and harassment of female protesters.[3] I offer these brief descriptions about the cultural politics of gender and sexuality in times of protest because they reveal the ongoing convergence of postcolonial Hong Kong with the forces that undergird global queer movements, rights discourses, and cultural politics.

As a former British colony, Hong Kong prides itself on the rule of law and its free market economy, even while it also exists as a SAR of the PRC, following the principle of "one country, two systems." This postcolonial doubleness—the precarious condition of living with the legacy of British colonialism under an increasingly authoritarian PRC—has produced a condition in Hong Kong that I term *queer globality*. As a conceptual framework, queer globality illustrates the convergent dynamics of the globalizing tendency of queer rights discourses, sexual practices, and pink dollar industries (tourism, customer service, and consumption-driven industries catering to LGBT customers) as these forces articulate themselves anew in the global modernities of queer Asian sites. Furthermore, queer globality as a condition of possibility in Asia points to the crisscrossing dynamism whereby queer cinema, literature, cultural industries, activism, and NGO networks often borrow genres, tactics, and strategies from existing models in other Asian cities and regions; hence, the need to imagine queer globality within the forces of regionalism across Asia is an urgent task for queer Sinophone studies at the current conjuncture.[4] In many ways, the invocation of queer globality here draws inspiration from the idea that doing queer theory in Asia also means "skipping the universal middle term of Anglo-American queer theory."[5] For scholars of queer Asian studies, engaging in meaningful dialogue with and comparison of queer cultures across global Asias is the first step toward provincializing the Eurocentrism of queer theory.

This chapter demonstrates that studying queer Sinophone cultures in Hong Kong requires the framework of queer globalities to move beyond the homogenizing tendency of the "global gays."[6] Exploring three distinct areas of inquiry—queer and trans rights, trans cinema, and an art exhibition—I argue that neoliberal and global Asian sites like Hong Kong offer diverse expressions of queer globalities and Sinophone regionalism that are distinct from any linear trajectory of queer liberalism. While queer diaspora studies and queer of color critique offer important insights into the dangers of queer liberalism—including how liberal institutional inclusions of LGBT subjects into the workplace, military, and homonormative gay marriage structures have reproduced racial inequality, transphobia, and Islamophobic homonationalism—what the intersectional theory of queer diaspora studies and queer of color critique might offer for queer Asian studies, and vice versa, is often left unexamined.[7] This uneven production of knowledge means that queer theory from Asia is often off the radar of academic knowledge production in Euro-America. In their "Introduction" to the groundbreaking *Social Text* special issue "What's Queer about Queer Studies Now?," David L. Eng, Judith Halberstam, and José Esteban Muñoz offer the politics of epistemological humility as an acknowledgment of the uneven academic knowledge production of queer theory globally. They write, "Such a politics must also recognize that much of contemporary queer scholarship emerges from US institutions and is largely written in English. This fact indicates a problematic dynamic between US scholars whose work in queer studies is read in numerous sites around the world. Scholars writing in other languages and from other political and cultural perspectives read but are not, in turn, read."[8] My theorization of queer globality and Sinophone regionalism in Hong Kong constitutes a humble attempt at overcoming the current imperial division within queer theory.

The first part of this chapter provides a critical legal analysis of contemporary LGBT and transgender rights in Hong Kong. Considering Hong Kong as a site of queer globality and regionalism reveals the uneven conditions of Hong Kong as a magnet for foreign investment and global capitalism that lacks progressive LGBT rights in all spheres of life. Caught between the three masters of British colonialism, the PRC, and global capitalism, Hong Kong's political discourses of LGBT rights show a gradual incorporation of queer liberal tolerance in the areas of transgender self-determination and spousal visa rights while retaining an enduring resistance to gay marriage in government policy. By mapping Hong Kong's queer legal discourses and practices across multiple colonial and global forces, I point to the uneven queer globalities and Sinophone regionalism of Hong Kong when the city confronts both the limits and the possibilities of Eurocentric queer liberalism.[9]

Next, I offer a queer transnational analysis of *Tracey* (2018), a Hong Kong arthouse film directed by Jun Li that won several awards in Hong Kong and Taiwan. *Tracey* narrates the complex gender identity and sexual desire of Tai-hung, a boy who falls in and out of love with his adolescent first crush, Ching (another gay boy in his high school); marries a woman later in life and begins a family; and eventually identifies as a transgender woman called Tracey. However, Tai-hung/Tracey's transgender and male-to-female (MTF) identity as Tracey does not result in a heteronormative sexual desire for "straight" men. Tracey sexually experiments with a Singaporean pansexual character, Bond Tann, who is fighting his own battle to seek legal burial rights in Hong Kong for his now-deceased husband Ching, Tai-hung's adolescent gay crush. Overall, *Tracey* maps the condition of becoming trans through multiple queer temporalities (past, present, and future), various transnational spaces (the UK, Hong Kong, and Singapore), and distinct geopolitical LGBT and sexual rights discourses (the UK versus Hong Kong). While the LGBT Action Plan (2018) in the UK indicated a proactive public consensus to treat LGBTQ subjects as "normative" citizens—like discourses of queer liberalism in the United States[10]—the Hong Kong government tends to tackle LGBTQ rights with tokenistic and reactive measures only when social issues are brought to legal proceedings. Reckoning with these material limits of queer lives, *Tracey* visualizes Sinophone Hong Kong as a city of queer globalities where queerness evinces precisely the uneven experiments of working out trans and queer identities in the relative absence of full legal protection, gay marriage, and queer liberalism.

The final section of this chapter maps the emergent connection between cinema, activism, and museum exhibition. Another recent Hong Kong film, *A Woman Is a Woman* (2018), directed by Maisy Suen, could not be more different from *Tracey* in its Sinophone local sensibility. This film narrates the struggles of a married trans woman, Sung Chi Yu, and a feminine high school boy, Chiu Ling Fung, who considers undergoing sex reassignment surgery (SRS). In November 2020, the film's producer, Mimi Wong, also successfully launched a series of transgender photo exhibitions and public workshops inspired by the film, and the exhibition traveled to Taiwan in November 2022.

By composing a messy archive of legislating queer and trans rights in Hong Kong, by visualizing queer temporality and complex personhood in trans cinema, and by framing trans photography as activism, this chapter demonstrates how unfixing the category of transgender in Hong Kong demands a theory of unruly comparison. Signifying transness in a global and postcolonial city-region like Hong Kong challenges trans and queer scholars to move beyond what Halberstam terms the "metronormativity" of queerness, which posits urban cities like New York City and San Francisco as queer meccas of the globe. "This term reveals the conflation of 'urban' and 'visible' in many normalizing narratives of gay/lesbian subjectivities."[11] Similarly, Aren Z. Aizura observes that Eurocentric and imperial logics of trans mobility often reinforce the United States as *the* site of trans modernity: the United States' "transgender exceptionalism tracks a logic through which the US nation fantasizes its superiority and tolerance toward transgender life, against other nations and cultures deemed to be intolerant, barbaric, and transphobic or homophobic."[12] By reckoning with both the Euro-American legal frameworks of desiring queer liberalism for transgender subjects while showing the messy processes of representing trans personhood in Hong Kong, I illustrate how transness as a form of unruly embodiment indexes its own incommensurability and untranslatability within Hong Kong, thus pointing to Hong Kong itself as a queer unruly region for signifying transness differently. Overall, this chapter illuminates the *trans* of transgender as a prefix that highlights transnational movement, trans-mobility, and trans-medial creativity in Sinophone Hong Kong.

Righting Wrongs in a Global City: On Transgender and Gay Rights in Hong Kong

Two major legal cases concerning the right to marriage for transgender individuals and the rights of spousal benefits for lesbians and gay men who married elsewhere were decided in Hong Kong in the 2010s. *W v. Registrar of Marriages* (2013) adjudicated transgender people's rights to marriage, and *Leung Chun Kwong v. Secretary for Civil Service* (2019) centered on same-sex spousal benefits for civil servants. Both deserve separate lengthy analysis, but I approach both cases as offering critical insights into the global dimensions of queer intimacies. In both cases, Hong Kong's status as a postcolonial region without political independence plays a crucial part in legal jurisprudence about gender and sexuality by interpellating LGBT folks as the "included out" subjects; that is, they are included as biopolitical subjects but excluded from exercising fundamental rights in the domains of privacy, marriage, and equal protection at the workplace.[13] Comparing transgender and gay rights thus highlights the way Hong Kong as a postcolonial, cosmopolitan city imagines its own sexual and legal future under the lingering presence of British rule of law and the increasing legal constraints and referentiality of the PRC, not to mention the context of liberal tolerance discourses associated with global human rights.

W v. Registrar of Marriages marked a milestone for LGBT rights in Hong Kong: the Court of Final Appeal (CFA) gave transgender individuals the right to marry according to their self-identified gender rather than their biological sex assigned at birth.[14] The legal battle of Miss W, whose birth name remains confidential, began in 2008 when she hired a lawyer to inquire of the Registrar of Marriages whether she could legally enter into marriage with her boyfriend. The Registrar denied her request, reasoning that Hong Kong at that time (and still as of this writing) does not recognize same-sex marriage and W's birth certificate indicated her sex as "male" rather than her post–sex reassignment gender "female." After a litigation process that lasted five years, the Court of Final Appeal finally overturned the Registrar's decision on May 13, 2013, and affirmed the right of Miss W to enter into a heterosexual marriage. In analyzing the legal precedents and the global legal discourses under which the W case acquired new queer meanings, Howard Chiang demonstrates how the W case based its legal rationale on the British precedent overturning of *Corbett v. Corbett* (1971), in which a British aristocrat petitioned to nullify his marriage to a transsexual woman, April Ashley. In that case, the British court upheld its transphobic ruling based on the logic that Ashley "cannot reproduce a person who is naturally capable of performing the essential role of a woman in marriage."[15] In other words, the British court at that time regarded sexual intercourse leading to procreation as essential to the definition of marriage. However, in 2002 an emerging European consensus found the institution of marriage was no longer strictly tied to heterosexual procreative sex. In particular, in *Goodwin v. United Kingdom* (2002), postoperative MTF Christine Goodwin claimed that the existing marriage law violated her right to marry in terms of Articles 8, 12, 13, and 14 of the European Court of Human Rights. In granting the right to marry in European contexts, the court held, "The applicant in this case lives as a woman, is in a relationship with a man and would only wish to marry a man. She has no possibility of doing so. In the Court's view, she may therefore claim that the very essence of her right to marry has been infringed."[16]

While the legal victory of Miss W in Hong Kong in 2013 followed neatly this particular European consensus in the adjudication of transgender rights through the rhetoric of queer liberalism, we must take into consideration

Hong Kong's status as a SAR that is geopolitically fragile under the PRC.[17] Specifically, while *W v. Registrar of Marriages* (2013) granted the right to heterosexual marriage for postsurgical transgender people confirmed by a medical panel, it framed the legal victory within the confines of the heterosexual institution of marriage, dissociating it from any future advancement for same-sex marriage in the postcolonial region. In fact, Justices Geoffrey Ma and Robert Ribeiro, who delivered the final ruling, stated baldly: "We should make it clear that nothing in this judgment is intended to address the question of same-sex marriage."[18] Furthermore, one concurring opinion, by Judge Kemal Bokhary, pointed out the often overlooked fact that the PRC, of which Hong Kong is now geopolitically a part, had already issued a marriage license to one MTF from Chengdu, Sichuan, back in 2004.[19] Hence, the relatively "late" liberal and legal progress for postcolonial Hong Kong in legalizing transgender peoples' right to heterosexual marriage in 2013 marked a pragmatic move to "catch up" not only with the rest of Euro-America but also with the PRC, whose political system is often seen as far less transparent and liberal than that of Hong Kong.

Chiang argues that the W case demonstrates an evolving and particularly queer Sinophone example in which multiple referentiality to the West, to China, and beyond is at play. "Whether the alibi for taking the transformation of the legal system in Hong Kong seriously is Europe or China, the message remains clear: the extraordinary geopolitical position of Hong Kong makes a seemingly straightforward issue of human right (i.e., marriage) fundamentally difficult to grasp without assigning global giant powers such as China or Britain an epistemologically and ontologically privileged position."[20] In other words, the desire to establish a transgender right to heterosexual marriage emerges within the haunting presence of British law and its overturning, global queer liberalism, and the PRC's own legal changes within a broader Sinophone and postcolonial context. Yet Justices Ma and Ribeiro's opinion that Hong Kong's recognition of transgender individuals' right to heterosexual marriage should not be interpreted as setting a precedent for legalizing same-sex marriage underscores a paradox. It points out that while Hong Kong as a fragile postcolonial region has in recent years selectively adopted certain features of queer liberalism in order to play "catch up" with both the West and China, its gradual chipping away of legal transparency and political autonomy in the aftermath of the 2014 Umbrella Movement and during its current political crisis might mean that same-sex marriage and more substantive civil rights for sexual minorities and queers are indefinitely on hold. Queer globalities in the arena of law, intimacy, and sexuality reveal that Hong

Kong's sexual minorities must come to terms with, and undertake their activism within, these often-fraught tensions.

Queer globality names the critical encounters between local legal and institutional structures in Hong Kong and global claims to queer rights and intimacy. The fact that Hong Kong is geopolitically part of China means that its queer liberalism—however compromised—and legal progress cannot explicitly challenge the legitimacy of "One China," that is the PRC. Though the CFA problematically displaced the question of gay marriage in the W case, it took up the same question again three years later when civil servant Angus Leung, a senior immigration officer, sued the Secretary for the Civil Service and Commissioner of Inland Revenue for infringing on his and his husband's rights to spousal benefits and taxation benefits due to their sexual orientation. Leung joined the government sector in 2003; he met his partner, Mr. Adams, in 2005 and subsequently married him in New Zealand in 2014. As a civil servant, Mr. Leung had a contract of employment with the government subject to the Hong Kong's Civil Service Regulations (CSRs); and under the clauses of CSRs 900 to 925 and 950 to 954, Leung was entitled to certain medical and dental benefits provided by the government. In Leung's email exchanges with the Civil Service Bureau after his marriage, the Secretary denied any need for Leung to update his marital status because, as was explained, his same-sex marriage "falls outside the scope of marriage under the Marriage Ordinance and is not recognized for the purpose of administrating staff benefits under CSRs by the Government."[21] In May 2015, Leung's attempt to e-file his income tax return with his husband's name on the form was rejected with the reasoning that a "same-sex marriage is not regarded as a valid marriage for the purposes of the Inland Revenue Ordinance."[22] When the case was adjudicated in the Court of First Instance, the judge ruled in favor of Leung regarding spousal benefits, stating that the decision of the Civil Service Bureau "unlawfully discriminated against the applicant based on his sexual orientation."[23] However, regarding tax-filing benefits, the court sided with the Inland Revenue department. The Court of Appeal subsequently handed down another decision on June 1, 2018, stating that both the CSR and taxation clauses serve legitimate purposes in the social context of Hong Kong and that preserving heterosexual marriage is a legitimate aim.

On May 7, 2019, however, the CFA issued a powerful ruling that basically displaced the preservation of heterosexual marriage as a legitimate reason and purpose for rejecting and harming minority rights. In building the case for respecting same-sex intimacy and privacy, the court held that "reliance on the absence of a majority consensus as a reason for rejecting a minority's claim was inimical in principle to fundamental rights."[24] Furthermore, the court noted that the extension of employment and tax benefits to same-sex married couples does not actually undermine the institution of marriage. As a result of Leung's legal victory, couples who enter into same-sex marriage in countries where it is legal are now entitled to the same benefits and allowances that the Hong Kong government would provide for heterosexual married couples. In addition, same-sex couples who marry outside of Hong Kong can also file income taxes together. The conventional clauses in relevant government documents that make references to "husband and wife" would also need to be amended to the inclusive language of "a married person and his or her spouse."[25] By granting civil servants who enter into gay marriages outside of Hong Kong the same spousal benefits traditionally accorded to heterosexual married couples, and by giving all LGBT married couples the right to file taxes together, the Hong Kong government thus queerly destabilized the regional legality of what *marriage* means discursively and materially. The Angus Leung case thus frames Hong Kong as a queer region whose subjects might accrue the cultural capital and benefits of gay marriage *outside* the geographical confines of Hong Kong and make claims through the legal discourses of global same-sex intimacy, privacy, and rights. This legal victory also means that gay men and lesbians who are economically privileged and well-equipped with knowledge of queer tourism and the global gay wedding industry will be those most likely to benefit from this ruling. Queer globality captures the messy friction and unpredictable outcomes through which claims to queer liberalism, rights, and belonging are unevenly applied and negotiated in the postcolonial queer regionalism of Hong Kong.[26]

Tracey: Visualizing Transgender Identity through Transnational Queer Temporalities

What does it mean to live a transgender life beyond the predictable queer liberal trajectory of overcoming oppression and reaching sexual liberation? *Tracey* presents a particularly Hong Kong transgender cinematic narrative that offers clues. The film's emphases on transnational queer spaces and temporalities implicate Hong Kong as a region of queer globality, namely a postcolonial global financial hub that prides itself as "Asia's world city" where queer liberalism and substantive rights are unevenly applied and contested. *Tracey* opens with a breathtaking panorama of a scenic lake where three young boys are playing in the water. The scene is narrated by Tai-hung, the protagonist, who is now the successful owner of an antique eyeglasses store

FIGURE 3.1. Anne disciplines the "promiscuous" sexuality of her domestic worker Parti. Stills from Jun Li's *Tracey* (2018).

in Hong Kong. From his voiceover, we learn that Tai-hung keeps having the same dream of Ching, Chi Jun, and himself playing by the lake in a bygone summer, already twenty-five years ago. This opening nostalgic visuality is juxtaposed with the present when Tai-hung is awakened by a phone call in the early morning from a Singaporean man, Bond Tann, who breaks the tragic news that Ching—Bond's lover and Tai-hung's teenage romantic crush—has just passed away in the UK. Bond will be bringing his lover's cremation urn back to Hong Kong for a proper burial. Troubled by her husband Tai-hung's sudden sobbing, Anne knocks on his door and offers to share the bed with him as a comforting gesture. Her husband kindly rejects the offer, hinting that they no longer regularly sleep together. Soon after this scene, Anne tells her son Vincent that their Indonesian female domestic worker Parti is "secretly" having sex with a Pakistani man at the infamous Chungking Mansions on the weekends, which she knows because she found a bag of condoms in Parti's drawer (figure 3.1). Responding to his mother's surveillance of racialized sexuality in the domestic sphere, Vincent claims that it is natural for every human being to have erotic desire.

By interweaving dense layers of temporality (past and present), geography (the UK, Hong Kong, Singapore, Indonesia, and Pakistan), and spaces (the domestic home versus supposedly "perverse" spaces outside), the opening sequence captures powerfully the visuality of queer globalities, wherein Hong Kong emerges as a global city for queer desire not because it fully embraces queer liberalism like the United States, Australia, and other sites of queer liberalism but precisely because different kinds of sexuality, desire, memories, and bodies are slowly coming into view. Hong Kong marks a uniquely Sinophone region of queerness. These queer bodies and desires—whether local, transnational, interracial, or migratory—are also highly relational and mediated through incommensurable geographies and the aesthetics of unruly comparison. If, for Anne, her husband's queerness results from his refusal to seek heteronormative sexual pleasure with her, her domestic worker Parti is equally queer even though she is a so-called heterosexual subject; Parti's queerness is expressed through her refusal to be disciplined as a chaste, sexless, and domestically behaving racialized worker for the middle-class family. By queering both the temporality of Tai-hung's memory and a contemporary transgender identity crisis and linking seemingly incommensurable spaces within and outside of Hong Kong, *Tracey*'s visual opening indexes what Howard Chiang and I elsewhere term "queer regionalism," which "signals greater attention to less orderly, bilateral, and horizontal intra-regional traffics of queerness across different countries and regions in Asia."[27]

Tracey unravels the queer time and space of Sinophone Hong Kong through a visuality of erotohistoriography. Extending my reading of Elizabeth Freeman's concept of erotohistoriography from chapter 1, here I explore how the trans body *remembers* different moments in a person's life that altogether unsettle a queer liberal narrative of overcoming repression and arriving at trans freedom. Freeman writes, "Erotohistoriography admits that contact with historical materials can be precipitated by particular bodily dispositions, and that these connections may elicit bodily responses, even pleasurable ones, that are themselves a form of understanding."[28] In particular, the opening scene described above highlights Tai-hung's discomfort with heterosexual intercourse, his gradual awareness of her identity as Tracey, and how her sensorial awareness as a trans woman is constantly haunted by the unconsummated queer romance with Ching. Here, Tai-hung/Tracey's body "in transition" serves as the sensorial repertoire of erotohistoriography, where various moments in his/her life are mediated by bodily sensations. Furthermore, the film's trajectory bypasses the predictable narrative of queer liberation wherein an LGBT, queer, or trans subject adopts a Euro-American modernity by becoming a subject with full realization of sexual freedom and self-determination.[29] The film chronicles the transgender trajectory of Tai-hung from a "responsible" married heterosexual man in the closet to a trans woman who still keeps strong ties to her family while finding alternative kinship networks that harken back to the communities and bonds of traditional Cantonese culture.[30]

Tracey also highlights disjointed temporalities and the interwoven dialectic of tradition and modernity through another important queer character, Brother Darling (Ben Yuen). Shortly after picking up Bond at the airport, Tai-hung decides that it is his duty as a close friend (and teenage crush) of Ching's to assist Bond (as Ching's legitimate husband) in seeking the legal rights to burial. Tai-hung recruits the help of his son-in-law Jeffrey, who happens to be a famous lawyer in Hong Kong. Jeffrey discusses the case of same-sex legal rights to burial with Tai-hung within the space of a traditional Hong Kong teahouse, where the live performance of Cantonese opera has been a main feature of leisure and entertainment for decades. One major performer at the teahouse is Brother Darling, who as an older man still retains the past glorious title of "red thread sister," a reference to a famous female Cantonese opera star, Hung Sin Nui [紅線女]. When Brother Darling comes onto the stage, his high-pitched, feminine voice with wide vocal range enthralls the audience. He turns out to be an old friend of Tai-hung's, a former coworker in an old dim sum teahouse in Central (the main financial district on Hong Kong Island) many years ago, when Tai-hung was still attending high school.

Here the traditional Cantonese teahouse turns out to be a microcosm of queer globality. By purposefully inserting the discussion of contemporary LGBT rights and legal redress into the relatively traditional space of opera singing and the leisure of the gentry class, *Tracey* powerfully destabilizes the neat dichotomy of tradition versus modernity and the public versus the private. That is, what is considered a controversial and public legal issue infiltrates the space of an old teahouse, one that is fast becoming a tourist space precisely because it represents a nostalgic "tradition" of Hong Kong, including the gendered and classed dynamics of working-class waiters serving tea and dim sum to the privileged class. And just as his former childhood friend and sweetheart Ching's death awakens Tai-hung's sudden desire to deviate from his heteronormative married life that is already abstinent, the queer voice of Brother Darling points to the messy, disjointed, and intersecting sources of globality and modernity. Queer globality is thus constituted *simultaneously* by cultural elements seemingly belonging to the "tradition" of Hong Kong (the old teahouse) and the emerging "modern" issues of LGBT rights. By framing Brother Darling as a queer pioneer of transgender identity formation for Tai-hung, then, *Tracey* refuses to succumb to a teleological narrative that assumes transgender subjects emerge only via the global flow of the transgender rights movement from Euro-America in the 1990s to contemporary Asia. In fact, if recent work in queer Sinophone history has taught us anything, the debate on transgender identity and gender variance began

FIGURE 3.2. Brother Darling (*left*) and Tracey (*right*) dance at a club in Lan Kwai Fong. Still from Jun Li's *Tracey* (2018).

in Cold War Taiwan, from which contemporary Hong Kong might be understood as a site of coeval Sinophone queerness and transgender formation.[31]

As a film about the crisscrossing of multiple notions of rights, temporality, spatiality, and "cultural" sources of transgender history, *Tracey* ends on an illumination of transgender being as a form not simply of gender embodiment for Tai-hung but of gender and sexual ambiguity, erotic opening, and transformation of the heterosexual family as well. Specifically, Tai-hung emotionally confronts his transgender identification in two scenes. The first takes place as he tries to console the crying Bond, who is remembering his time with Ching and who eventually makes out with Tai-hung; in this moment of erotic heat, Bond discovers that Tai-hung wears a bra every day under his male dress shirt. The second scene comes when Bond, Tai-hung, and Chi Jun visit Brother Darling's home in an old-style walk-up flat. There, both Tai-hung and Brother Darling put on nice makeup and decide to go for a night of trans confirmation in the bustling clubbing district of Lan Kwai Fong, known for its cosmopolitan, expat, and queer scenes (figure 3.2). During a dance fiesta, Brother Darling suddenly blacks out from exhaustion. Tai-hung then carries Darling's body into a taxi to rush to the hospital, and just at that moment Vincent, Tai-hung's son, spots his dad in drag as Tracey. While the first moment of trans coming out confirms Tai-hung as a trans woman who does not identify as a gay man, the second moment marks a point of no return, when Tai-hung can no longer hide his trans identity from his heteronormative family. By the end of the film, Tai-hung, now Tracey, repairs her broken relationship with her son and daughter, while Anne, her ex-wife, comes to terms with the fact that Tai-hung is gone, and that she can still care for her former husband in a different way.

If transgender is conventionally understood as an umbrella term that encompasses all sorts of gender embodiments and identifications that defy the coherence between chromosomal sex and gender identity, in what sense does *Tracey* as a film invite a more capacious understanding of both transness and queerness? How does the film play on the prefix of "trans" to name the processes and embodiments of transition and transformation both individually and relationally?

Beyond tracing the incoherence between the sexed body and the gendered self, the film also narrates ongoing discontents with existing legal regimes in Hong Kong that do not recognize same-sex marriage or the queer rights of individuals who simply do not fit into rigid legal categories. In addition, *Tracey* demonstrates how transgender indexes its own potentiality, queer globalities, and transformative agency. If Tai-hung has begun the journey of becoming Tracey by the end of the film, isn't Anne equally on an unfinished journey of reckoning with the complexity of gender? Anne has to affectively overcome the rigid and binary gendered personhood and heteronormative regimes where sex is assumed to take place only within the domestic sphere and between married heterosexual couples.[32] As Anne learns to love first Tai-hung and now Tracey, the film hints at the ways that being trans can be not only a self-transformation but also a relational category of social transformation for Tai-hung, Tracey, and those deeply affected by them. As a film about Hong Kong (Tai-hung, Brother Darling, etc.), Indonesia (Parti), the UK (Ching), and Singapore (Bond), *Tracey* demonstrates the extent to which Hong Kong serves as an unruly Sinophone region of queer globalities, where various notions of becoming queer and transgender coexist across local, transnational, and global spaces and across entangled queer temporalities.

A Woman Is a Woman: A Cinematic View of Queer Sinophone Regionalism

If *Tracey* tells the trans narrative of Tai-hung becoming Tracey through a cinematic aesthetic of queer globalities, the film *A Woman Is a Woman* (2018), directed by Maisy Suen, at first glance seems unmistakably local by comparison. It narrates a double-transgender narrative by pairing the struggle of a married trans woman, Sung Chi Yu, with that of a frustrated feminine high school boy, Chiu Ling Fung, who is considering undergoing SRS in the near future. To make things more complicated, Sung's stepdaughter Lai Kei is romantically attracted to Chiu, and the film maps the trans personhood of Sung and Chiu through a deep illumination of local belonging, a contestation of conventional kinship structure, and a phenomenological rethinking of trans embodiment.[33] More than simply an exemplar of local arthouse cinema, the film opens up multiple views of the local and the regional that is Hong Kong while queering essentialist understandings of trans bodies in general. In addition, its extra-cinematic afterlife in a photo exhibition and trans community activism enables what Gayatri Gopinath terms "a queer regional imaginary."

Queer Sinophone regionalism as a concept describes both the status of Hong Kong as a special administrative region of the PRC and how the city is embedded in multiple power relations of heteronormative kinship, religious communities and discourses, emergent queer and transgender discourses, and legal claims to sexual autonomy and privacy. In other words, while the official status of Hong Kong as a Chinese region and "Asia's world city" (the official branding of the 2001 HKSAR government campaign of "Brand Hong Kong") tends to indicate its ongoing processes of Mainlandization and lack of judicial and cultural autonomy, queer Sinophone regionalism instead imagines more rhizomatic and unruly practices of queer embodiment, desire, and minor-to-minor relationality. This queer Sinophone regionalism "suggests the possibility of tracing lines of connection and commonality, a kind of South-South relationality, between seemingly discrete regional spaces that in fact bypass the nation."[34]

A Woman Is a Woman opens with a disorienting depiction of being trans and queer in Hong Kong that evokes trans performativity of the body in multiple local and regional inflections. The camera follows the bodily gestures of Chiu Ling Fung, the genderqueer feminine boy: dressed fully in black, spandex leggings and loose upper shirt, her hair is medium length while her face is painted with a dramatic red eye shadow. While Chiu dances behind the curtain for a theatrical performance at her school, Sung Chi Yu walks into the room and takes a seat. Chiu is performing a silent theatrical act known as Pantomime, pulling the string without a visible rope or prop to be seen. At the end of the silent act, she falls onto the ground. By depicting the act of Chiu falling down while climbing up the rope, this scene symbolically comments on the many obstacles that a trans subject must overcome in their life.[35] The queer choreography of Chiu, the genderqueer boy, paired with the relatively stable identity of Sung Chi Yu as a trans woman at a later stage in life, demonstrates transness itself as a constant process of transition in the

Butlerian sense of performativity as citationality.[36] Beyond the conceptual understanding of transgender and other gender identities as performative acts that accrue their fiction of authenticity over time, the film also invites us to *read* the heterogeneity of being trans in Sinophone Hong Kong. Indeed, the bodily gestures and queer choreography in the opening scene evoke transgender as a gendered embodiment that is rehearsed, performed, contested, and reaffirmed repeatedly, often against the multiple hegemonies that condition trans possibility in the regional locale of Hong Kong.

Besides the heteronormative scripts of everyday life such as attending school, riding on public transportation, and attending school parents' meetings that might pose obstacles to both trans subjects in the film, *A Woman Is a Woman* also subtly names the multiple hegemonic forces (i.e., religious conservatism, heteronormative kinship, and institutional authority at school) that seek to make ordinary life and gender politics, to borrow a provocative phrase from queer filmmaker Yau Ching, "as normal as possible" in Hong Kong.[37] Queer Sinophone regionalism names the confinement and concrete modality of living with and against heteronormative patriarchy in Hong Kong. Specifically, early in the film narrative, Sung Chi Yu is captured through the mobile camera's frame as walking backward on the bridge connected to the IFC (International Finance Centre) Mall in Central, an iconic landmark of finance and elegant lifestyle consumerism in Hong Kong. As we see her body and hair only from the back, she narrates: "For a long time, I felt that my body and my life did not belong to me. The life of Sung Chi Yu actually started at the age of twenty. I changed my phone, moved house, and changed jobs. I took twenty years to recreate my own life." Right after this internal monologue by Sung, we see Chiu speaking about her ambivalent life as a gender nonconforming high school boy. She observes, "I always seem to have stolen the life of another person. I have stolen the life of a person called Chiu Ling Fung. Each day, I am just operating the body of Chiu Ling Fung. I am living at a distance from the real world."

While Sung's first trans narrative reveals a trans woman who has gone through SRS to "realign" biological sex and socially recognized gender (to use the conventional medical terminology), the fact that she is walking backward seems to suggest that transness marks a phenomenology of gender that never quite arrives and that always traffics in a state of mobility and transition. Or is Sung's feeling of her body "moving backward" indicative of the discomfort of all bodies in general within the constraints of gender normativity? As Gayle Salamon perceptively argues, "the production of normative gender itself relies on a disjunction between the 'felt sense' of the body and the body's corporeal contours and that this disjunction need not be viewed as a pathological structure."[38] Similarly, Chiu speaks of an almost stereotypical view of transgender personhood as existing in "the wrong body" and as never belonging in a cruel world of gender conformity. Both Sung and Chiu's internal monologues, told amid intricate camera work of looking from the back, evince what Halberstam terms the *transgender gaze*. In examining the ways in which transgender characters appear in Hollywood cinema in such films as *The Crying Game* (1992) and *Boys Don't Cry* (1999), Halberstam demonstrates how these films attempt to show transgender persons as flexible subjects in postmodernity, challenging the heteronormative and linear temporality ordered by the sequential logic of past, present, and future. Halberstam writes, "The transgender gaze becomes difficult to track because it depends on complex relations in time and space between seeing and not seeing, appearing and disappearing, knowing and not knowing."[39] The notion of the transgender gaze unpacks the different registers in which the camera makes Sung and Chiu appear and disappear within the urban density of Hong Kong as well as reveals how trans subjects seek to reclaim queer autonomy and personhood in public spaces such as shopping malls, public schools, and the home.

Beyond offering a phenomenological rethinking of gender variance and trans personhood through self-narratives, the film is heavily invested in mapping the queer Sinophone regionalism of Hong Kong in spatial terms. Specifically, it indexes the queer urban density of Sinophone Hong Kong by placing trans subjects within spaces of heteronormative hegemony such as schools, public bathrooms, church and religious meetings, and the domestic spaces of family gatherings. In turn, it shows how trans subjects must redefine the meanings of these spaces for queer purposes. Denise Tse-Shang Tang, in her study of lesbian desire and eroticism in the urban density of Hong Kong, has urged us to examine lesbian desire through the intersectionality of gender, race, class, age, and capitalism across different periods of Hong Kong history. Tang writes, "I call this mode of spatial practice as everyday erotics in density to describe the way of navigating sexual desires in relation to urban development and colonial modernity, where becoming a woman with lesbian desires means not only carving out one's alternative erotic space but also disengaging with traditional gender roles in one's life course and redefining gender and sexuality for an older generation of women."[40] While Tang's work reveals the changing meaning and possibility of women identifying as lesbians and exploring queer desire in Hong Kong across the divide of colonial modernity in the past and neoliberalism in the present, the concept of "everyday erotics in density" is also highly perceptive in naming trans practices of navigating the Sinophone regionalism of Hong Kong. *A Woman Is a Woman* offers multiple views on how trans subjects navigate through urban density and confinements while hinting at possible modes of deviation and queer disorientation.

The character Sung Chi Yu as a married trans woman is particularly revealing in the ways that she reproduces heteronormative models of femininity while gradually accepting and asserting her trans personhood. Specifically, in the early parts of the film when her husband, Chi Hung, does not yet realize her trans identity, one bathroom scene shows Sung soaking a menstrual pad with red ink to simulate the experience of menstruation and avoid possible suspicion. Eventually, Chi Hung finds out that Sung was a "man" in the past by digging through her old photographs. Feeling cheated by his wife, he calls out Sung as a "man." In a most dehumanizing manner, Chi Hung yells at her: "You took advantage of me when you knew I was a divorced man with a daughter and really needed a woman. You lied to me on purpose. In these ten years, I have been fucking a man every night! I feel extremely disgusted!" While Chi Hung yells, the camera focuses on Sung's emotional facial expression through a close-up shot, pointing to the ways in which heteronormative ideas of domesticity strip away her femininity and claim to womanhood through the typical mechanism of "gender revelation" in cinema. In Halberstam's framework of the transgender gaze, popular Hollywood films often dramatize moments of crisis when a trans character's "biological gender" is revealed. The trans character's horror of being exposed also aligns the viewers empathetically with trans ways of seeing through a transgender gaze.[41]

Beyond the strictures and violence of everyday erotics in urban density, the film offers a parallel view of Chiu Ling Fung as she breaks the school's gender binary uniform code by wearing a dress on casual wear day, confronts the school principal, asserts her decision to undergo SRS in the future, and rebels against her parents who insist that she pray every night at the dinner table. Her traditional father, who insists that she must behave in a masculine manner—in alignment with her biological sex—eventually resorts to locking her up in her room. By the end of the film, Chiu convinces the principal to provide a gender-neutral bathroom, with the help of a more understanding social worker at school. Unfortunately, Sung still cannot convince her husband to reconcile and accept her gender as a trans woman. *A Woman Is a Woman*, echoing the straightforward message of the film's title, seems to conclude with the idea that *a woman is a woman* no matter what the biological sex of a person might be. Through a queer lens, the film also names trans modes of becoming and making do with the confinement and possibilities of the urban density of Sinophone Hong Kong.

Once released, *A Woman Is a Woman* traversed the normative boundary of genres and artistic divisions through screenings at both arthouse theaters and educational venues such as the Hong Kong Lesbian and Gay Film Festival, Hong Kong Film Archive, and university campuses like the University of Hong Kong (HKU) and the Chinese University of Hong Kong (CUHK). Furthermore, the producer Mimi Wong, herself one of the most outspoken transgender activists and educators in Hong Kong, successfully secured funding from various NGOs to curate a related photography exhibit that was accompanied by a series of workshops titled Transcendence. I conclude this chapter by reflecting on my own participation as an audience member at public film screenings of *A Woman Is a Woman* and in my role as an "accidental translator" at one of the Transcendence workshops.

Transcendence: Queering the Divides of Photography, Museum Space, and Activism

I started following Mimi Wong's activist work after I attended one of the first public screenings of *A Woman Is a Woman* in the summer of 2019. The screening took place at the theater of the Hong Kong Film Archive in Sai Wan Ho, a primary site for researching Hong Kong cinema and screening arthouse films. The theater that night was not too crowded, and I found myself quite relaxed within the well air-conditioned space. Once the film began, I was immediately surprised to see that the shooting location for Chiu Ling Fung's high school was none other than my alma mater, Munsang College in Kowloon City! My mind was immediately aroused by both the possibilities and limits of trans cinema and visuality. How might trans visuality and filmmaking in Hong Kong radically alter our conventional mapping of memory, space, and belonging? For myself at least, the film queerly disrupted my adolescent memories and enabled the possibility of queering the public-school setting, in this case a relatively elitist high school in Hong Kong with a heavy Protestant Christian influence.

Meanwhile, the actress who plays Sung Chi Yu is the 1990s Cantopop diva Amanda Lee, known for her trademark melancholy songs and campy style. Though Lee is not publicly identified as queer or transgender, her coarse and gender-ambiguous voice somehow makes her portrayal of the trans character very convincing. Here, a certain disidentification of Cantopop female stardom and trans cinema emerged, which unsettled many Hong Kongers' public reception of Amanda Lee and her star image.

Both amused by the queering of my own memory of Munsang College and surprised by Amanda Lee's queer acting, I was eager to listen to the audience's interactions with Maisy Suen and Mimi Wong. One male attendee noted that while the acting was good and the subject matter socially urgent, the film was just not as entertaining as Jun Li's film *Tracey*. He asked the filmmaker directly: "Why can't your film be more like *Tracey*?" To this somewhat rude and startling question, Wong responded, "It was not our intention to make a melodramatic film about the trauma of being transgender. The message of my film is clear enough—a woman is a woman." Suen followed up that, while *Tracey* is indeed commercially successful, the transformation of Tai-hung to Tracey is almost too quick. It does not seem realistic for many transwomen and transmen. I raised the question about Amanda Lee's status as a Cantopop diva and what she felt about acting in a transgender role; the filmmaker and producer said this was not a main concern either for them or for Lee. Other audience members found the narratives of the main protagonists Chiu and Sung very convincing and true-to-life. The film's realistic portrayal of the ordinary lives of transwomen in Hong Kong was in part inspired by Mimi Wong's own life story. She lived socially as a man for many years and was married before coming out as transgender and undergoing SRS.[42] Given the heavy dose of cinematic realism and almost documentary-like narratives and visual elements of the film, it is not surprising that *A Woman Is a Woman* has been warmly received at arthouse and LGBT film festival circles. After successful screenings of the film locally, the film went on to screen publicly in Japan, Taiwan, and at local universities in Hong Kong.

In the summer of 2020, Mimi Wong announced that she would enhance the visibility of the film by launching a related project, a trans photo exhibition and public event. Entitled Transcendence, the multimedia event, held November 21–30, 2020, featured workshops in which trans individuals shared their experiences with attendees, a public film screening of *A Woman Is a Woman* followed by Q&As, and a daily exhibition of photography featuring trans people in fabulous and stylized poses. Given my experience of watching the film, and after having introduced myself to Mimi, I shared this event with students in my queer theory course at HKU and attended the events on the first two days. On the evening of the first day, I attended the human library, which featured two self-identified transwomen, Alice and Pinky, and was moderated by Mimi Wong.[43] Given that Hong Kong was in the middle of another wave of COVID-19, with another round of strict social distancing measures mandated by the government, the seating capacity was limited and fewer than twenty people showed up. Instructed by Mimi, we formed a circle while sitting a little bit apart from each other, a queer way of making do with the pandemic!

Alice first shared her story of overcoming social discrimination at her workplace. While she could afford the medical expenses of hormone therapy and breast implants and enjoyed relative freedom given her stable income as an engineer, she was traumatized by the fact that her workplace would not let her use the female bathroom, and of course her workplace did not have designated gender-neutral bathrooms either. Furthermore, she was denied a salary raise without a clear reason. The fact that Hong Kong does not yet have antidiscrimination laws and policies on the books to ensure equal protection to individuals regardless of sexual orientation and gender identity means that many transphobic and homophobic employers can discriminate against their employees in both subtle and obvious ways.

Around halfway into the human library sharing session, while Alice was still talking, a middle-aged South Asian man joined the group and sat next to me. Next, Pinky started sharing her story, but Mimi interrupted when she realized that the man next to me did not understand Cantonese. Since Mimi knew my background as an academic based at HKU, she turned to me for help. I gladly translated Pinky's testimony into English in a low voice. With an interest in fashion, Pinky liked to wear pink and to dress in a more provocative Lolita fashion. Her trans self-fashioning and confidence lightened up the atmosphere in the room. Pinky presented a more transnational story. She grew up in Hong Kong, studied abroad in Australia, and returned to Hong Kong after college. Her first part-time job was working as a cashier at a McDonald's. She related an incident of discrimination when her boss prohibited her from using the female bathroom. Her boss and colleagues even went so far as to lock the bathroom door.

While I did my best to translate a bit of Alice's life story and Pinky's full story during Pinky's human library session, I wondered if anything was "lost in translation." During the Q&A session, the South Asian man (whose name I cannot recall) began with a tone of affirmation. He said while addressing Pinky: "If I were your father, I would love you no matter what. It doesn't matter whether you are transgender or not. Being trans does not define you." Other audience members nodded in agreement. After the session, he and I chatted casually, and I found out that he learned of the event through some South Asian community announcements about diversity. I found out about the event by having already been exposed to the activist work of Mimi Wong beforehand. Alice and Pinky, I assume, came to the event wanting to share their stories as part of the Hong Kong stories yet to be heard, perhaps with some aim of reaching out to non-trans communities. I came to this event and subsequent Transcendence exhibits with the idea of eventually writing about this in my own work. We all had different reasons and priorities in attending a local trans event, and our social identities and solidarities were formed not through sameness but through differences.

The Transcendence photo exhibition and human library events critically highlight the queer Sinophone politics of incommensurability in Hong Kong. Sinophone theorist Shu-mei Shih has written extensively on feminism, transnational encounters, and the politics of incommensurability. In her much-cited essay "Towards an Ethics of Transnational Encounter, or 'When' Does a 'Chinese' Woman Become a 'Feminist'?," Shih points out how academic compartmentalization of knowledge often places Chinese women and feminists in different positions. Through a provocative exposition of multiple paradigms of feminism, transnationalism, and affect, Shih arrives at a logic of "transpositional and transvaluational relationality" that must vigorously question the positions of the self and the other.[44] In a more recent work that revisits the ethics of transnational encounter in postcolonial feminism when it travels to Sinophone Asia and Taiwan in particular, Shih notes that Gayatri Spivak, despite her previous writings on subalternity and "learning to learn from below," has imposed a universal Asian value of respect for older women during her arrogant encounters with Taiwanese feminists.[45] Through a critical analysis of the writings of Taiwan indigenous feminist A-Wu, Shih concludes that incommensurability and commensurability are, in fact, flip sides of the same coin, and transnational feminists must learn to communicate both within and across both forces. Shih writes: "Looking back at the encounter between Spivak and the local feminists, what was missing was precisely this generous spirit of critical reciprocity that *takes incommensurability as an incomplete translation, starting from the presupposition of translatability*."[46]

Drawing on Shih's work on transnational feminism and issues of translation and incommensurability, I show that my own invocation of "transnationalizing transgender" is itself an incomplete translation marked by gaps, tensions, desire, and silence. Mimi Wong, Alice, Pinky, and the films *Tracey* and *A Woman Is a Woman* cannot and do not claim to fully translate what the category of *trans* signifies in contemporary Hong Kong any more than I could translate fully the testimonies of Alice and Pinky to the ethnically marked South Asian man sitting next to me. It is not an "accident" that Mimi picked me to translate the message, given my privileged background as an English-speaking academic in Hong Kong. Recognizing the ethics of incommensurability in Sinophone Hong Kong might be the first step toward imagining some form of queer and trans solidarity.

To visualize trans solidarity and incommensurability in action, let us turn to the Transcendence photo exhibit itself. I first encountered the photo exhibit when it was hosted at the Kowloon Union Church in Yau Ma Tei.[47] By working with a local church that might be open to LGBTQ topics, Mimi Wong and her team challenged the existing divide between the religious and LGBT communities in Hong Kong, allowing Transcendence to indeed queerly transcend differences by sexualizing and queering the church as a potential space for queer exhibition. While some scholars of museum studies have critiqued the Western fetishism of colonized and ethnic others in museum displays of colonial, ethnic, racial, and sexual differences, an emergent body of work has also turned to the museum as a possible feminist and queer space.[48]

While some of the models in Transcendence, such as Alice and Mimi Wong, had previously participated in the human library sessions, reencountering them as fabulous subjects framed in large photos evoked a sense of trans affirmation, survival, and fabulosity that might not have been found elsewhere in mainstream Hong Kong mass media and culture, which tended to particularize trans subjects as deceitful, pathological, mentally ill, sexually promiscuous, and so on. In Transcendence, a name card with information accompanies the photo of each trans model. Alice's placard included the message: "My church thought I was against the wish of God and ousted me. I hope the art show can improve the understanding of the general public towards transgender people." One photo of Alice shows her wearing a bright orange sweater with nicely coiffed hair and staring back at the imagined viewer. Her look is one of confidence and queer defiance (figure 3.3).

The placard that introduces Mimi Wong reads: "I was asked to sign a mutually agreed upon separation agreement when I came out at work. I was asked to pay a whole year's rent in advance due to the mismatch between my ID card's gender and my appearance. I had no job offers after my sex reassignment surgery because my past credentials showed that I was male. I hope the art show can send a loud and clear message that we are not inferior." Next to this information, we are greeted by a photo of Mimi in high femme queer style, wearing a dress with a rosy, flowery design (figure 3.4). With her eyes closed and exhaling in a state of ecstasy, Mimi's photographic self-image challenges the viewer to imagine what exactly she is thinking at that moment. Trans photography of the self and trans queer fabulosity operate through the

FIGURE 3.3. Alice with a look of queer defiance. From the *Transcendence* photo exhibition. Reprinted with permission by Mimi Wong.

logics of transparency and opacity simultaneously. They perform unruly visions with queer fierceness.

This chapter began with the recognition that the dominant frameworks of postcolonialism and area studies often overlook the significance of Hong Kong as a site of queer regionalism. The concepts of queer globalities and Sinophone regionalism show how an Asian global city like Hong Kong is trafficked within multiple political powers and discursive references—the postcolonial city has historically served as the intermediary of global capitalism and for years practiced the British rule of law. Thus, its postcolonial "return" to the PRC also implicates its unevenness within the global discourse of queer liberalism. If queer liberalism assumes that LGBT subjects are to some extent "post–gay rights" and that we enjoy equal rights and citizenship like any heterosexual citizen in a democratic society, the fact that Hong Kong is an Asian global city that lacks substantive civil rights for LGBT subjects thus

FIGURE 3.4. Mimi Wong in high femme fabulous style. *Transcendence* photo exhibition. Reprinted with Permission by Mimi Wong.

points to the necessary incompleteness, alterity, and ethics of difference in queer transnational encounters. Legal battles for transgender rights to marriage and same-sex spousal benefits for civil servants in court cases like *W v. Registrar of Marriages* (2013) and *Leung Chun Kwong v. Secretary for Civil Service* (2019) demonstrate that the Euro-American legal discourses of rights to privacy, same-sex marriage, and sexual tolerance will always be unevenly and creatively applied, tested, and transformed in a queer region like Hong Kong. Similarly, the film *Tracey* demonstrates the heterogeneous lifeworlds that Tai-hung lives through in his transformation to Tracey and the queer globalities that emerge through his/her past romance, current domestic life, and fluid sexual desire with Bond. In this sense, queer globalities connect disparate and often incommensurable geographies and temporalities through the aesthetic of unruly comparison. *A Woman Is a Woman* points to the erotics of urban density and how trans subjects navigate these fraught terrains and tensions in everyday life in a locally inflected Sinophone mode, while the Transcendence photo exhibit and workshop reveal the queer incommensurability in Sinophone Hong Kong. Most daringly, they gesture toward queer unruly visions and trans fabulosity that defy heteronormative ways of seeing Hong Kong.

As a global city that finds itself at the crossroads of the legacy of British colonialism, global capitalism, and China's geopolitical authoritarianism, Hong Kong reveals the necessity of overcoming the theoretical divisions of area studies, Hong Kong studies, and queer theory. While the dominant theoretical language of queer theory tends to orient around issues of deconstruction, performativity, shame, affect, and so on, area studies often supplies regional specificity, historical analysis, and the anthropological "raw materials" that queer theory bypasses. And as a small postcolonial city under the shadows of British colonialism and a rising neoliberal and powerful China, Hong Kong is often marginal to both Eurocentric queer theory and the China-centric agenda of area studies. When we theorize in the plural (globalities) and the regional, Hong Kong emerges as an indispensable site for understanding precisely the unevenness, unpredictability, and global connections that challenge accepted models of chronology, temporality, and "area." Queer theory, practiced without the baggage of either Eurocentrism or China-centrism, can come to terms with other visions of queer globality through region-to-region and minor-to-minor Sinophone articulations. This turn to imagining queer globalities and Sinophone regionalism in Hong Kong also means that "diverse frames of reference cross our horizon, multiply our perspectives, and enrich our subjectivity" beyond the imperialist eyes of queer Eurocentrism and liberalism.[49] Theorizing a queer Hong Kong through trans visuality evinces discrepant processes of queer globality and regionalism. Ultimately, imagining transgender in Sinophone Hong Kong through an unruly comparative lens can powerfully disrupt the metronormativity of queer studies and the transgender exceptionalism of Eurocentric trans imaginary.

4

QUEER SINOPHONE INTIMACIES

Visualizing Queer Migrant
Domestic Workers

In the previous chapters, I explored questions of queer literary and cinematic archives, South-South queer minor transnationalism in Hong Kong cinema, and the potentiality of transnationalizing transgender in Sinophone Hong Kong. This chapter further expands the analytical potential of queer Sinophone studies by examining the emergent body of documentary activist films and fiction films on migrant domestic workers in the Sinophone locations of Hong Kong and Taiwan. My goal is threefold. First, an exploration of queer intimacies among migrant domestic workers in Sinophone cinema expands the purview of what counts as *queer Sinophone cinema*. While the existing body of works on queer Sinophone studies center on cultural productions written, spoken, and filmed in Sinitic languages such as Mandarin, Cantonese, Hokkien, and so on, Sinitic languages spoken by ethnic minorities born in or recently migrated to Hong Kong and other Sinophone spaces are marginal to the field. Queer Sinophone films about migrant domestic workers carry the potential of "defetishizing Chineseness" and "racializing area studies."[1] Second, by comparing Hong Kong and Taiwan through an exploration of queer desire as portrayed in recent films about queer migration, labor, care work, and sexuality, queer Sinophone studies can revise and *queer* dominant generalizations about the right to the city, neoliberalism as exception, and global care chains, all of which tend either to particularize nonwhite domestic workers as the "new slaves" of global cities in Asia or to universalize these marginalized subjects as new subjects of global human rights.[2] Finally, this chapter mobilizes the conceptual framework of *queer Sinophone intimacies* to attend to modes of resistance, alliance, solidarity building, feminism, and queer desire among both Southeast Asian domestic workers and their Sinophone allies in Hong Kong and Taiwan, pointing to a minor transnational network of desire that transforms the emergent Sinophone public spheres.

The study of Hong Kong cinema before the emergence of Sinophone studies had always already been concerned with globalization and transnationalism. Specifically, Poshek Fu and David Desser write, "The accepted model of a national cinema seems hardly to apply to the Hong Kong situation — a Chinese community under British rule, a cinema without a nation, a local cinema with international appeal. Perhaps a postmodern model is more appropriate — a transnational cinema, a cinema of pastiche, a commercial cinema, a genre cinema, a self-conscious, self-reflexive cinema, ungrounded in a nation, multiple in its identities."[3] Echoing Fu and Desser's view, Esther Yau likewise categorizes Hong Kong films as "small speedboats breaking the waves alongside a daunting fleet of Hollywood *Titanics*, charging ahead on the basis of their irreverent imagination, their unique mix of cultural references, and their reinvention of generic elements."[4]

While Hong Kong film scholars express genuine interest in debunking the national paradigm, the study of ethnicity and non-Sinitic languages in Hong Kong cinema tends to escape their analytical purview. Furthermore, the study of ethnic minorities in Hong Kong is often carried out by social scientists interested in questions of immigration and ethnicity, ethnic neighborhoods, and governmental policies of inclusion and assimilation in general.[5] An examination of the dominant tropes for the representation of ethnic minorities in Hong Kong and Sinophone cinemas as well as the modes of visuality that deviate from these tropes can open up new ways of visualizing queer Sinophone Hong Kong.

Thus before mapping the three interventions I have outlined above, I show the ways in which foreign domestic workers have been problematically represented in Hong Kong and Sinophone cinema through the discourse of liberal humanism. This section scrutinizes Fruit Chan's film *Little Cheung* (1999), Joanna Bowers's documentary film *The Helper* (2017), and Oliver Chan's film *Still Human* (2018) as cultural texts that simultaneously gender, racialize, and fetishize the figure of the migrant domestic helper as always maternal and caring toward Han-Chinese and Cantonese-speaking Hong Kong families and children. While *Still Human* attempts to confer liberal humanism on the beautiful domestic helper Evelyn Santos, it ultimately reinforces an overtly optimistic narrative of upward social mobility for Santos through the masculinist story of self-recovery and rejuvenation of her boss, Leung Cheong-wing, who is also a disabled man. The final part of the chapter turns to recent documentary films that portray queer sexuality and desire of migrant workers in Sinophone Taiwan and Hong Kong, including Susan Chen's *Lesbian Factory* (2010), its sequel *Rainbow Popcorn* (2012), and Baby Ruth Villarama's *Sunday Beauty Queen* (2016).

By unpacking the heteronormatively maternal and racializing mechanism of representing Southeast Asian migrant domestic workers in Hong Kong films and pairing them alongside alternative queer Sinophone visuality, I demonstrate how queer migrant workers disrupt the dominant liberal humanist regime of visuality in their unruly queer subjectivities. Their queer incommensurabilities within Hong Kong are linked to their transnational mobility across multiple "homes" in both Sinophone societies and Southeast Asia. The chapter ends with an analysis of queer survival and homemaking practices that *queer* heteronormative notions of domesticity by studying the Filipina butch organization Filguys Association Hong Kong and its printed materials. Unruly comparison offers a methodology for dissecting dominant liberal humanist visuality alongside visualities that seem too minor and inconsequential. Queer Sinophone intimacies reframe visual aesthetics as "the grounds of uncommon, illiberal sensibilities."[6]

Visualizing the Racial Other: Global Care Chains and Sinophone Cinema

From the curious inclusion of a domestic "helper" in films about working-class Hong Kong life—from *Little Cheung* to *The Helper*—a stereotypical view emerges of the domestic worker as a caring helper, a heroic mother (who is missing in action in her home country but sending money *over there* through remittances) but also an easily replaceable figure.

Fruit Chan's *Little Cheung* uniquely sees the foreign female domestic worker as part and parcel of globalization, neoliberalism, and class inequality in post-1997 Hong Kong. The third installment of a series of films that symbolically comment on the fate of Hong Kong at the eve of the 1997 handover to the PRC, *Little Cheung* forms part of Chan's "1997 Trilogy." (*Made in Hong*

Kong [1997] and *The Longest Summer* [1998] are the earlier installments.) Fruit Chan as a local filmmaker is often categorized under the label of "independent filmmaking," and he tends to make films with a trilogy in mind. (In fact, the next chapter of this book discusses the queering of Sinophone borders in his "Prostitute Trilogy" films.) Briefly, *Little Cheung* narrates the overlooked aspects of poverty, crime, and Triad activities that form the underbelly of the otherwise glossy image of Hong Kong as a global city. Told from the perspective of a nine-year-old boy who works occasionally for money at his father's *cha chaan teng* (Hong Kong-style fast food café and restaurant popular among the locals), the film portrays the lives of ordinary folks and a family of illegal immigrants from the Mainland. They live within a few blocks of Portland Street, an extremely dense and crime-ridden red-light district in Mongkok, itself one of the most densely populated districts in Kowloon. The mischievous child figure and protagonist Little Cheung often runs around the flat in his white underwear only. But he is not a typical spoiled middle-class boy from Hong Kong. One of his lines in the opening sequence reads almost like a theoretical statement on globalization. He states matter-of-factly: "I already understood a lot when I was nine. My father owns a restaurant to make money. Our Filipino maid is here to make money. My mother plays mah-jong in the mah-jong parlor for money. And Brother Cheung also goes on the TV charity fundraisers for money. Of course, I'm no exception." Here, the young boy equates his part-time job as a delivery boy for his father's restaurant with the work done by his live-in Filipina domestic helper, Ami, as a form of exchange labor in a capitalist society. And the fact that he puts Brother Cheung, the stage name for the famous Cantonese opera singer and star Cheung Gor, into the same equation suggests that all forms of labor in a capitalist society like Hong Kong are entangled and exchanged for money. Thus, even his mother's leisure activity of playing mah-jong is a form of work according to this logic.

However, what escapes Little Cheung's childish view here is precisely the fact that domestic work performed by his maid Ami *is* a differently gendered and racialized form of labor compared to his own part-time job, which he can choose (or not) freely. Linguistically, the local and racist term that Little Cheung uses to refer to his maid, *bun mui* [賓妹], carries the connotation that she is a lower-class woman from the Philippines. Symbolically, the term has the tendency to reduce the full humanity of a person to merely a woman from a particular Southeast Asian region.

While Fruit Chan's film might suggest a simplistic view of the abstraction of all forms of labor under capitalism due to unending processes of exchange and appropriation of surplus value, the film nevertheless visualizes moments when Ami speaks back to the imagined Sinitic language–speaking Hong Kong viewer with a sense of irony and defiance. One Sunday evening when the whole family gathers for dinner together at the restaurant, Ami confronts Little Cheung's father, her boss: "In fact, I can sue you in court, you know? Sunday is my holiday." To this, the father casually responds by complaining that she has to bring it up every Sunday during meals. But Ami doesn't take any of his bullshit: "It is your Hong Kong government's law." A few moments later, Little Cheung's grandmother tells him about her tough life as a child back in the day in Mainland China. Ami interrupts this intimate conversation between grandmother and grandson by telling her, "You need to tell your son to pay me. I work overtime without compensation on Sundays." The grandmother then loudly orders her to "shut up!" Ami is also simultaneously speaking to a relative from the Philippines on the phone and remarks sarcastically: "I don't understand! Hong Kong people are crazy!" But her second sentence in fact injects a sense of Sinophone cacophony into the first sentence. When Ami utters the word "crazy," she uses the Cantonese slang *chi sin* [黐線 / crazy]. The phrase describes the condition when two phone lines stick together, causing a communication jam in a landline phone. In everyday Cantonese usage, it means someone or a situation is insane. By describing the family that she works for and lives with as *chi sin*, her statement points to the capitalist illogic and unfreedom of Hong Kong, despite its claim to be "Asia's World City."

Whereas *Little Cheung* shows the domestic worker both inhabiting stereotypical ideas of servitude and exploding in momentary defiance, *The Helper* seeks to refashion the domestic helper into a figure of liberal humanism capable of achieving her dream within a Hong Kong that appears to the viewer as becoming more global and multicultural. I draw here on Lisa Lowe's definition of liberal humanism as "a project that includes at once both the universal promises of rights, emancipation, wage labor, and free trade, as well as the global divisions and asymmetries on which the liberal tradition depends, and according to which such liberties are reserved for some and wholly denied to others."[7] Specifically, *The Helper* demonstrates the ways in which a modern liberal Hong Kong subjectivity, domestic bliss, and freedom are possible only due to the hard work and material and immaterial labor provided by the many domestic "helpers." However, to the extent that Bowers's film acknowledges the violence of liberal humanism, which distributes rights and economic freedom unevenly, it ultimately reproduces another hierarchy of freedom and liberal individualism by positioning white British femininity and motherhood above the local Hong Kong women in human value; in turn, Hong Kong women are positioned above the Filipina domestic helpers in the film.

The Helper affirms the politically correct value of multiculturalism in its opening sequence. Bowers begins the film with an open-ended question: "What is a helper?" The camera turns to various Hong Kong residents of virtually all races, including an African NGO worker, a Cantonese girl, and a white boy. The NGO staff member Carine Kiala states, "In Africa we have aunties who help around the house, but when I first arrived in Hong Kong the idea of a foreign domestic helper who is also a live-in maid was totally foreign to me." The local Cantonese girl gives her answer: "A helper is like, um . . . a person that helps a family and does some chores, and it's like another mommy to the kids." A Filipina then defines the term in this way: "A domestic helper for me is—we are the ones who are in charge of the house when the boss is not around." She smiles confidently while offering this definition. The next speaker, an American white boy, says, "A helper is someone who brings the family together." Then the husband in an interracial couple jokingly says, "I call her my Hong Kong granny!" Another middle-class, English-speaking Asian woman remarks, "I work. My husband works. So when we're both gone, she's not helping, she's doing." This segment ends most powerfully with a concluding statement by the famous democratic politician Emily Lau Wai-hing, the first woman directly elected to the Legislative Council of Hong Kong in 1991. Lau remarks: "They touch all our lives." While this plurality of voices affirms the indispensability of Southeast Asian domestic workers to Hong Kong both personally and economically in an upbeat manner, it also translates the affect of liberal humanism by making the simple but powerful statement that domestic workers are all humans just like us, the viewers— presumably privileged local Cantonese Hong Kongers and foreign expats who have the time to consume an arthouse film about domestic helpers! In other words, the film operates in the classic vein of documentary filmic activism in attempting to give voice to the "voiceless" and disenfranchised.

In her book *Immediations*, Pooja Rangan argues that documentary cinema, especially the genre of participatory documentary, relies on the rhetoric of rescue mission and emergency to carry out its goal of exposing inequality and saving the "other" who is often too powerless to speak on his/her own. Rangan observes that "the aesthetic of feral innocence and other humanist tropes of documentary immediacy exploit the concrete material circumstances and labors of disenfranchised individuals—and do so in a manner that reinforces their status as other."[8] In other words, while documentary films often orient around the desire to speak for the voiceless, the mechanism of the camera's intrusion into private spaces of emotional outburst, the effacement of the filmmaker's positionality, and the claim to truth altogether reproduce the unequal dynamics between the filmmaker and the filmed subjects. In *The Helper*, the approach is more complex, as the white female filmmaker and the white expat women and families who hire domestic helpers acknowledge from the start that they thrive in Hong Kong in large part thanks to the work and maternal sacrifice of their Southeast Asian live-in domestic helpers. The film also includes statistics, such as the fact that domestic helpers contribute around HK$13.8 billion to the economy of Hong Kong, approximately 1 percent of the total GDP in 2016.

One of the oldest domestic helpers in the film, Analyn, comes from Quezon City, the most populous city of the Philippines. She offers one of the most emotional testimonies in the film: "In Manila, I can work there, yeah, but the problem is salary's very low compared to here [Hong Kong]. My eldest son, he finished already his college education in hotel management. And by early next year my youngest son will finish his degree in engineering. And I can say that I am the best and very proud mom with them, you know." As Analyn shares her trauma of separation from her sons (the husband is very much missing from the picture), the camera captures her aging body carrying a large suitcase as she is about to return to Hong Kong to work so she can pay for her younger son's college education. Her white female employer in Hong Kong, Angela Newby, offers this compliment: "If we didn't have Analyn, I wouldn't be able to go to work feeling as confident and relaxed as I do. Having her means that me and my husband can work full-time and know that our children are safe, being well looked after, loved, and cared for." At the end of this filmic sequence, Analyn is seen playing on the beach with a white little boy, the son of her employer, a strange but very common sight in Hong Kong public areas. Analyn states matter-of-factly: "I am taking care of the kids, which are not my own children, but I treat them like my own. And I think they saw that. They trusted me so much."

By giving almost equal amounts of screen time to Analyn and her white female employer, Bowers seems to offer both subjects the same level of respect and the power to convey their messages of motherhood, love, and maternal sacrifice. Furthermore, by showing Angela's acknowledgment of the indispensable contributions of Analyn to her family both economically and personally, the film successfully delivers the multicultural and inclusive message that Hong Kong families of all racial backgrounds simply cannot survive without the hard work of domestic helpers. In other words, *The Helper* is fully aware of the stark inequality that is foundational to the gendering of global-ization, or what sociologist Rhacel Salazar Parreñas terms "the international division of reproductive labor," which "refers to the three-tier transfer of re-productive labor among women in sending and receiving countries of mi-gration. Whereas class-privileged women purchase the low-wage household services of migrant Filipina domestic workers, these women simultaneously purchase the even lower-wage household services of poorer women left be-hind in the Philippines."[9]

But while *The Helper* quite honestly translates the human dimension of feminization of care work and the international division of reproductive la-bor, it also tends to flatten the asymmetry of power by showing Analyn and Angela as equally loving mothers. Simply put, it falls short of scrutinizing the material and global conditions that unevenly distribute (im)mobility to the two racially different female subjects. While Angela is a white expat worker who is marked as a desirable global talent for Hong Kong's global finance and related industries, a "brain gain" for Hong Kong, Analyn's worth is measured by her "talent" in repetitive domestic chores and her trustworthiness.[10]

Even as the film attempts to give voice to the voiceless by narrating the grief of domestic helpers who are separated from their children in the Philip-pines, it also unfortunately reinforces a gendered and racial hierarchy of li-beral humanism wherein white women occupy the top position, followed by local Cantonese-speaking Hong Kong women, sexually respectable do-mestic workers who are mothers, with the sexually free and "promiscuous" pregnant domestic worker occupying the lowest rung of the ladder. This hi-erarchy is established not only through the white female employers who are interviewed in the film but also by positioning a British woman, Jane Engel-mann, as a "feminist teacher" to the domestic workers. Engelmann is cur-rently the performing arts director and composer at an international school in Hong Kong. One key narrative thread that drives the documentary film is the training of and eventual successful and emotional performance by The Unsung Heroes, a choir masterminded by Engelmann and composed solely of English-speaking Filipina domestic workers. Once the group's rehearsal vid-eos appeared on YouTube, they began to receive public recognition and were invited to perform two songs, "Kiss You Goodnight" and "Find Your Voice," at the big local music and arts festival, Clockenflap. While Engelmann comes across as a very humble woman who, like Angela Newby, is fully aware of her own privileged subject position, there are moments in the film when she tries to assert empathy with the domestic helpers who are mothers because she, *like them*, was also a vulnerable mother of a single-headed household raising two boys when she first arrived in Hong Kong. In other words, the fact that Engelmann is now a musical director implies that she is the ideal feminist heroine who is ready to teach the nonwhite domestic workers how to survive in Hong Kong. She literally can help these Southeast Asian domestic maids to "find [their] voice."

The other ranks in this imaginary feminist global sisterhood are illustrated through attention to the work of Jessica Chow, a Cantonese-speaking Hong Kong woman who is the senior case manager of Pathfinders, a local NGO that assists foreign domestic workers in emergency situations who might need legal and humanitarian interventions. And how convenient that Bowers's film indeed includes such a story of a poor domestic worker in need of rescue! Chow, who occupies a kind of middle rank in the feminist hierarchy, appears in the film mostly in her role finding shelter and financial support for Nurul, an Indonesian maid who becomes pregnant while under contract, implying that she is *too* sexually free during her one day off (Sundays). Nurul's employer has terminated her contract, and eventually the hospital where she delivers the baby charges her HK$100,000, ten times the rate for local residents, due to her non-visa status in Hong Kong. At one point in the film, the camera pans through the spaces of Chungking Mansions where South Asian and African small business owners, traders, illegal drug dealers, and hostel owners are located, implying that Nurul will fall into the temptation to sell her child if she decides not to keep her daughter upon delivery. By contrast, Liza Avelino, an empowered and optimistic domestic worker, becomes an avid local hiker and eventually climbs Mount Everest successfully. In his trenchant critique of the myth of liberalism and feminist empowerment in the film, Christopher Patterson writes, "The makeshift community space of the domestic worker areas is here seen as an extension of the Philippine slums. The film captures Avelino's literal uplift, filming her climbing Mount Everest (she makes two attempts) with groups of white westerners, literally climbing upwards from the 'degrading' space of migrant community."[11] In other words, the film performs a strict hierarchal mapping of liberal humanism and feminist empowerment. By relegating the "sexually perverse" Nurul to a position of victimhood, the film assumes heterosexual motherhood within marriage and aspiration for upward mobility as the prerequisites for liberal feminist empowerment. Ultimately, it reinforces the imperial divide of humanism by inventing victimized subjects that documentary humanitarianism can then "give voice" to, to borrow Rangan's notion of immediation again.

While the award-winning 2018 Hong Kong film *Still Human* questions some
stereotypes about migrant domestic workers from Southeast Asia, it resur-
rects the central feature of liberal humanism by imagining friendship and
possible romance between a Filipina domestic worker, Evelyn, and a disabled Hong Kong middle-aged man, Leung Cheong-wing. Directed by Oliver Chan and produced by Fruit Chan, *Still Human* both reproduces and
complicates the liberal humanist project of "giving voice" to the voiceless in
Sinophone cinema about migrant domestic workers. Leung (played by the
award-winning actor Anthony Wong) used to work as a team leader at construction sites; however, a few years ago he was hit by a heavy object that fell
from a building, resulting in the permanent immobility of his legs and neces-
sitating life in a wheelchair. His newly-hired domestic worker from the Philippines, Evelyn Santos (played by the newcomer Crisel Consunji, who is not
a domestic worker in real life) learns upon her arrival that her new employer,
whom she first calls "Sir," can communicate only in Cantonese or very broken English. Meanwhile, Evelyn soon meets other Filipina domestic workers in Hong Kong and establishes friendships with them. They teach her to
act "stupid" as a mode of passive resistance so that her boss will not ask her
to perform more demanding tasks. They even teach her to pretend she does
not know how to ride on the Mass Transit Railway (MTR), the major public
transport network in Hong Kong. Leung is a very street-smart man despite
his immobility, and he soon threatens to fire Evelyn if she keeps acting stupid
and not performing her tasks properly. Meanwhile, Leung is marginalized by
everyone in his immediate family, including his sister, Leung Jing-ying, who
is estranged from him because he disapproved of her marriage with a hair-
dresser (a job considered working-class in Hong Kong). Soon, Leung and
Evelyn establish deep trust, especially after he makes fun of her for aspiring
to become a photographer but then realizes and regrets his insensitivity. As
Leung becomes more humane toward his domestic worker, Evelyn starts calling him by his first name, Cheong-wing. He even buys a high-tech camera for
her after he finds out that photography is her true passion. Eventually, Leung
enables her dream by encouraging her to compete for a Hong Kong photography prize, and Evelyn wins the honorable mention prize with her affectively
raw photography of Hong Kong urban landscapes, ordinary people, and poverty. Evelyn also helps Leung realize his dream by convincing his son, who is
studying overseas in North America, to return home and spend the summer

after graduation with his father in their home at the public housing Oi Man Estate in Ho Man Tin.

Given this emotionally powerful message of hope, dreams, and multicultural inclusion, the film won numerous awards locally and abroad, including best actor for Anthony Wong and best new performer for Crisel Consunji at the thirty-eighth Hong Kong Film Awards, the Hong Kong equivalent of the Oscars. While some reviews expressed concerns about the humanitarian rescue impulse of the film and particularly the way it presents the disabled man Leung Cheong-wing as a savior for the economically and socially powerless Evelyn, a more complex reading must interrogate the entanglement of liberal humanism, disability, race, and queerness. Specifically, I argue that the humanitarian savior mentality of the film is possible only through the exotic commodification of Evelyn's innocence and racialized beauty. In turn, Evelyn's racialized subjectivity and her desire to achieve her dream is what ultimately enables Leung, the disabled and differently marginalized subject, to regain his masculinity and thus his heterosexuality as well. Evelyn's relatively powerless position in relation to Leung's disability emerges early on. In the opening sequence, the camera focuses on the messy interior of Leung's flat in the public housing estate, with clothes thrown all over the floor. The next shot shows him rolling down the hilly road on his electric wheelchair and stopping at the bus stop to wait for the arrival of Evelyn, his new domestic helper. Given his broken English, he even mispronounces Evelyn's English name as *Lin* in Cantonese, which means *lotus*. On the way home, he warns her not to play any tricks on him and tells her that if she decides to switch to a new employer later, she must inform him a month ahead of time because he was screwed over by his last maid, Mary. Shortly after they arrive at the unpleasant flat, Leung uses the Google translate function on his phone to demand that she gives him her passport. He insists that this is "only for your safety." On her first night in a small room, Evelyn takes a picture of her new surroundings and uploads it onto Facebook, with a heading "this is just a shelter, not a real home." While Leung might hold more power over Evelyn due to his role as the boss, his linguistic incompetence in English and physical immobility render him less free than Evelyn. From the start, the film introduces the paradox and intersectionality of heterosexuality, disability, race, class, and gender.

While the film restores Leung's masculinity through the liberal humanist promise of giving voice to the voiceless maid, a cinematic discourse that "seeks to redeem dehumanized lives as a first-order principle," other moments allow a critical interrogation of heterosexuality as a system of compul-

FIGURE 4.1. Cheong-wing's sister (*right*) questions his relationship with Evelyn. Still from Oliver Chan's *Still Human* (2018).

sory able-bodyism that is mutually constituted through racism in the context of Sinophone Hong Kong.[12] Leung's sister illustrates these intersecting oppressions. During Evelyn's first year in Hong Kong, she prepares for a Lunar New Year celebration with Leung. And when Leung's sister visits and stays for lunch, she shows her usual contempt for his surroundings at the public estate flat. At this point in the film, Leung has already bought the new camera for Evelyn as a birthday present, and the two are developing an intimacy beyond the employer-maid relationship. But their relationship is also more ambivalent than a normative heterosexual romance as the two never openly declare their love for each other (perhaps due to internalized stigma about Leung's disability). Still, the sister is shocked by the fact that Evelyn is allowed to eat with them at the dining table; most Hong Kong families force their Southeast Asian maids to eat in the kitchen. Evelyn cleverly retreats into the kitchen at this moment. In another scene, Leung's sister runs into her brother and Evelyn as Evelyn rides happily on the back of his wheelchair—a game they often play together that provides some of the most uplifting parts of the film. However, the sister uses this occasion as an excuse to criticize Leung: "Am I supposed to call [Evelyn] my sister-in-law now? How can you do it with any woman, let alone a *bun mui*? How disgusting!" (figure 4.1).

As noted in my analysis of *Little Cheung*, the phrase *bun mui* in Cantonese reduces the whole humanity of Filipinas to their identity as domestic workers.

But the sister's racist remark also disciplines Leung's sexual desire, suggesting that his disability has stripped him of any right to carry on a romantic relationship. Queer disability studies can unpack the complex crossing of race, heterosexuality, queerness, and liberal humanism in the film.[13] Specifically, the shock expressed by Leung's sister about their possible "miscegenation"— she makes clear that even if he were to enter into a romance, it should be with a local Cantonese woman, not a Southeast Asian maid—requires that we return critical race theory to queer disability studies.

My call to rethink disability studies through queer of color critique is also inspired by the recent work in crip colonial critique that sees imperialism and coloniality as rehabilitative logics that assume the "savagery" of the queer colonized subject. Sony Coráñez Bolton writes, "Crip colonial critique is a queercrip heuristic through which we grasp the racial-sexual and racialized gendered relations of disability within the developmentalist telos of colonialism more broadly."[14] Extending Bolton's work to consider the racial and sexual logics of ethnonationalism in Han-Chinese-centric Hong Kong, a queer Sinophone reading must unpack how Leung's liberal humanism and his rehabilitation of masculinity through altruism still fall short of breaking the taboo of interracial relationships in contemporary Hong Kong. The Han-centric tendency of local Cantonese Hong Kongers to look down on domestic workers from Southeast Asia also stems from the fact that the latter are temporary sojourners who are ineligible for permanent residency, even after a stay of seven years (the required residency for "ordinary residents" to achieve "permanent resident" status) or more in Hong Kong. What ultimately marks Leung and Evelyn's potential romance and friendship as *queer* is not simply the fact that he is disabled but also the very fact that their interracial romance already operates at the limit of racial, gender, and sexual norms in contemporary Hong Kong.

Lesbian Desire and Documentary Activism: Queering Domesticity in *Lesbian Factory* and *Rainbow Popcorn*

If Sinophone Hong Kong films such as *Little Cheung*, *The Helper*, and *Still Human* demarcate the limits of liberal humanism through racial and gendered fetishism, recent documentary films that center on the queer desire and sexuality of domestic workers in Sinophone Taiwan and Hong Kong offer other ways of seeing beyond liberal humanism. Susan Chen's *Lesbian Factory* (2010), its sequel *Rainbow Popcorn* (2012), and Baby Ruth Villarama's *Sunday Beauty Queen* (2016) all present new possibilities for visualizing queer Sinophone intimacies.

Lesbian Factory is a queer activist documentary that narrates the years-long struggle of a group of Filipina factory workers who were fired by Fast-fame Company when the Taiwan computer manufacturer decided to relocate its production site to Mainland China in 2004. Once news of the decision reached the Taiwan International Workers Association (TIWA), a local NGO at the forefront of advocating for women and migrant workers' rights, they intervened, listening to the workers' complaints and beginning the legal procedures to ask Fastfame to pay the workers' unpaid wages. But what begins as a conventional documentary that attempts to "give voice to the voiceless" soon transforms into something altogether queer when the filmmaker, Susan Chen, starts noticing several pairs of lesbian couples at meetings, lunches, and interviews. In other words, Chen provides a rare cinematic record of both ongoing violence by global corporations against migrant workers from Southeast Asia and the queer genders and desire that become visible within anti-capitalist activism.

Film criticism by Feng-Mei Heberer theorizes the cinematic aesthetic of *Lesbian Factory* as sentimental activism, "the simultaneous repetition and radical decentering of liberal rights discourse and its sensorium of human legibility."[15] While Heberer focuses on how the film mobilizes and ultimately queers the liberal rhetoric of humanism, individualism, and social justice toward radical ends, my approach to the film and its 2012 sequel *Rainbow Popcorn* offers a queer Sinophone lens that examines how the migrant workers queer a heteronormative vision of domesticity beyond the "global care chain" and "international division of reproductive labor" frameworks. I show how meanings of home are always multidirectional when workers are confronting the threat of separation between lovers, seeking sexual pleasure within a tight same-sex dormitory space, and negotiating with lesbian femme lovers who might choose heterosexual marriage over lesbian love after "returning home" to the Philippines (as shown in the sequel *Rainbow Popcorn*). A queer Sinophone analysis of the minor transnational journeys of activism, queer desire in urban density, and lesbian entanglements with heteronormative kinship structures thus enables us to theorize the complexity of queer migration. Ultimately, the films visualize the queer Sinophone intimacies of migrant workers as they navigate across Sinophone and non-Sinophone global spaces.

Lesbian Factory begins with the cinematic language of rights, liberal humanism, and social justice in ways that might seem to subordinate the role of the filmmaker through a humanitarian documentary framework. However, this conventional mode of cinematic humanism is juxtaposed with the intensity of queer affective communities among the migrant workers. Specifically,

FIGURE 4.2. Migrant workers chanting a protest slogan in accented Mandarin. Still from Susan Chen's *Lesbian Factory* (2010).

the film opens with a few workers holding up protest banners in English that read: "Fastfame Company Abused Migrants! No Salary! No Food! No Jobs! Please Help!!!" But immediately following a shot that captures a group of migrant workers taking a photo in front of the banner, the camera suddenly shifts to capture a butch-looking worker, Lan, in a black jacket dancing in a macho way and just having fun. Lan will become one of the most active faces of the worker strikes later on. The next scene returns to the group holding the banner. On the count of three the workers all shout loudly in Tagalog-accented Mandarin: "工人鬥陣，車拼相挺," which roughly translates into English as "workers are fighting bravely just like two cars driving fast together" (figure 4.2). Phonetically, this Chinese slogan pronounced by the marginalized Filipina workers points to the cacophony of Chineseness, namely the plasticity of the Sinophone as a living and open linguistic community.[16] Extending the notion of linguistic plasticity and the nondeterminism of the Sinophone, I suggest that the language of rights, representation, and equality that is often expressed by Taiwan citizens and activists in the post–martial law era of political liberalization is here queerly appropriated by the migrant workers, who demonstrate the underbelly of what liberal humanism in Taiwan actively denies. What is queer here is as much the strangely accented Mandarin as the appropriation of political slogans by those subjects who are denied political status in the first place.

Beyond linguistically queering the Sinophone, *Lesbian Factory* also unsettles heteronormative visions of home, domesticity, and kinship among Southeast Asian female domestic workers and immigrant brides in contemporary Taiwan. Feminist sociologist Pei-Chia Lan details how, as modernization enables Taiwan women to enter white-collar professions through access to higher education, the state and heteronormative discourses have not relieved women of care and reproductive work (i.e., biological reproduction like child-bearing and social reproduction like cooking, cleaning, and elderly care). Thus, the notions of "care deficit" and "bride deficit" propel Taiwan's signing of global recruitment programs to import Southeast Asian female domestic workers to relieve working careerwomen from care work.[17] Meanwhile, there is an increasing demand for foreign brides from Southeast Asia, especially from countries like Vietnam and Indonesia, by rural Taiwanese men who have been left behind by urbanization and often deemed undesirable by urban women in the marriage market, which favors hypergamy. Perversely, the increasing media and public visibility of the ethnic migrant bride and the accompanying language of eugenics by state officials often accuse ethnic wives of being unhygienic; as a result, they are seen as unfit mothers compared to Han-Chinese Taiwanese mothers. Lan argues, "Foreign brides and foreign maids are 'outsiders within' in Taiwan—they are considered class others and racialized aliens despite their intimate contacts with Taiwanese households and their physical presence in the national population as temporary residents or future citizens."[18] Still, while Lan's work on the racialized and gendered effects of the global transfer of care work in Taiwan crucially shows how the fragile Taiwanese state in international post–Cold War globalism enacts its own hierarchy of human rights and citizenship, this strand of feminist sociology unfortunately produces another form of heteronormativity, assuming all Southeast Asian migrant women and workers to be heterosexual.[19] It also does not examine the ways in which transnational mobility and the relative autonomy of the Sinophone host countries and regions like Singapore, Taiwan, and Hong Kong might offer migrant workers more opportunities to experiment with queer gender identity and sexual desire.[20]

Lesbian Factory, in its most playful and daring mode, challenges viewers to come to terms with Filipina queer embodiment and desire in Sinophone locations. Specifically, the documentary turns the leftist and activist space of the workers' temporary dormitory into a tight space of erotic playfulness and declaration of queer love. Around three minutes into the film, Chen says in a voiceover, "Originally, we only wanted to faithfully record the process of activism, but as we keep on filming, pairs of *tongzhi* [LGBT] couples appear in the camera's frame. Given its touching nature, this documentary accidentally becomes a story of love." Intriguingly, Chen uses the Sinophone phrase *tongzhi*, which in the past carried a connotation of socialist comradeship but has become a word of community building and solidarity for LGBT-identified Sinitic-language communities in the post-1990s period.[21]

Further, Chen's intimate and intrusive camera and voiceover often directly capture the migrant subjects. The outspoken butch activist Lan declares her love for Pilar, her femme (*po*) lover, in front of other fellow workers and members of TIWA.[22] When asked "Where is your girlfriend?" Lan replies, "There! The very fat one!" She goes on to offer the first testimony of love in the film (many more follow): "You know? I love her very much. You know why? When we have finished working for one year in Taiwan, she said she wanted to go home. Then I said I wanted to stay because my family needs me to send remittance money. And she [Pilar] said: OK, I will stay with you." As Lan finishes her testimony with a big smile, the female workers at the back, who are with Pilar, cheer for Lan and clap hands. An unidentified feminine voice jokingly describes Pilar: "Look at her now, she is pregnant!" In another interview segment, the filmmaker, Chen, asks Pilar why she loves Lan, and Pilar says it is because Lan spends time with her. Lan then adds: "I give her all." Chen inquires: "What's that 'all'?" And Lan replies with a funny face and sly look: "My body!" (figure 4.3). The rest of the film is full of these moments of banal jokes, erotic innuendos, and emotional testimonies.

Discursively, the Taiwanese state and biopolitical governmentality frame both female migrant domestic workers and new immigrant brides as "foreigners within" who must be constantly disciplined, reformed, and civilized—the workers must be desexualized and the mothers modernized. In contradistinction, the queer love, erotics, and solidarity expressed in these cinematic representations of affective community point to queer Sinophone intimacies. These queer forms of intimacy reorder heteropatriarchy and the racist organization of the intimate and the domestic by visualizing other ways of living and desiring, even while migrant workers live on the fringe of Sinophone host countries. Queer Sinophone intimacies are akin to what Neferti X. M. Tadiar calls remaindered life: "modalities of living that exceed the necessary

FIGURE 4.3. Pilar (*left*) and Lan (*right*) express their love and desire in front of the filmmaker. Still from Susan Chen's *Lesbian Factory* (2010).

reproduction of the becoming-human as a resource of disposable life for capital."[23]

Rainbow Popcorn further queers heteronormative notions of domesticity and home by excavating the queer minor transnational trajectories of the Filipina migrant workers several years post–*Lesbian Factory*. The film begins with a scene of a funeral in which the caption informs the viewer that Alice, one of the queer migrant workers, has passed away at the age of thirty-two. (The film later hints that Alice died by suicide.) The rest of the film traces the parallel stories of multiple pairs of lesbian lovers originally seen in *Lesbian Factory* by tracking their diasporic dispersals after leaving Taiwan; they now live in places like Dubai and Manila and on other Philippines islands such as Mindanao. One of the older butch lesbians, Pher, tells the filmmaker, Chen, that her lover, Gie, went to Dubai in 2006 and that she (Pher) soon followed her there. But by the time the sequel was filmed, they had already broken up. Luckily, Pher found a new girlfriend, Lhiean, in Dubai, who was also more financially independent and could support Pher while she was unemployed.

One aspect of queer diaspora and romance that recurs throughout *Rainbow Popcorn* revolves around lesbian love, breakup, and heterosexual mar-

FIGURE 4.4. A bittersweet reunion of queer migrant workers in a hotel room.
Still from Susan Chen's *Rainbow Popcorn* (2012).

riage. Another butch lesbian, Ellen, went to Bahrain after leaving Taiwan; later, after having had a stroke, she came back to the Philippines. The film narration reminds viewers that Ellen and her femme lover, Elsa, were one of the most loving pairs filmed in Taiwan back in 2004. Indeed, Ellen's screen presence in *Lesbian Factory* sometimes rivals that of Lan with her cheerful personality and stocky body. But in 2008, Elsa suddenly decided to marry and give birth to a child. Perhaps traumatized by the breakup and financial losses due to her illness, Ellen looks a lot older and darker in skin tone in the second film. Eventually, the filmmaker follows the life trajectories of almost every couple from *Lesbian Factory*, and they all gather in a small hotel room in Pangasinan, a coastal province in Luzon. Here, each queer migrant subject takes a turn asking questions of other members of the group. What is even queerer is that Elsa's current husband is also in the mix of the Filipina lesbian reunion! (See figure 4.4.)

By tracing the entangled lives of all the queer migrant workers after their first meetings in Taiwan and their ordinary and sometimes traumatic love lives in the years post–*Lesbian Factory*, *Rainbow Popcorn* shows how queer Sinophone intimacies partake of minor transnational routes. While the film at times seems fragmentary, incoherent, nostalgic, and even melancholy, it never portrays its subjects as victims or merely as the "servants of globalization," to borrow Parreñas's provocative phrase again. Commenting on the queer potentials of both films, Feng-Mei Heberer observes that they "center migrant working-class women and trans and gender-nonconforming individuals from the Global South as historical protagonists in the global struggle for equal rights and social justice."[24]

Beyond serving as the transactional medium of global capitalism and as participants in the global care chain, queer migrants' complex life trajectories, romantic breakups, and indeed "messy" lives illustrate what Martin F. Manalansan terms "messy mismeasures": queer intimacies beyond capture by modern state regimes of biopolitics, governmentality, and measurement.[25] Queer migrant workers who find new homes in Dubai or who return to the Philippines only to find that their past "home" has changed dramatically due to further neoliberal deregulation and gentrification thus reveal the messy aspects of minoritarian lives. Queering domesticity and multiplying the notion of "home" thus offer an analytic for describing these messy entanglements of queer minor transnationalism. Indeed, "mismeasures are messy engagements that are performed in order to move, live, and survive. Mismeasures are those that thrive in spaces of the wild and the undomesticated. They are about impossible lives made livable through various fabulous and creative narratives that are spun and woven by minoritarian subjects."[26] If my cultural archive of queer Sinophone intimacies seems a bit messy, it might be that the roots and routes of queer migration by these subjects are in fact beyond the biopolitics of measurement. In the spirit of unruly comparison, I now turn to some more messy queer visual archives and narratives by analyzing the Hong Kong documentary film *Sunday Beauty Queen* and queer magazines published by the Hong Kong queer Filipina group Filguys Association.

Making Queer Homes in Sinophone Hong Kong

Sunday Beauty Queen moves beyond the rhetoric of liberal humanism by documenting the ordinary violence and discrimination that Filipina domestic workers face in Hong Kong and by offering visions of queer Sinophone intimacies and homemaking. The film begins with the bustling urban noises of Hong Kong as the camera pans through jewelry shops, cosmetic stores, and walk-up bookstores on Nathan Road, one of the busiest streets on the Kowloon side of the city. The next shot captures a few domestic workers waiting at the bus stop; one asks another "How do I look?" only to receive a harsh and funny reply, "Your makeup is melting!" Soon, the camera zooms in on the skyscrapers in Central from a low angle, perhaps implying the position of domestic workers looking at the major financial district of Hong Kong from an economically marginalized perspective. The next scene shows a bunch of domestic workers in the process of applying makeup and getting ready for some exciting event. One domestic worker, Rudelie Acosta (who is soon to be terminated by her employer), tries on a pair of bright orange high heels and performs a catwalk. The end of this opening sequence features a cultural anthropologist, Dr. Ju-chen Chen, speaking to the filmmaker, Baby Ruth Villarama, during an informal interview. Chen explains how she encountered a group of lively Filipinas who organize and compete in a beauty pageant. She tells Villarama that at first she asked the contestants why they didn't rest on Sunday, their only holiday free from work, but soon she realized that her question was silly: "This is life for them."

The disorienting perspective of the camera demonstrates contemporary Sinophone Hong Kong to be a global city in its capitalist aspiration, but one that fails miserably to treat Southeast Asian domestic workers fairly. Domestic workers in Hong Kong can rest only on Sundays (or whichever single day of the week their employers might assign under special circumstances) and face a two-week visa termination policy after being fired by employers. This precarity stems from the 2013 *Vallejos v. Commission of Registration* decision: locating domestic workers as "not different in kind, but only in degree, from the pre-existing categories of excluded persons, for instance, Vietnamese refugees and imprisoned or detained persons," the judgment barred domestic workers from any citizenship claim and from any residency status not contingent on their employment.[27] In this way, their existence in Hong Kong illustrates what John Erni terms the "included-out" aspect of cultural citizenship. Erni writes, "As a political concept, included-outness is not something that severs but something that bridges: a sense of inclusion that is in very close proximity to the sense of exclusion, perhaps a sense of the double-take in relation to what happens in experiencing, or sensing, our citizenship or right of autonomy."[28] Erni's concept of the *included-out* clearly points to the vulnerability and marginalization of migrant domestic workers in Hong Kong, and it provides an instructive hermeneutic for analyzing *Sunday Beauty Queen* and previous documentary films on the figure of "the domestic helper." Despite the ongoing violence and inclusive exclusion faced by domestic workers, these workers also embody different ways of being in the world through queering heteronormative notions of domesticity and capitalist regimes of productivity.

FIGURE 4.5. Leo plays multiple roles within the community. Still from Baby Ruth Villarama's *Sunday Beauty Queen* (2016).

The queering of domesticity and capitalist calculations of productive measurement is evident in *Sunday Beauty Queen* in the representation of the butch lesbian beauty pageant organizer Leo, who has also been a domestic worker for many years in Hong Kong. In the film narrative, he (Leo uses masculine pronouns) plays multiple roles, such as the loving "aunty" to Yoanna Leung, the twelve-year-old daughter of his employer; a community organizer for the beauty pageant; and a "helper" and "Daddy Leo," when other foreign domestic workers get terminated and have nowhere to go. Leo seems to enjoy an exceptional arrangement in which his employer allows him to live outside of her home, while most Southeast Asian domestic workers must follow the live-in arrangement mandated by the government. By showing Leo's multiple subject positions and the tension between his feminized role as domestic helper for his employer and his masculine role as Daddy Leo to his lover and the beauty pageant community (which is, by and large, composed of heterosexual female contestants), the film queers a normative model of domesticity defined by maternal caring and household chores (figure 4.5).

To be sure, Leo's identity as a domestic worker is still measured by capitalist logics of exchange value, bodily objectification, and abstraction. During an early segment of the film, when the filmmaker interviews Leo's employer of the past eight years, Bonny Lee, the viewer gets a sense of how the two negotiate a perfect solution for work and family within the single-family Lee household. (It is implied that Bonny Lee is the head of the family because we never see the husband, who is absent even in wedding portraits in the bedroom.) Bonny remarks, "Leo is a huge help for the family! He takes care of everything, and it is so comfortable when I get off work and just relax. He took care of my daughter when she was small, that was a big relief." Here, the cinematic representation of a female-headed family indicates the increasingly diverse composition of households in Hong Kong, in which the traditional and Confucian model of the husband as breadwinner is no longer the only possibility. While Bonny seems egalitarian with Leo by treating him as part of the family, she at times also asserts a businesslike personality. One conversation about buying the proper poultry for cooking illustrates the complex boundaries of domesticity in the Lee family. During dinner one night, Bonny asks Leo why the pork in the soup does not taste very good. Leo tells her that he asked the butcher to sell him the best part of the pig used for making soup. Bonny further probes: "But did you tell him the exact part for pork, you know the pork rib, for soup?" Leo replies, "Yes, I told him that I need the part for making soup." Bonny follows up with doubt, "Did you say it in English or Chinese?" Leo smiles, "Yes, I said soup/*tong*" [Cantonese for soup]. This gastronomic compartmentalization of the body parts of a pig for different uses (some for making soup, some for pork chops, etc.) subtly echoes the similar compartmentalization of a domestic worker like Leo. Namely, at home he must carry out household duties well, and while going to the local wet market, he must learn how to speak Cantonese properly to avoid being cheated by the sellers. Leo's smart response shows that years of residing in Hong Kong have given him a certain familiarity with Cantonese. Using English or Cantonese depending on a specific occasion and balancing domestic responsibility and public commitment to the beauty pageant, Leo's embodiment exemplifies a queer Sinophone remaking of home.

Here, I borrow Gopinath's theoretical insight of "queering the home." Excavating a vibrant corpus of queer diasporic cultural productions such as novels, films, and music in South Asian public cultures, Gopinath argues that "non-heteronormative sexualities travel within and away from the space of home and transform the very meanings of home in the process."[29] Likewise, Francisca Lai's pathbreaking work on queer Indonesian migrant domestic workers shows how their butch and femme lesbian relationships in Hong Kong do not actually relieve the women of their daughterly duties to their families back "home" in Indonesia. In other words, queer migrant domestics create multiple senses of home across the Sinophone diasporas of

Hong Kong and back home "over there." Lai suggests that "a transnational perspective that looks comparatively at current, past, and future locations of 'home'—imagined and otherwise—can help us to better understand the sexual subjectivities and same-sex oriented gendered sensibilities of Indonesian domestic workers in Hong Kong."[30] Both Gopinath's queer diasporic approach and Lai's ethnography of queer gender embodiment by migrant domestic workers show how meanings of home, belonging, and desire are multiply reconfigured within the realms of cultural representations and everyday materiality of queer racialized subjects.

Taking up this potential of queering the home and centering Leo's subjectivity in *Sunday Beauty Queen*, we can thus unpack the dense and mobile meanings of home and domesticity as Leo travels between his employer's home and his own queer home on the outskirts of the city. Around twenty minutes into the film, the camera follows Leo's footsteps as he commutes on the MTR. In the subway compartment, Leo tells the viewer that he works from 10:00 a.m. to 7:00 p.m. each day, and on any given Sunday, he is working hard to sustain the beauty pageant and the community of Filipina domestic workers in Hong Kong. While the film caption reveals that "he's one of the few allowed by his employer to have his own home in Hong Kong," his home in what appears to be Yuen Long, in the western part of the New Territories, seems "rough" and chaotic. The entrance to the building is located in a back alley, but Leo is renting the flat with elevator access at a bargain price of only HK$5,500 (around US$700) monthly. As Leo enters the flat, he greets his femme lover with the term of endearment *Mother*, probably because many other Filipinas in the local community call him *Daddy Leo*. Leo then jokes with Mother that they renamed the "Beauty and the Beast" theme of heterosexual pageantry "Beauty and the Best" when the competition first began and that "the lesbian was the Best."

During the film, when a female contestant walks onstage, she is often accompanied by a butch-looking masculine "groom." In its most daring mode, *Sunday Beauty Queen* queers the heteronormative logic of domesticity attached to the modern nuclear family in Hong Kong while challenging dominant knowledge about Southeast Asian domestic workers, which tends to reinforce the heterosexual and maternal model of the global care chain and the international division of reproductive labor. Through its queer Sinophone visuality of alternative homemaking, the film dares us to see beyond the confines of capitalism and liberal humanism that either maternalizes migrant domestic workers through logics of care or universalizes their suffering through a theory of global disposability. Tadiar also suggests that "the idle practices of social enjoyment can also be viewed as a time of recovery and restoration, a time for the restoration of life-times lost in the production of time for others. While these times of waste can be viewed to thereby support the reproduction of waged reproductive labor, within such times of reproduction can also be gleaned times exceeding sustenance, times 'freeing' experience from the emancipated subjectivities of labor, times of flourishing and elaboration that cannot be subsumed in the life-times of disposability reproduced."[31] In its queer alternative rendering, *Sunday Beauty Queen* alludes to "analytical and empirical openness to the possibilities of migration, gender and emotion that will enable a more expansive and effective politicization of global domestic workers by refusing to render their affective status as 'natural' and inevitable."[32]

An Alternative Archive of Queer Sinophone Intimacies

While documentary and fiction films powerfully visualize queer Sinophone intimacies beyond the strictures of heteronormativity and liberal humanism, a handful of queer and lesbian Filipina networks in Hong Kong produce print materials such as pamphlets and magazines that offer another window into the often-overlooked domain of queer Sinophone culture. Filguys Association Hong Kong is one of the longest running organizations founded by LGBT-identified Filipinos. While its community members are not composed solely of migrant domestic workers, many indeed work now or once worked as domestic workers in Hong Kong. Filguys was founded in 2006, and since then it has successfully hosted community events, including a "best couple" competition, outreach programs during the LGBT Pride Parade, and private wedding ceremonies. For example, during its fourth anniversary it held the "Filguys' Couple of the Year" contest (figure 4.6). The association's magazine features a front page that lists its founding members (Marrz Saludez Balaoro, Irene Coles Peji, Ian Bojo, Pia Bagaoisan, Elsa Lacar, and Berna Morales, among others) and gives a welcome message from its founding President, Balaoro: "Four years ago, twenty founding members welded their efforts to form the first Filipina lesbian organization in Hong Kong with the aim of boosting morale and catering to the needs and welfare of lesbians and other overseas Filipino Workers (OFWs). A lesbian victim of physical assault by a homophobic man in 2006 gave rise to this unity. The death of Hilda Mali Montilla, who was brutally killed by her jealous husband, pushed us to reaffirm our commitment to further our cause to promote and protect our rights and general well-being of Filipino lesbians in Hong Kong." Balaoro fur-

SEARCH FOR FILGUYS' COUPLE OF THE YEAR 2010 FINALISTS

COUPLE # 1 - JAY & EDARLYN

COUPLE # 2 - MARZ & YOLLY

FIGURE 4.6. Filguys' "Couple of the Year" contest winners. Courtesy of Queer Reads Library. Reprinted with permission by Filguys Association Hong Kong.

ther calls on all LGBT Filipinas with the following inspirational message: "The vision to stand up as who we are, with pride and dignity not only for lesbian rights but joining the overall struggle of the Filipino people to have a humane life for all is the ultimate goal of this progressive organization."[33]

Balaoro's uplifting message of hope and fighting for equal protection and rights should not be narrowly understood as an appeal for liberal human-ism. Rather, the material efforts by Filguys to advocate on behalf of, and work alongside, fellow queer and lesbian Filipinos through modes of affirmation, survival, and pleasure point to minoritarian tactics and disidentification in Sinophone Hong Kong. If Hong Kong's official policy of immigration and rights of abode deny Southeast Asian migrant workers the right to become legal citizens, Filguys' determination to remain active and build for longevity and survival actualizes bottom-up and horizontal networks of alliance. The very fact that it participates in the annual LGBT Pride March and Queer Migrant March, in addition to holding workshops at LGBT-friendly hotels like Eaton Hotel, indicates its multiple platforms of activism, solidarity building, and homemaking. A queer Sinophone unruly comparison perversely juxtaposes a dominant liberal humanist framework of seeing migrant domestic workers with alternative queer visuality. Queer Hong Kong as method can imagine queer survival, longevity, activism, and resistance through cultural productions like *Lesbian Factory, Rainbow Popcorn, Sunday Beauty Queen*, and printed materials from Filguys' archives. Such a queer Hong Kong method challenges the Han-centrism and raciality of queer Hong Kong culture while simultaneously exposing the heteronormative and racialized modes of representing "minorities" in dominant Hong Kong media. Through the visuality of queer intimacies, these cultural forms actualize the place-based practices of queer Sinophone articulation and homemaking by seeing queerly beyond the visual regime of liberal humanism.

TRESPASSING THE
SINOPHONE BORDER
On Fruit Chan's Prostitute Trilogy

With the global COVID-19 pandemic; the resurgence of populism in Europe, Asia, and the United States in recent years; and the 2022 Russian invasion of Ukraine, the question of borders has assumed new significance. The academic field of border studies tends to reinforce a certain disciplinary separation between the humanities and social sciences. While the social sciences offer historical and international security-based accounts of the shifting boundaries of border, existing theory on borders and borderlands in the humanities often reveals the psychic and social violence imposed upon the classed, gendered, racialized, and sexualized minorities who are most likely to be policed and detained at national borders by security regimes.[1] For example, Gloria Anzaldúa offers the following poetic evocation: "Borders are set up to define the places that are safe and unsafe, to distinguish *us* from *them*. A border is a dividing line, a narrow strip along a steep edge. A borderland is a vague and undetermined place created by the emotional residue of an unnatural boundary. It is a constant state of transition."[2]

For Anzaldúa, borderlands and borders are not simply spatial limits imposed by heteronormative nationalism and border patrols; they are also the liminal psychic conditions and sources of resistance of those who simply do not fit into "normative" and binary personhood. Anzaldúa introduces the figure of the *mestiza* as an embodiment of the feminist and queer potential to rupture hegemonic constructions of boundaries: "She [the *mestiza*] communicates that rupture, documents the struggle. She reinterprets history and, using new symbols, she shapes new myths. She adopts new perspectives toward the dark-skinned, women and queers."[3] In short, the queer *mestiza* figure exemplifies both the social violence enacted upon racialized queer subjects and their possibility of resistance against such state-imposed heteronormative structures.

Extending Anzaldúa's work and drawing on recent feminist and queer approaches to border studies, what might a queer Sinophone inflection on border and borderland look like?[4] How might it unsettle the conventional spatial and temporal logics of Hong Kong, situated in between the triangular geopolitics of Britain, the PRC, and global capitalism? Furthermore, building on Lily Wong's recent work in queer Sinophone studies that traces the affective embodiments of the border-crossing sex worker figure, how might a queer Sinophone approach to sex work in Hong Kong cinema unsettle existing frameworks of Hong Kong studies, area studies, and queer theory?[5] In this chapter, I turn to the films of Fruit Chan, specifically to the three films in his "prostitute trilogy."

In his classic breakthrough film, the independent and award-winning *Xianggang zhizao* [香港製造 / *Made in Hong Kong*] (1997), Fruit Chan narrates the marginalized working-class protagonist Autumn Moon's life through a series of misfortunes and entanglements with crime that ultimately result in his death. The film begins with Moon discovering a suicide letter written by a high school girl, Susan, whose despair resulted from an unconsummated affair with a married PE (physical education) teacher. Since discovering the letter, Moon has had a wet dream every night while suffering from nightmares about Susan. Eventually, he falls in love with Ping, a working-class girl with a fatal kidney disease. Ping's family borrows money from the local Triad, and in attempting to help Ping and her family get out of a distressing situation, Moon promises to "save" her and join the local Triad to carry out assassination tasks. At one point, Moon also attempts to murder his own father because of his extramarital affair and for having abandoned his family. Before the ultimate failed assassination that leads to Moon's death, a campy musical score is played in the background while Moon dances half naked in torn, cheap jeans. A film about a failed murder, a failed romance, disability, patricide, delinquency, and frustrated youthful sexuality—is there something queer about Fruit Chan's independent Sinophone classic?

Made in Hong Kong introduces several key themes that Fruit Chan continues to explore in subsequent films, such as 1997 Hong Kong's postcolonial return to the PRC, transnationalism and border-crossing, female sexuality, marginalized working-class communities, and Hong Kong localism. Chan's cinematic oeuvre, as I demonstrate, intervenes in existing debates on borders, Chineseness, female sexuality, and queer desire in Sinophone cinema. What would it mean to unsettle the notion of Chineseness from the vantage point of Sinophone Hong Kong cinema? How might a rigorous study of the heterogeneous subjectivities of the sex worker figure reveal the porousness and instability of the border of the Chinese nation and the regional border across Hong Kong and the Mainland?

Fruit Chan is a Hong Kong independent filmmaker with a grassroots sensibility, and his three films on the plight of the border-crossing female sex worker are often universalized as representing "the aesthetic form of the global city."[6] This chapter departs from previous studies on Chan's films that tend to universalize the suffering of Hong Kong sex workers and marginalized working-class communities as tropes of postcolonial crisis in post-1997 Hong Kong. Likewise, nationalist articulation of Chineseness often maps onto sexually moral and politically progressive female subjects in the history of Chinese cinema in modernist and socialist films such as *Xin nuxing* (新女性 / *New Women*, dir. Cai Chusheng, 1935) and *Qingchun zhi ge* (青春之歌 / *Song of Youth*, dirs. Chen Huai Ai and Cui Wei, 1959), while in contemporary Hong Kong cinema the prostitute figure in *Yanzhi kou* (胭脂扣 / *Rouge*, dir. Stanley Kwan, 1987) symbolizes the bygone glorious past of 1930s colonial Hong Kong. In *Rouge*, the prostitute/ghost Ruhua's return to Hong Kong in the 1980s epitomizes the crisis of spatial disappearance and urban postmodernity. How might queer theory and Sinophone studies disrupt this tendency to associate the prostitute figure with politics, morality, and modern nationalism? How might the female sex worker be read as queer through her destabilization of the border of Chineseness?

Given the increasingly porous border between the Mainland and Hong Kong and the nationalist logic of seeing Hong Kong as part of the Greater Bay Area in both the PRC's economic infrastructure and, indeed, in Xi Jinping's recent speech on restoring order in post-2019 Hong Kong (after the 2019 protests), Sinophone studies emerges as ever more important in its emphasis on multidirectional critique. Shu-mei Shih, in her original formulation, provocatively predicts that "as Hong Kong's integration into China is more and more thorough, Hong Kong may inevitably cease to be a Sinophone community on the margins of China and Chineseness but partake more constitutively in the imagination of new forms of Chineseness within China."[7] While Shih's diagnosis of Hong Kong's precarious condition under the shadow of China-centrism is quite perceptive, I stress that the value of queer Sinophone studies lies precisely in its critical attention to the complexity of cultural forms that defy the hegemonic formulation of Chineseness, whether in its nationalist or long-distance diasporic variety. Chris Berry's concept of "cinemas of the Sinosphere" is also instructive here, as this notion shifts from "a language-based to a cultural-based definition of multiple cinematic ways of being Chinese. . . . Unlike the old Sinosphere in which China was the centre of the known world, we are now experiencing a multipolar world of overlapping and competing world orders."[8] To this end, I deploy queerness here less as the Anglo-American-centric critique of identity politics but as a critique that troubles any fixation of Chineseness and sexual positionality. Here, I build on the recent work in queer Sinophone and transpacific studies that tracks the ever-morphing figuration of the sex worker and the queering of the geographical border across China and the United States. As Lily Wong writes, by "detecting these assemblies through the affectively charged figure of the sex worker, Chineseness is deterritorialized from fixed, and often exclusionary, authenticity discourses."[9]

Using a similar approach that tracks the heterogeneous morphology of the sex worker subject as she unsettles geographical and ideological assumptions of Chineseness through both the invocation and undoing of borders, this chapter examines Fruit Chan's "prostitute trilogy," which consists of *Durian Durian* (2000), *Hollywood Hong Kong* (2001), and *Three Husbands* (2018). While *Durian Durian* portrays the friendship between Yan, a sex worker, and Fan, an illegal immigrant girl in Hong Kong, the portrayal of Yan's more peaceful life back home in Northeast China also subverts the stereotypical idea that Hong Kong is a more desirable city of social mobility for young Chinese women. I read Yan as a queer Sinophone subject who critiques the ethos of capitalist upward mobility in contemporary Hong Kong from a feminist perspective in Northeast China. *Hollywood Hong Kong* further queers the border of the PRC and Hong Kong through the global border-crossing travels of the sex worker Hung Hung. In this section, I mobilize queer Sinophone studies to track the multiple power dynamics embodied by Hung Hung, who is controlled by the mysterious Hong Kong rich pimp Peter while she herself gains an upper hand over the working-class male clients in the soon demolished Tai Hom Village. The multidirectional critique of queer Sinophone studies emerges most powerfully in the last film of Chan's trilogy. *Three Husbands* most daringly symbolizes the geopolitical tension within Hong Kong by showing how the female protagonist, Ah Mui, negotiates the power dynamic between her first, second, and third husbands, thus subtly queering the triangular relationality among Hong Kong's British colonial legacy, Chinese nationalism, and Hong Kong's Sinophone localism. In other words, the film shows how Ah Mui and her sexual attachments to the "three husbands" both conjure the well-worn geopolitical metaphor of Hong Kong being sandwiched between the three masters of British colonialism, China-centrism, and global capitalism, while it ultimately undoes any easy attempt to read the figure fully by the queer Sinophone fracturing of subject position. This deconstruction of border and Chineseness is evident through the cinematic obsession with imageries of water, ocean, sailing, and belonging to nowhere in general.

Overall, Chan's cinematic aesthetic offers an analytic of unruly comparison: it frames the sex worker as a queer, unruly figure who both embodies the new geopolitical anxiety of China-centrism in postcolonial Hong Kong while envisioning this figure as a conduit for unknowing Hong Kong-ness through the queering of border.

Durian Durian: Queering the Fetishism of the Mainland Prostitute

Durian Durian unsettles and queers the spatial borders between Mainland China and Hong Kong by visualizing both the materialist dimension of Hong Kong's return to China under the doctrine of "One Country, Two Systems" and the affective merging of the two spaces by the sex worker Qin Yan's state of mind. The film begins with a panoramic long shot of the iconic Victoria Harbor from the view of Tsim Sha Tsui, while a melancholy score of the saxophone plays in the background. Soon, voiceover narration by the female protagonist, Qin Yan (often referred to as Yan), emerges. She tells the viewer: "My hometown is right by a river. When I was a kid I used to walk by the river because the school was on the other side. In Hong Kong, there's a harbor too. People cross it every day to go to work. You can take a ferry or cars there. Not like in my hometown. In the summer, we can take the boat. But when winter comes, we can only take cars or walk." As Yan narrates the similarities and differences between Hong Kong and her hometown, Mudanjiang, in the southeast part of Heilongjiang Province, the blue water of Victoria Harbor seems to become yellowish, resembling the "local color" of her hometown. Through cinematic techniques like the montage, fade-out, and dissolve, Victoria Harbor visually changes into Mudangjiang. Aesthetically, this opening sequence captures the liminal status of the female sex worker as a temporary sojourner. As mandated by the Hong Kong government border and custom regimes and the policy of controlling "illegal immigrants," any Mainland visitor must leave Hong Kong after ninety days; a longer stay can result in deportation. While the material and governmental aspects of immigration control mandate an absolute distinction of the local versus foreign and the legal citizen versus illegal immigrant, Yan's voiceover and the cinematic malleability and crossing of oceanic currents suggest that she can find bits and pieces of Northeast China in Hong Kong and Hong Kong in Mudangjiang. In other words, the film questions the biopolitical separation of borders through a cinematic provocation of queering oceanic borders, for the ocean indeed has no clearly demarcated border.

Beyond queering the physical border between the PRC and Hong Kong through the oceanic metaphor of crossing, the film also destabilizes the conventional and heteronormative fetishizing of the figure of the "Mainland prostitute." In Hong Kong cinema and mass media, it is not uncommon to find this highly exoticized figure, overlaid with meanings of backwardness, hypersexuality, and greed. Notably, *Long Arm of the Law* (1984), directed by Johnny Mak Tong-hung, narrates a group of ex-People's Liberation Army (PLA) men who have now become well-trained armed robbers targeting banks and aiming to "colonize" the wealth of capitalist Hong Kong just across the Shenzhen border. In the film, a narrative of gender transformation underlines the bygone romance between Pa Chung, one of the big-circle criminal robbers, and Ah Sheng, his former sweetheart in Guangzhou. Now working in the red-light district of Mongkok, Ah Sheng occasionally reminisces and savors the nostalgic memory of past romance while finding her current status as a Hong Kong prostitute more profitable and preferable. Other Mainland sex workers in the film are granted less humanity, often reduced to a state of animalistic existence whose only motivations in life are money and greed and whose only redeeming quality is their sex appeal.

Of course, this tendency to objectify the Chinese prostitute is historically and cinematically coproduced. Lisa Lowe's work on the gendering and racializing mechanism of Asian immigration to North America reminds us that the Page Act (1875), which banned Chinese women from entering the United States, often reduced all Asian women to the figure of "immoral prostitute" through its arbitrary enforcement.[10] In cinema, Rey Chow's notion of "primitive passions" reveals that from the golden days of Chinese cinema during the 1920–30s Shanghai modernist and left-wing cinema period, prostitutes remain gendered and sexualized figures of fetishism in such films as *Shennu* (神女 / *The Goddess*, dir. Wu Yonggang, 1934) and *Malu tianshi* (馬路天使 / *Street Angel*, dir. Yuan Muzhi, 1937).[11] Extending Freud's concept of the fetish and Marx's notion of commodity fetishism, Chow writes, "If the commodity stands for the alienation of human labour in industrialized society, the prostitute, by being at once the worker and the commodity, is arguably the paradigmatic case of *a commodified fetish in human form*."[12] Chow's reading of the prostitute figure through the frameworks of fetishism and human commodification also evokes the history of racialization, commodification, and social death that condition transatlantic slavery.[13] This connection suggests that any cinematic representation of the prostitute as a commodified sexual fetish is at once a racialized fetish insofar as the Mainland prostitute figure in Hong Kong conjures up the fear of a *foreigner within* the city who can potentially become a homewrecker. Chow further elaborates, in her reading of Chinese cinema's fascination with the prostitute figure, that the figure embodies a gender and class contradiction: "This is the contradiction, perhaps more peculiar to the media involving visuality, of *presenting 'lowly' or debased subject matters or characters in a cultural form whose effects tend to be spectacular and glamorous*."[14]

Chow's work here provides a useful point of departure from which to engage with Fruit Chan's trilogy insofar as Chan's three films both destabilize, queer, and to some extent reproduce myths and fetishism surrounding the sex worker figure. Returning to the cinematic analysis of *Durian Durian*, we might ask: How does Yan the sex worker and her border-crossing trajectory both reproduce and queer the fetishization of the Chinese woman as sex worker? If fetishism in both Freudian and Marxist conceptions hinges on the glamorization and erasure of the labor that goes into the production of the commodity that is sex work itself, how do Yan and her labor reveal the unglamorous and almost repetitive routines of sex work?

Durian Durian queers the cinematic fetishism of the prostitute by juxtaposing glamorous and exotic scenes of sexual intercourse with unglamorous scenes of waiting, shitting, eating, and enduring boredom in Hong Kong. Specifically, the first scene in which Yan (Qin Hailu) enters the camera's frame takes place in a dirty alleyway that is most likely located in the Mongkok district in Kowloon, famous for shopping, entertainment, and the thriving red-light district. Employing a conventional cinematic gaze through a tracking shot, in an example of what Laura Mulvey terms "scopophilia," the camera focuses on Yan's legs as she walks in front of her male pimp, Yiu. Their walk through the alleyway is seen from the perspective of the illegal child laborer Fan, who is underage for employment and without permanent resident status. Fan lives with her family in a small flat carved out of a normal-size flat to work around the pricey real estate market in Hong Kong. The next sequence again objectifies Yan as the camera slowly studies the back of her body from the shoulder to the waist, revealing her red panties peeking above her jeans. As she eats a lunchbox, a travel commercial is playing on television. At the same time, Yiu is using the toilet, and as he defecates he finds that Yan has not flushed the toilet paper with her feces on it. Instead, she has thrown the dirty toilet paper into the trash bin. Yiu questions Yan's poor hygiene: "It doesn't bother you? You are eating around it too!" Yan only stares at Yiu with a disapproving look. The next scene shows Yan putting on makeup in a local Hong Kong café. Just at this moment she receives a call to serve a male client at Victoria Hotel, an infamous love motel. Intriguingly, the first scene in the film depicting a sexual encounter between Yan and a male client skips the intercourse, focusing instead on the small talk between the client and Yan. While the camera shows the man's naked body in the shower, Yan, wrapped in a towel, counts the money she has received for the job. Relatively speaking, Yan's body here is fairly desexualized.

If Chow demonstrates that the visual fascination with the prostitute figure in cinema is contradictory in the sense that the viewer's fascination derives from the lewd and debased nature of sex work, *Durian Durian* exposes this contradiction with a queer twist. Indeed, by redirecting the cinematic fetishization of the prostitute's body to her unglamorous preparations before sexual intercourse takes place—shitting, sleeping, resting, eating, waiting, and so on—the film queers the will to know and the glamorization of the prostitute figure by granting the viewer access to what is usually unpleasant and hidden behind: the process that reproduces the commodity itself. These hidden yet vital processes point to the human labor of sex work in its most corporeal and thus most unglamorous forms. As Wendy Gan argues, "Chan removes the sensationalism of Yan's job through the portrayal of sheer repetition and routine. As we see Yan meet customer after customer, we recognize the set patterns of her job—from the familiar traipse to the motel accompanied by her pimp escort to her scripted greetings and exhortations to her customers to tip her well."[15] In other words, through the cinematic aesthetic of routine and repetition, Fruit Chan goes a long way in troubling the heteronormative male gaze toward the sex worker by recognizing that sex work is as repetitive and unglamorous as any other form of work in a capitalist society.

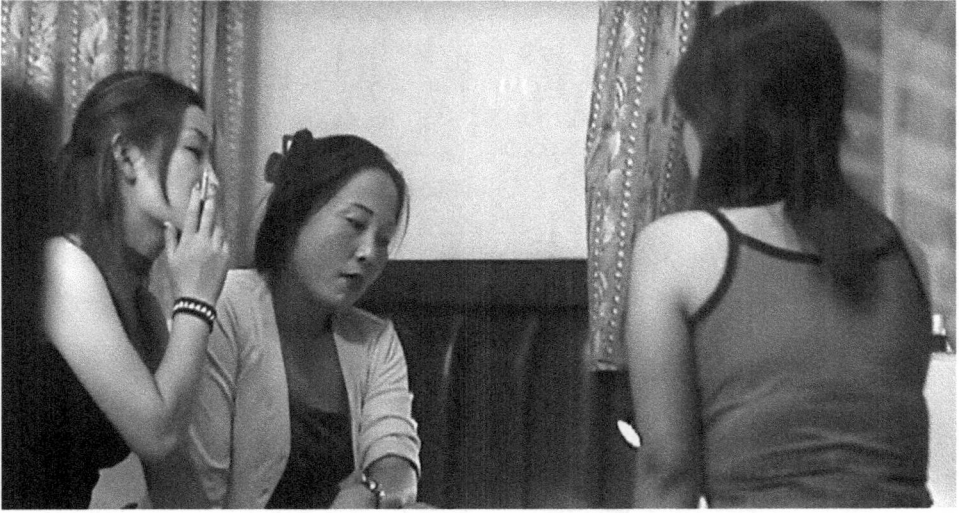

FIGURE 5.1. Yan (*left*) commiserates with fellow sex workers from mainland China. Still from Fruit Chan's *Durian Durian* (2000).

Durian Durian further queers the cinematic borders across Mainland China and Hong Kong by presenting a double narrative that disrupts the dominant view of the Mainland prostitute in Hong Kong as a victim of trafficking, which often reinforces a related assumption of Hong Kong people's moral and economic superiority over new Mainland female immigrants, given the latter's presumed criminality and susceptibility to illegal prostitution. The film further defetishizes prostitution by hinting at the possibility of a horizontal and cross-generational alliance among women. Specifically, one scene features Yan engaging in small talk with fellow sex workers from the Mainland, and they all concur that their Hong Kong male clients are petty and often tip stingily (figure 5.1). Beyond picturing a sisterhood among female sex workers, the film develops another narrative arc by showing the gradual development of friendship and intimacy between Yan and Fan (played by Wai-Fan Mak, the same actress who played an illegal child immigrant in Chan's previous film, *Little Cheung*). Before Yan leaves at the end of her legal stay in Hong Kong, she passes her home address in Mudangjiang to Fan. Fascinated by the pungent smell of durian, which is often nicknamed the "King of Fruits," Fan mails a durian to Yan, who has now moved back to Northeast China. Yan shares the fruit with her high school friends despite the sorrow of a recent divorce from her husband, Bai Xiaoming, which may (or may not) be directly linked to Yan's past profession as a sex worker in Hong Kong. By playfully associating the mobile trajectory of Yan from Northeast China to Hong Kong and back to her hometown with durian, the film evinces forms of queer Sinophone intimacy that she develops across the vast spatial distance of the Mainland and Hong Kong.[16] Furthermore, these minor and mobile intimacies defy the conventional framing of the sex worker as victim of sex trafficking by mapping female-to-female forms of network and solidarity beyond heteronormative desire. While lured by frequent calls from her female brothel madams in Shenzhen and Hong Kong, Yan by the end of the film decides not to return to Hong Kong, instead pursuing her hobby of opera singing and performance.

Previous feminist work by Shu-mei Shih on the representation of Mainland women in Sinophone mass media shows that Taiwanese mass media tend to negatively eroticize Mainland women as mistresses of Taiwanese men (often called the "Mainland sister" [*dalumei* / 大陸妹]), while Hong Kong media in the 1990s equally exoticized Mainland women from across the border as potential threats to Hong Kong's married families. Furthermore, Hong Kong media and the commercially successful series of films *Her Fatal Ways* (dir. Alfred Cheung, 1990–94) degrade another category of Mainland woman as the "Mainland cousin," the *biaojie*, whose femininity "tends to denote a set of mostly negative characteristics: backwardness, unfashionableness, lack of proper etiquette and culture, and an inclination to use bribery and connections."[17] *Durian Durian* considerably departs from this heteronormative script of gendered geopolitics. Ultimately, Chan's film visualizes the sex worker Yan as resourceful in Hong Kong, satisfied with her new life back in Mudanjiang, and reluctant to return to Hong Kong. In Yan's refusing to succumb to the lure of transnational capital through sex work and instead charting a new path for herself through horizontal feminist solidarity with other sex workers and Fan, the film ultimately maps minor-to-minor forms of mobility, solidarity, and belonging, namely a form of minor transnationalism within China.

Hollywood Hong Kong: Queering the Transnational
Borders of Sex Work

Hollywood Hong Kong (2001) takes up some of the queer potential of *Durian Durian* with its further exploration of the queer transnational mobility of the sex worker figure. The film begins with a medium shot of the Chu family, a family of butchers that includes a father, Mr. Chu (Glen Chin); an older son,

Ming (Ho Sai Man); and a little boy, Tiny. The chubby Chu family resembles the pigs they butcher for sale, and from the start the viewer is fully aware that the family lives in Tai Hom Village, a squatter village in Diamond Hill in Kowloon that was slated to be demolished in 2001 at the time of filming. Soon, we are introduced to another resident of the village, Wong Chi-Keung (played by Wong You-nam, of the Cantopop duo *Shine*), who wastes his time watching porn all day while dreaming of making it big in Mongkok, the commercial district famous for prostitution. In fact, he carries on his own small "business" by pimping out his casual girlfriend, Ah Lu. He even learns the digital skill of photoshopping to make Ah Lu look more like a Eurasian bombshell. Soon enough, Chi-Keung comes across an online ICQ (the most popular form of online dating software at the time) advertising "The Angel of Shanghai," an attractive woman named Hung Hung (Zhou Xun). At different points in the film, this woman also calls herself Tung Tung in order to disguise her true identity. Chi-Keung is erotically attracted to Hung Hung, and one night asks her out to the hiking trail overlooking Diamond Hill to have outdoor sex. While Chi-Keung treats the sexual encounter as a date, soon enough he starts receiving legal letters stating that Hung Hung is underage, and his sexual intercourse with her constitutes a statutory crime as it is illegal in Hong Kong to have sex with anyone under the age of sixteen. These scam letters demand money from Chi-Keung. It turns out that the two adult men in the Chu family, Mr. Chu and Ming, fall for the same scam after having sex with Tung Tung/Hung Hung; apparently a mysterious lawyer called Peter is the mastermind behind this legal scam and blackmail. Chi-Keung refuses to pay to settle the legal dispute, and he is chased by the urban Triad hired by Peter and the mysterious prostitute. By the end of the film, Hung Hung/Tung Tung leaves Hong Kong for Hollywood without facing any legal consequences or retribution from the Chu family or Chi-Keung, while Chi-Keung's hand is amputated by the mafia gang hired to punish him for not paying up for sex.

Given its genre of neo-noir, use of black humor, and themes of sex work, disability, and globalization through a sensationalist plot, it is not surprising that critics tend to read *Hollywood Hong Kong* as paradigmatic of the underside and horror of class inequality within globalization. Pheng Cheah argues that the film "positions Hong Kong within the circuit of global capitalism and unflinchingly portrays the inhuman consequences of global connectivity. What makes it exemplary in a manner that goes beyond the specific case of Hong Kong . . . is that it captures the aesthetic form of the global city."[18] But while the cinematic representation of the prostitute as a femme fatale who brings both desire and damage to the inhabitants of a poor working-class area like Tai Hom Village resonates well with an abstract idea of Hong Kong as a global city that conjures up both desire and fear, I interpret the film from the perspective of queer Sinophone studies by emphasizing the border-crossing transnational flexibility of Hung Hung/Tung Tung. Indeed, the very names *Hung Hung* and *Tung Tung* can be translated as *red red* and *east east* in Chinese. If we put the two words together, they carry multiple symbolic meanings. They can point to the very status of Hong Kong as a SAR of the PRC, with the red color implying the national flag. Indeed, the double identity of Hung Hung as Tung Tung farcically conjures up the haunting revolutionary heritage that imbues "The East Is Red" [東方紅 / *Dongfang hong*], a famous 1966 song that attests to admiration for Chairman Mao by fellow comrades during socialist China; but *Hollywood Hong Kong* adds a queer twist, since the savvy border-crossing sex worker looks nothing like a socialist female comrade.

The queering of border through Hung Hung's transnational mobility begins during her first sexual encounter with Chi-Keung. Arguably, their first meeting takes place virtually, as Chi-Keung finds her information on ICQ. Hung Hung's advertisement calls herself "white-haired girl" and "the Angel of Shanghai," while Chi-Keung's casual girlfriend, Ah Lu, belittles this glamorous competitor from the Mainland as the "Northern sister." The term *Northern sister* carries the negative connotation of an unrefined prostitute from the Northern region of China—a stereotypical figure that, by the late 1990s, had invaded Hong Kong media, often as a homewrecker destroying local Hong Kong families.[19] From the start, then, Hung Hung's identity is multiply fractured and queerly inflected. The Chinese "flavor" of the socialist "white-haired girl" who is socially upright and opposes the capitalist class now comes into conflict with the local ideological positioning of Mainland prostitutes as troublemakers who are savvy self-entrepreneurs. Crossing regional boundaries with no clear geographical origin of her own, Hung Hung is mysterious in a way that recalls Yan in *Durian Durian*, who tells different clients that she is from Hunan, Xinjiang, Shanghai, or simply from Hong Kong! Beyond the ambiguity of her geographical identity, Hung Hung also subverts the moral superiority of Hong Kongers over Mainland women by displaying herself as a savvy woman who is arguably more upwardly mobile, financially, than people like Chi-Keung, Ah Lu, and the Chu family.

The representation of Hung Hung as a street-smart sex worker-cum-businesswoman marks the rise of a new class of mobile Mainland Chinese women on Hong Kong screens and in public media, and "the sexual economies that would presume Mainland women as less modern than Hong Kong women are destabilized by the increasing mobility of women's economic activities across both sides of the border."[20] Specifically, Chi-Keung first meets Hung Hung at the Diamond Hill MTR station and agrees to pay her HK$1000 for sex. Chi-Keung promises to give her a "good time" but reaches orgasm too quickly. As they are having sex by the underground tunnel, Hung Hung looks up to the high-rise residential buildings in the Diamond Hill district, including the Plaza Hollywood, an unmistakable symbol of consumerism and the Hong Kong middle-class good life.

After the quick sex, Hung Hung questions Chi-Keung's virility: "Are you a tiger? A tiger's head, but a snake's tail." (The Chinese slang, which refers to someone whose ability and power are less than they appear, also foreshadows Chi-Keung's disabled body after his hand is chopped off by the mafia gang and reattached by an unlicensed female doctor in Tai Hom Village.) Hung Hung continues to belittle Chi-Keung by stating that she lives in a flat in the Hollywood high-rise and that he is worse than her, being born in such a poor place as Tai Hom Village. As she walks up the hiking trail with him after sex, she further claims that Shanghai is prettier than Hong Kong, thus underlining Shanghai's possible replacement of Hong Kong as the new global financial hub. Finally, after reaching the top of the mountain, Hung Hung puts her five fingers in front of her face and remarks that "Hollywood looks like Five-Finger Mountain." By spatially aligning the newly gentrified Hollywood high-rise in Diamond Hill with Five-Finger Mountain—the mountain in *Journey to the West*, under which the Monkey King is confined—Hung Hung again asserts her economic and moral superiority, implying that Chi-Keung is a mischievous local Monkey King forever trapped in Tai Hom Village. As Cheah observes, "Globality as symbolized by Plaza Hollywood bears heavily on the minds of those who live in Tai Hom Village as an ambivalent object of fantasy and anxiety."[21]

Hung Hung's assertion of the economic and moral high ground over and against Chi-Keung proves prophetic: the ending of the film shows that she has transcended the Sinophone border of Mainland China and Hong Kong by crossing the ocean to live in Los Angeles. The next scene shows a postcard addressed to Tiny Chu arriving at the Chu family's mailbox in Tai Hom Village. The sender turns out to be Hung Hung/Tung Tung, and the postage stamp indicates it has come from Los Angeles. The final scene shows the female protagonist, the embodiment of transnational femininity, libidinal desire, and fantasy, now wearing a casual shirt and short skirt that make her look like any other Chinese student studying abroad in California.

While Hong Kong cinema is replete with cosmopolitan female subjects who partake in various forms of exile, travel, and mobility that defy national and regional borders (films such as *Zhongqing senlin* [重慶森林 / *Chungking Express*, dir. Wong Kar-wai, 1994] and *Tian mi mi* [甜蜜蜜 / *Comrades: Almost a Love Story*, dir. Peter Chan, 1996] come to mind), what makes *Hollywood Hong Kong* truly queer *and* Sinophone lies in the way that the film directs our critical attention to the multidirectional dynamics of power and (im)mobility at play. Hung Hung could not have traveled to Los Angeles and remade her life without accruing money through sex work, scams, and exploitation of the local working-class men in Hong Kong. Hung Hung's cosmopolitan Chineseness is likewise conditional only to the extent that she follows the scheme set out by the mysterious capitalist pimp Peter. Ultimately, unlike the Hong Kong locals who are forever trapped in the soon-to-be-demolished Tai Hom Village, through sex work, illegal monetary scams, and economic savviness, Hung Hung/Tung Tung has become a truly border-crossing female subject, queering the Sinophone borders that once contained her. Her playground is no longer the Hollywood in Diamond Hill but the Hollywood in America.

Three Husbands: The Geopolitics of Queer Sinophone Hong Kong

Three Husbands is probably the most provocative of the three films in Chan's trilogy. The film both depends on the well-rehearsed postcolonial theory of Hong Kong as between colonizers and, through queer Sinophone visual aesthetics, unsettles any nationalist and geopolitical mapping of the global city. Specifically, my reading demonstrates how the film both invokes dominant metaphorical geopolitics of Hong Kong mediated by British colonialism, China-centrism, and global capitalism while showing how a queer Sinophone lens ultimately undoes these hegemonic positions. Queer Sinophone studies offers a clear-eyed analysis of the multiple layers of power dynamics and positionality in the film.

The opening scene, at a karaoke bar in Zhuhai, features hostesses/sex workers catering mostly to Hong Kong and Macau's sex tourists from across the border. Little Bro (Chan Charm-man), the male protagonist, and other Hong Kong men are greeted by prostitutes who hail from Heilongjiang, Henan, Guizhou, and Guangxi. While the prostitutes and clients are singing, Little Bro interrupts the cheerful noise by calling himself a descendant of Lo Ting [盧亭], the half-human, half-fish mythological figure who is said to have been the original inhabitant of Hong Kong.[22] This is the first of several times the film references Lo Ting.[23] Suddenly, Mainland officers enter the private karaoke room and arrest all the sex workers and clients. Little Bro is kind enough to bail out Sau Ming, a Cantonese-speaking prostitute who claims to come from Guangxi but later turns out to be from Hong Kong, even though he needs to borrow money from his friend in Hong Kong, Fatty (Sai Man Ho, who played the character Ming Chu in *Hollywood Hong Kong*). Though barely getting by financially, Little Bro has the tendency to try to "rescue" prostitutes.

Back in Hong Kong, Little Bro resumes his habit of visiting prostitutes. He becomes addicted to one particular sex worker, Ah Mui, who is visibly mentally impaired and manipulated by her current husband, referred to as Second Bro or Second Husband in the film. Ah Mui's mental illness is linked to her sexual insatiability in the film; she is addicted to sex, and Second Husband, a man almost twice her age, decides it would be profitable to market her as a sex worker on the boat that they sail and live on near Gin Drinkers Bay, the waterway in Kwai Fong near Tsing Yi. Little Bro meets her on the boat, eventually falls in love, and decides he wants to marry Ah Mui and adopt her new-born child as his stepson. It turns out that the baby is actually the son of her incestuous biological father (First Husband). Despite being very poor, Little Bro bails out Mui from a life of prostitution, paying her second husband HK$80,000 to divorce her. Once Mui moves into the small public housing flat owned by his grandmother where Little Bro lives, she remains melancholy, as she is used to having sex on the boat instead of on land. To quench Mui's sexual desire, Little Bro comes up with creative ideas such as having sex on a blown-up, floating mattress, sneaking into a moving truck in which they fuck on colorful plastic balls, and even sticking an eel into Mui's vagina. Unable to satisfy Mui's thirst for sex, Little Bro/Third Husband eventually arranges with Second Bro/Second Husband to again sell Mui as a sex worker on the boat. Eventually, the shipboard prostitution scheme is discovered by the sea patrol, who mandate that the three husbands, Mui, and her baby leave Gin Drinkers Bay immediately. The group sails to Tai O, a fishing village on the western side of Lantau Island. Believing that Mui is also a descendant of Lo Ting and is in fact a demonic fish-and-human figure, the three husbands decide to find out the truth of Mui's mythological ancestry in Tai O. While there, they continue to sell Mui for sex to the local men, while the women and wives of the village try to hunt her down. By the end of the film, the three husbands and Mui are sailing to nowhere and approaching the newly built Hong Kong-Zhuhai-Macau Bridge that will begin operation in October 2018.

Whereas in the two preceding films the prostitute figure represents emergent transnational Chinese femininity by traveling and defying national and regional borders, here the prostitute's interspecies body seems to represent Hong Kong itself. The term *interspecies* refers to "relationships between different forms of biosocial life and their political effects. It is a capacious framing paradigm that names the articulation of human/nonhuman binaries and human/animal/plant taxonomies as interrelated even as these continue to operate in both congealed and differentiated modes."[24] Following the dominant logic of Hong Kong postcolonialism with a queer Sinophone twist, Mui functions as an allegorical Hong Kong subject caught between two colonizers. Whereas British colonialism since 1842 affected Hong Kong's economic structure through laissez-faire capitalism, free market ideals, and relative freedom in terms of the uses of Chinese and English in official language policy and social life, the return to the motherland evoked in many Hong Kong locals a fear of the implementation of the socialist system and ideological "colonization." Therefore, while the phrase *between colonizers* might be historically inaccurate, it quite provocatively captures the collective fear of Communist China's takeover in the late 1990s. At the time of writing this book, Hong Kong has experienced what some cultural critics term a "second return" to China, and the large-scale civil disobedience, protests, and social movements of 2003, 2014, and 2019, coupled with a state-mandated zero-COVID policy in 2020, mean that Hong Kong people in general are sensing the ideological, political, and cultural effects of Mainlandization more and more on a daily basis.

Given existing discourses on Hong Kong postcoloniality as a subtle (or not so subtle) form of triangulated cultural-economic colonization, it is tempting to read Mui, with her three husbands, as an embodiment of Hong Kong serving the three masters of Chinese nationalism, British colonialism, and global capitalism. However, geopolitical allegory can be overly simplistic if we map China, the UK, and globalism symbolically onto the three husbands. What is so *useful* about Mui is precisely her ability to generate surplus value, something that the incestuous First Bro (her biological father), fisherman Second Bro, and working-class Little Bro lack. Furthermore, none of the husbands seems to be the perfect candidate to stand in for either Chinese nationalism, British colonialism, or globalism. I suggest that the interspecies figuration of Mui as Hong Kong via her role as a prostitute remains logical only if we approach her multivalent subjectivity through a queer Sinophone critique. A queer Sinophone reading highlights Mui's status as shuffling constantly in between the human and the nonhuman, mobility and immobility, and power and powerlessness.

Mui's mobile subjectivity (her status of living between sea and land), queer insatiability, and interspecies embodiment rupture the referentiality of Chineseness or Hong Kong-ness. This queer rupture leads to an understanding of Mui's queer Hong Kong liminality as a form of queer Sinophone articulation and multidirectional critique. This multidirectional critique resides in Mui's hypersexuality, in which her constant urge for sexual pleasure amid a watery, vibrational context leads to the defiance and queering of multiple borders and boundaries.[25] Specifically, when Mui moves into the small public housing flat owned by Little Bro's grandmother, they fuck vigorously a few times a day, with their "private" bedroom separated by only a curtain from the dining room. Soon enough, the neighbors complain about the noise, and eventually one male neighbor is lured by Mui to engage in casual sex; her fluid and vibrational sexuality and constant desire for pleasure disturbingly disregard the boundaries between public and private, normative and nonnormative.

If Mui emerges as a symbolic figure of Sinophone Hong Kong localism, it is a form of localism that is multidirectional in its queer disorientation and desire.[26] For example, once Little Bro/Third Husband finds that she is not satisfied with sex at home and being tied to living on land, he exploits multiple occasions for quick sex, including the most perverse scene of the film in which they sneak onto a truck and have sex in a half-opened container while the driver steers the vehicle across the busiest street in the financial district of Central. Cinematically, the camera films Mui and Little Bro in a state of orgasm through an aerial view where they can see the street, pedestrians, and high-rise buildings in motion from the moving truck, while other people would only spot the couple's nudity if they were to occupy an elevated visual position somewhere near the truck (figure 5.2). Aesthetically, Fruit Chan's cinematic gaze queers the masculine visuality of verticality and aerial view by displaying a mode of queer Sinophone cognitive mapping, which "provides a cinematic language to express how queer subjects in Sinophone films navigate time-space compression, gentrification, and the heteronormative gendered division of the public and the private."[27] *Three Husbands* pushes the multidirectional critique of queer Sinophone studies to its visual limit in the sense that any attempt to search for Mui's ancestral origin (is she a descendant of the mythical creature Lo Ting?) and to *cure* her mental disability and sexual addiction remains futile. Here, queer cognitive mapping takes on a vibrating journey. The final sequence of the film, in which Mui wears a red dress (which might be symbolic of the Communist PRC) and stands at the bow of the boat alongside her three husbands facing the Hong Kong–Zhuhai-Macau Bridge, articulates an uncanny queer Sinophone visuality. Mui, the queer Hong Kong prostitute subject, is facing the uncertain future of Hong Kong across the oceanic currents of further economic and cul-

FIGURE 5.2. Mui and Little Bro have sex in the bed of a truck driving through Hong Kong's financial district, Central. Still from Fruit Chan's *Three Husbands* (2018).

tural entanglement within the state-mandated "success story" of the Greater Bay Area.

Fruit Chan's ironic representation of a queer female sex worker sailing to nowhere amid the increasing economic tidal wave of Chinese capitalism and economic integration of Hong Kong into the PRC is evident through a minor female subject: Sau Ming, the sex worker from Hong Kong who pretends to be from Guangxi at the beginning of the film. By the end, Sau Ming rides on a cross-border bus, perhaps following the "advice" by Xi Jinping and then-Chief Executive of Hong Kong Carrie Lam to open herself to new opportunities on the Mainland. Whether sailing across an unknown seascape or embarking onto new economic sexscapes in the Mainland, both Ah Mui and Sau Ming embody protean Sinophone positions that ultimately undo any fixity and assumption of the border of Chineseness.

By considering the border-crossing queerness in the cinematic representations of the prostitute in Fruit Chan's prostitute trilogy, we come full circle with the theoretical challenge and promise of Hong Kong cinema as a site of vibrant queer Sinophone critique. While Yan, the transnationally mobile female sex worker in *Durian Durian*, challenges gendered geopolitics that denigrate and fetishize Mainland Chinese women as backward, *Hollywood Hong Kong* further visualizes the flexible citizenship of the prostitute Hung Hung/Tung Tung as she crosses regional and transpacific borders, moving from the PRC to Hong Kong to the United States. Finally, *Three Husbands* demonstrates the extent to which any attempt to essentialize Hong Kong through dominant geopolitical allegories—such as the city being between colonizers or under the three masters of Chinese nationalism, British colonialism, and globalism—is doomed to fail. Instead, one must come to terms with the multidirectional critique of queer Sinophone studies. Queer Sinophone visuality in the work of Fruit Chan unsettles our constant fixation on queerness, Chineseness, and Hong Kong-ness. Ultimately, Chan's prostitute trilogy daringly queers the analytical borders of China studies, Hong Kong studies, and queer theory through the Sinophone aesthetic of unruly comparison.

EPILOGUE

Throughout this book, I have invoked the concept of unruly comparison in three specific senses. First, unruly comparison envisions queer Hong Kong cultures through, paradoxicaIly, the politic of unknowing Hong Kong itself through opacity and conceptual openness. It argues that the dominant mode of comprehending Hong Kong through metaphors as a former British colony, as a global city, a late capitalist city within the PRC, and as a special administrative region between colonizers tends to restrict Hong Kong's worldliness within the China-centrism of area studies and the Eurocentrism of queer theory. Drawing on two decades of transnational queer studies scholarship, my book advocates for a model of queering Hong Kong and other similarly marginal regions of the world by understanding them beyond postcolonial anomaly and capitalist exceptionality.

Second, unruly comparison expands the spatial and temporal units of comparison by connecting Hong Kong to the rest of the world through "deep time" and minor transnational scales. It takes up the question of translation and incommensurability from the discipline of comparative literature and cultural studies to treat Hong Kong as a protean site for exemplifying racial, gender, class, and queer incommensurability and differences internally while extending this elastic scale of comparison to other regions, temporalities, and archives outside of Hong Kong. My approach of relational comparison places Hong Kong in asymmetrical comparison across histories of colonialism, imperialism, war, diaspora, migration, and neoliberal capitalism. In turn, this unruly approach opens up the queer worlding potential of Hong Kong literature and cinema (chapter 1); the South-South queer transnationalism that reckons with neocolonial complicity (chapter 2); the queer globalities of global human rights in trans visuality in Hong Kong (chapter 3); queer Sinophone intimacies among Southeast Asian migrant domestic workers (chapter 4); and the cinematic visuality of unruly queer border-crossing by sex workers (chapter 5).

Third, by reading across racial, gender, class, and sexual differences *within* Hong Kong and extending them to other transnational geographies and temporalities (Israel-Palestine, Southeast Asia, Taiwan, Mainland China, the UK, and more), a queer unruly comparison unknows Hong Kong by not presuming the Han-centric raciality and localism of a proper gay Hong Kong subject. By not privileging a conventional approach that centers on Cantonese gay men and lesbians as the default subjects for queering Hong Kong, a queer Sinophone approach also disrupts the China-centrism of Chinese studies, the Han-centric raciality and localism of Hong Kong studies, and the unspoken trans and racial exclusion of scholarship on queer Hong Kong. By unfixing the "proper" gay Hong Kong subject through the queer Sinophone ethic of unruly and asymmetrical comparison, I see my work as actively in conversation with Travis S. K. Kong's approach of transnational queer sociology and Denise Tang's project of studying the erotic density and transnational mobility of aging lesbians across Hong Kong, Taiwan, Singapore, and other marginal Sinophone regions overshadowed by a rising China.[1]

In this epilogue, I demonstrate how a queer Sinophone ethic of unruly comparison offers a minor transnational approach for reading across the asymmetrical power dynamics of homelessness, subalternity, displacement, British imperialism, and rising China-centrism. I turn to Jun Li's latest film *Zhuo shui piaoliu* (濁水漂流 / *Drifting*, 2021) as an unlikely queer Sinophone text that accentuates feeling of homelessness, loss, unbelonging, queerness, and subterranean resistance in post-2019 protest Hong Kong and read it in comparison to the award-winning young Hong Kong poet Eric Yip's poem "Fricatives." While Li's film hails into being Hong Kong's queer undercommons[2] through a not-so-subtle critique of post-2019 Hong Kong as a police state— queering homelessness by imagining queer kinship among homeless men, a mentally challenged youth, a sex worker, and a former Vietnamese refugee—Yip's poem further connects Hong Kong youth, queerness, linguistic impurity, and interracial imperial desire by writing a post-2019 queer Hong Kong diaspora from within the former imperial center of Britain.

Li's *Drifting* recently won the award for Best Adapted Screenplay at the fifty-eighth Golden Horse Awards in Taiwan. The film centers on the story of the protagonist, Ho Kei-fai, played by veteran actor Francis Ng. In the film, Ho is often referred to as Brother Fai, a well-known unhoused man who lives on Tung Chau Street in Sham Shui Po, one of the most densely populated working-class neighborhoods on the Kowloon side of Hong Kong that is infamous for being populated by drug addicts and sex workers. Just when Brother Fai is released from prison, his belongings, including a much-treasured photograph of his dead son, are suddenly confiscated by the police and cleaners from the Food and Environmental Hygiene Department (FEHD). His fellow rough-sleepers Master, an older, respected Vietnamese refugee who is also homeless; Chan Mui, a former female club dancer and sex worker; and others decided to file a lawsuit with the help of the social worker Miss Ho. When the government and FEHD agree to settle the case with an individual payment of HK$2000 to each plaintiff, Brother Fai refuses to accept the payment and demands a formal apology from the government. Throughout the course of the film, Brother Fai also befriends a young man named Muk. Muk suffers from speech disorder and mental health issues, both of which the film suggests are linked to the years he spent separated from his mother. Fai forms a genuine bond with Muk and treats the young boy almost like his own son. By the end of the film, Fai's temporary home is set on fire during a particularly cold and dry winter.

While some initial film criticism and journalistic commentaries praise Jun Li's film for its simplicity and cinematic realism in portraying poverty, gentrification, and homelessness in a matter-of-fact manner, I deploy a queer Sinophone approach here by pointing to the ways that the filmmaker visualizes *homelessness with queerness* through a cinematic appraisal of the dehumanizing effects of neoliberal capitalism and gentrification, on the one hand, while seeing queer intimacy among the homeless as engendering an undercommons, on the other. The film debunks the myth of individualism and the dominant Hong Kong economic ideology of hard work and self-sufficiency (otherwise known as the Lion Rock spirit) by showing how gentrification and urban redevelopment in Sham Shui Po also led to the further marginalization of homeless people, beggars, drug addicts, and sex workers, namely, the surplus population destined for necropolitical expulsion. The visualization of gentrification emerges early in the film's narrative. In the establishing shot, the camera pans from the cityscape of Kowloon through a kaleidoscopic scanning of newly built high-rise residential buildings. Immediately following this shot, the camera adjusts to a low-angle shot that positions Brother Fai and Master at the center of the frame. Master offers to "treat" Fai with a drug injection just after Fai's release from the prison. The next scene shows the police and FEHD officers ordering Fai and the homeless gang to stand aside for regular street cleaning. As the officers indiscriminately clear all of Fai's belongings (including his family photo and Hong Kong identification card), Fai can only put up a fight by verbally cursing the officers.

While this scene depicts how the police officers and government workers clear the belongings and homes of homeless people in Hong Kong without prior notice, it also symbolically alludes to the very dehumanization of homeless folks like Brother Fai, Master, and Chan Mui as deviant subjects who can be expulsed with impunity. The confrontation between the homeless and the police force also brings up the more political question whether the police are acting on behalf of the state and exercising excessive force. One police officer, in fact, shouts at Brother Fai that "we police don't need you to teach us how to properly do our job!" This was, in fact, one of the most frequent warnings directed by the police toward protesters during the 2019 Hong Kong protests, which the government and official discourse have recently branded as a "color revolution" and "black riots" since most protesters wore black clothes and masks to avoid surveillance. In an affectively charged mode, the cinematic representation of the confrontation between the homeless and the police thus evokes a more general sentiment that many pro-democracy Hong Kongers feel about living in the city at the current moment: a queer sense of disorientation and unbelonging. Alternatively, the very acts of Brother Fai verbally assaulting the officers and rescuing his only photograph of his son serve as a reminder that he is not simply a piece of rubbish that can be easily discarded.

The film critiques the violence of neoliberalism and gentrification not by re-conferring liberal humanism on Brother Fai and his friends. Instead, Jun Li shows the possibility for horizontal solidarity and queer intimacy among homeless subjects and those who experience mental health issues who are otherwise made invisible by "normal" Hong Kong citizens and the government. This horizontal intimacy is most evident in the father-son-like relationship between Brother Fai and Muk. Muk first offers to carry the bed frame with Brother Fai when he sees him dragging the heavy item across the street. The Fai-Muk kinship bond also offers a sarcastic critique of real-estate hegemony and capitalism in contemporary Hong Kong. Specifically, as Brother Fai suffers from chronic foot pain, Miss Ho convinces him to stay hospitalized. One night, Fai escapes the hospital with the help of Muk, and the young boy even secretly infiltrates a construction site, operates the crane, and elevates Fai to see an ariel view of Shum Shui Po at night. From there, Fai and Muk piss onto the ground. When the police officers find out that someone is pissing from above, Muk helps Fai escape by running around and evading the police's chase. This scene visualizes what Michel de Certeau calls the power of the weak through tactical intervention by the powerless, who must "seize on the wing the possibilities that offer themselves at any given moment."[3] If real-estate hegemony rests its capitalist and phallic power through the regime of verticality and elevation, Brother Fai's momentarily elevated vision positions him as a perverse urban parasite that suspends the regime of neoliberal dehumanization of the homeless.

Furthermore, queer Sinophone intimacy and alliance also operate in a less obviously confrontational manner: mapping queer female desire and fractured kinship across Hong Kong and the Vietnamese diaspora. In one scene, Chan Mui (played by veteran erotic film actress Loletta Lee) reveals to Brother Fai that she may soon move in with another homeless woman, Aunty Lan, when the government assigns a public housing unit to them. In a heartfelt conversation with Fai, Chan Mui expresses her doubt about whether Aunty Lan will relocate together with her. In another easily overlooked scene in the film narrative, Chan Mui massages Lan's foot to alleviate her pain from a recent injury. The two women exchange ambivalent smiles that suggest that their relationship might signify something queerer than sisterhood among urban dwellers in a homeless community. In a different scene, the social worker, Miss Ho, is able to identify the long-separated son of the homeless Vietnamese Master. Master's son, Thang Quang, now lives in Norway and has grown up as a successful architect. In a highly emotional dialogue between father and son during a virtual meeting set up by Miss Ho, Master confesses that he failed to relocate to Norway from the refugee camp of Hong Kong in the past (most likely during the 1980s) due to his criminal activities in the detention center. The next day after this virtual reunion, Master takes his own life by jumping into the ocean. By weaving together several narrative threads, namely the homosocial kinship between Brother Fai and Muk, the queer lesbian intimacy between Chan Mui and Aunty Lan, and the fractured transnational kinship between Master and his son due to the Vietnam War and refugee relocation, *Drifting* gestures toward an analytic of unruly comparison. This queer optic of unruly comparison recognizes the immense cultural, racial, and sexual incommensurability within Hong Kong by expanding it toward other regions, histories, and archives. The film embodies a queer Sinophone visuality that ultimately unknows what a proper Hong Kong subject might be in an era of homelessness (both metaphorical and materialist), subalternity, political suppression, and global migration.

The closing credits of the film state that the screenplay is based on an actual legal dispute between the homeless community in Sham Shui Po and the government in 2012. Tragically, two homeless men died before the government issued any formal apology. The opening sequence also quotes from the feminist philosopher and queer theorist Judith Butler's writing: "Such bodies both perform the conditions of life in public—sleeping and living there, taking care of the environment and each other—and exemplify relations of equality that are precisely those that are lacking in the economic and political domain."[4] In its manifold visualizations of homelessness, the brutal processes of neoliberal dehumanization, and the subterranean formation of the queer undercommons, *Drifting* offers a powerful vision of unruly comparison that unsettles Hong Kong across the asymmetries of China-centrism, the Vietnam War, refugeehood, and diasporic displacement.

My approach of deploying unruly comparison as an analytic that reads differences and connections across the asymmetries of imperialism, colonial legacy, China-centrism, and neoliberal capitalism thus links *Drifting* with "Fricatives" in an unlikely manner. Both the film and the poem allude to queer deviant subjectivities rendered impossible and unthinkable within post-2019 Hong Kong. Eric Yip's poem, however, further pushes the limits of comparison across language, migration, queerness, and Hong Kong itself. The speaker is presumably a Hong Kong young man who has newly arrived in Britain. He is instructed by a certain Mrs. Lee "to speak English properly" and to "learn / the difference between *three* and *free*."[5] The poem also references the United States when it invokes the famous prison escape:

> Three men
> escaped from Alcatraz in a rubber raft and drowned
> on their way to Angel Island. (ll. 2−4)

In the next line, the speaker confronts the reader with a terrifying mental image of a man whose testicles have been beaten:

> Look
> at this picture. Fresh yellow grains beaten
> till their seeds spill. That's threshing. That's
> submission. (ll. 5−8)

The speaker alludes to his Hong Kong diasporic identity by remarking sarcastically:

> Nobody wants to listen
> to a spectacled boy with a Hong Kong accent.
> You will have to leave this city, these dark furrows
> stuffed full with ancestral bones. (ll. 10–13)

While the first part of the poem offers the reader some clues on the diasporic identity of a Hong Kong boy who left the city for the West (possibly the UK or the United States) and who speaks with an accent, the rest of the poem provides more vivid descriptions of blood and violence that recall scenes of the police's use of excessive force on protesters in the summer of 2019 in Hong Kong. The speaker instructs readers on possible topics for writing about Hong Kong for a curious Western audience:

> You will speak of bruised bodies
> skinnier than yours, force the pen past batons
> and blood, call it fresh material for writing. (ll. 14–16)

The last portion of the poem self-reflexively comments on the title of the poem:

> You're lucky enough
> to care about how the tongue moves, the seven types
> of fricatives, the articulatory function of teeth
> sans survival. You will receive a good education
> abroad and make your parents proud. You will take
> a stranger's cock in your mouth in the piss-slick stall
> of that dingy Cantonese restaurant you love and taste
> where you came from, what you were made of all along.
> *Put some work into it*, he growls. *C'mon, give me*
> *some bite.* (ll. 17–26)

The poem ends with the speaker stating that he is taking his mother, who visits him in October, to the same Cantonese restaurant and ordering dim sum in English.

> They're releasing
> the students arrested five years ago . . .
> The television replays
> yesterday on repeat. The teapots are refilled. You spoon

served rice into your mouth, this perfect rice.
Steamed, perfect, white. (ll. 29–34)

Structurally, the poem moves seamlessly between the art of mastering a language (English) and the act of mastering sex, and in this particular case, the act of learning submission to perform oral sex on a stranger. That the sexual act takes place in Chinatown with the accented Hong Kong boy assuming a submissive role resonates with what queer theorist David L. Eng terms "racial castration." Namely, within the Western cultural imaginary of feminizing Asian masculinity and the historical formation of the Chinese "bachelor societies" in North America during the Chinese Exclusion Era (1882–1943), Asian men have been emasculated and rendered deviant both racially and sexually.[6] While the speaker never names the racial identity of the stranger on whom he performed oral sex, the ending of the poem, which erotically conflates rice with semen as "steamed, perfect, white" may possibly allude to his sex partner being white. Regardless of whether the sexual encounter is interracial or not, the poem ultimately portrays a politically engaged Hong Kong young man in the process of learning English and coming into sexual awakening of himself as queer, all the while staying alert to the latest political developments in Hong Kong. The unruly convergence and comparison of race, sexuality, queerness, immigration, and geopolitics in Yip's daring queer poetics not surprisingly has resulted in the young poet winning first prize in the 2021 National Poetry Competition in the UK.

While a straightforward reading of the film *Drifting* would reduce it to a cinematic exemplar of class segmentation and the social realism of homelessness, an unruly comparative approach demonstrates how in fact a seemingly local community in Sham Shui Po already evinces incommensurable differences, worldliness, and intersectionality. The purposeful asymmetrical juxtaposition of queer kinship and alliance among Brother Fai, Muk, Master, and Chan Mui (namely a socially and racially incommensurate group) offers a relational comparison that recognizes both the internal differences within Hong Kong while connecting this elastic Sinophone community to other regions, histories, and archives. If the political unconscious of state and police violence serves as a subtext in *Drifting*, the queer Hong Kong diaspora in the UK narrated by the speaker in "Fricatives" demonstrates queer Sinophone subjectivity as a dense repertoire for thinking the entanglement of language, race, migration, and queer desire. At once racially castrated, linguistically impure, and politically deviant, the queer Cantonese speaker offers a queer Sinophone imaginary in a drifting poetic vision that ultimately unknows both Hong Kong-ness and queerness. In this conjoined queer optic offered by Li's film and Yip's poem, we see a queer Hong Kong method that constantly unknows the relationality between queerness, Hong Kong, and the Sinophone.

Notes

INTRODUCTION

1 Hong and Ferguson, "Introduction," 3.
2 Chiang, "(De)Provincializing China," 20.
3 On the concept of wake work, see Sharpe, *In the Wake.*
4 Hung, *City on the Edge,* 15.
5 Hung, *City on the Edge,* 14.
6 On the concept of minor transnationalism, see Lionnet and Shih, *Minor Transnationalism.*
7 Gopinath, *Unruly Visions,* 7.
8 Muñoz, *Cruising Utopia,* 1.
9 Standing Committee of the National People's Congress, "The Law of the People's Republic of China on Safeguarding National Security in the Hong Kong Special Administrative Region."
10 Chan, "Hong Kong Protests."
11 Tang, "Where Are You Going?," 32.
12 Mirzoeff, *The Right to Look,* 1.
13 On parasite as a Sinophone concept, see Tan, "Parasite."
14 Dimock, *Through Other Continents,* 3–4.
15 Cheah, *What Is a World,* 11.
16 On the concept of "a small place" as a point of departure for critiquing the legacies of colonialism and the tourist gaze, see Kincaid, *A Small Place.* I am also inspired by Evelyn Blackwood's work on queer desire and locality in West Sumatra, Indonesia. See Blackwood, "Transnational Sexualities in One Place."
17 Apter, *Translation Zone,* xi–xii.
18 On the concept of disappearance, see Abbas, *Hong Kong.* On theorizing Hong Kong as caught between colonizers, see Chow, "Between Colonizers." For the phrase "lost in transition" as a framework to describe Hong Kong's postcolonial economic transition into the orbit of China's postsocialist capitalism, see Chu, *Lost in Transition.* For the provocative idea of Hong Kong serving the three masters of British colonialism, Chinese nationalism, and global capitalism, see Erni, "Like a Postcolonial Culture."
19 Melas, *All the Difference,* xii. Melas's emphasis on figures of incommensurability is illustrative of the broader debate about distant reading (Franco Moretti), (un)translatability (Emily Apter), planetarity (Wai Chee Dimock, Gayatri Spivak), and worlding (Pheng Cheah) in the fields of comparative literature and world literature.

While all these models aim at overcoming the field's entrenched Eurocentrism, they also perceptively emphasize the worlding aspects of literature, its longevity beyond the temporality of the nation and empire, and its rupturing of East-West comparison.

20 Chuh, *Difference Aesthetics Makes*, xi.

21 Shih, "Comparison as Relation," 79. See also Bernards, *Writing the South Seas*.

22 Lowe and Manjapra, "Comparative Global Humanities," 26.

23 See Tadiar, *Remaindered Life*.

24 Doyle, *Inter-imperiality*, 1.

25 See Eng, *Racial Castration*; Ferguson, *Aberrations in Black*; Muñoz, *Disidentifications*; Gopinath, *Impossible Desires*; Manalansan, *Global Divas*; Reddy, *Freedom with Violence*; Puar, *Terrorist Assemblages*.

26 Wilson, "Queering Asia," paragraph 8.

27 In addition to the groundbreaking scholarship on queer diaspora by Eng, Gopinath, and Manalansan, the scholarship on Black queer diaspora also decenters Blackness through transnational and global configurations. See Allen, "Black/Queer/Diaspora at the Current Conjuncture," 215: "To follow the routes of black/queer/diaspora is to interrogate dynamic, unsettled subjects whose bodies, desires, and texts *move*." See also Ponce, *Beyond the Nation*; and Walcott, *Queer Returns*.

28 Chow, *Age of the World Target*, 68.

29 In raising these questions, I am joining scholars who think with the tension generated between queer studies and area studies. See Arondekar and Patel, "Area Impossible."

30 Liu, *Queer Marxism*.

31 Liu, *Queer Marxism*, 5.

32 Chiang, *Transtopia in the Sinophone Pacific*, 73–74.

33 Liu, *Specter of Materialism*, 17.

34 For a queer temporal approach to Chineseness, see Martin, *Backward Glances*. For spatial and transnational queer approaches that fracture the meanings of Chineseness, see Kong, *Sexuality and the Rise of China*; and D. T.-S. Tang, *Conditional Spaces*.

35 For foundational works in queer Sinophone studies, see Chiang and Heinrich, *Queer Sinophone Cultures*; and Chiang and Wong, *Keywords in Queer Sinophone Studies*.

36 Shih, *Visuality and Identity*, 4.

37 Recently, historians who study "New Qing History" have begun the work of deconstructing Han-centric notions of China. See Mullaney et al., *Critical Han Studies*; Crossley, *Translucent Mirror*; Elliott, *Manchu Way*; and Perdue, *China Marches West*.

38 Ang, *On Not Speaking Chinese*.

39 Ang, *On Not Speaking Chinese*, 36. See also Tan, *Rethinking Chineseness*. Another strand of Sinophone studies questions the notion of linguistic nativity at the core of Chineseness. See Tsu, *Sound and Script in Chinese Diaspora*.

40 Chow, "Introduction," 24.

41 Muñoz, *Disidentifications*.

42 See Lionnet and Shih, *Minor Transnationalism*; see also Boutaghou and Jean-Francois, "Introduction."

43 See K.-H. Chen, *Asia as Method*. My concept of queer Hong Kong as method also builds on recent scholarship in queer Asian studies that explores an earlier historical formation of "global queering" that is coeval with the emergence of gay capital cities in the West, as well as comparative studies of Hong Kong and Singapore through an emphasis of disjunctive queer modernities. See Jackson, "Capitalism and Global Queering." On disjunctive queer modernities in Asia, see Yue and Leung, "Notes Towards the Queer Asian City."

44 K.-H. Chen, *Asia as Method*, 107.

45 Hoskins and Nguyen, "Introduction," 3. See also L. Wong, *Transpacific Attachments*; and Metzger, *Chinese Atlantic*.

46 Works originally published in Chinese will appear in pinyin first, followed by the title in Chinese with an English translation. Subsequent mentions of the same work will refer to the translated English title only.

47 See Parreñas, *Servants of Globalization*.

48 See Halberstam, *Female Masculinity*, 13: "A queer methodology, in a way, is a scavenger methodology that uses different methods to collect and produce information on subjects who have been deliberately or accidentally excluded from traditional studies of human behavior."

49 Gopinath, *Unruly Visions*, 18.

1. QUEER HONG KONG AS A SINOPHONE METHOD

A large portion of chapter 1 appeared as "Queer Hong Kong as a Sinophone Method," in *Sinophone Studies across Disciplines: A Reader*, ed. Howard Chiang and Shu-mei Shih (New York: Columbia University Press, 2024): 193–208.

1 Ghaziani and Brim, "Queer Methods," 14.

2 Love, "Close Reading and Thin Description," 404.

3 Arondekar, *For the Record*, 4.

4 Spivak, *Critique of Postcolonial Reason*, 175.

5 Bardoloi, "An Ecosystem of Incentives and Policies."

6 Meyer, *Hong Kong as a Global Metropolis*, 60.

7 Lowe, *Intimacies of Four Continents*, 101–33. It is worth pointing out that Lowe devotes one chapter to Hong Kong as the colonial site where both the recruitment and transfer of coolies and the interracial intimacies and differentiation of European and Chinese bodies are simultaneously at work. These forms of colonial and imperial intimacies cover debates of "free" and unfree labor, vagrancy, and the unequal regulation of prostitution and venereal diseases.

8 For a trenchant critique of how both postcolonial theory and area studies are complicit with US empire and fail to critique racism domestically and Asian colonial modernity and imperialism abroad, see Shih, "Racializing Area Studies, Defetishizing China."

9   Zhu [朱耀偉], *Xianggang yanjiu zuowei fangfa* [香港研究作為方法 / Hong Kong studies as method].

10 Muñoz, *Cruising Utopia*, 1.

11 Chiang, *Transtopia in the Sinophone Pacific*, 4.

12 Chen, *Asia as Method*, 3.

13 One exception to this is Gina Marchetti's call for theorizing Hong Kong as a feminist method, in which "considering Hong Kong as 'method' demands a nuanced appreciation of the way in which the process of decolonization is inflected by gender as well as race and ethnicity." Marchetti, "Hong Kong as Feminist Method," 60.

14 Shih, "Race and Relation," 141.

15 Butler, *Bodies that Matter*.

16 For queer of color critique, see Muñoz, *Disidentifications*; and Ferguson, *Aberrations in Black*. For queer diaspora studies, see Manalansan, *Global Divas*; Gopinath, *Impossible Desires*; and *Unruly Visions*. For queer Sinophone studies, see Chiang and Heinrich, *Queer Sinophone Cultures*.

17 For an analysis of Hong Kong as a site of colonial intimacy where both discourses of free trade and violent governmentality converge, see Lowe, *Intimacies of Four Continents*, 101–33.

18 My invocation of the minor is indebted to the theory of minor transnationalism. See Lionnet and Shih, *Minor Transnationalism*.

19 Chen [陳冠中] and Li [李歐梵], "Xianggang zuowei fangfa" [香港作為方法 / Hong Kong as method], 137.

20 Williams, *Marxism and Literature*, 132.

21 For a theory of the minor, see Lionnet and Shih, *Minor Transnationalism*.

22 Ye, "*Zishu nü* [自梳女]: Dutiful Daughters." See also Stockard, *Daughters of the Canton Delta*.

23 *She Is a Woman, I Am Also a Woman* is the 1994 Taiwan edition of the 1991 novel *Thereafter*, published in Hong Kong.

24 Wong N. Y. [黃念欣], *Wanqi fengge: Xianggang nu zuojia san lun* [晚期風格:香港女作家三論 / Late style: Three essays on Hong Kong women writers], 223–42.

25 Lau, "The 'Little Woman' as Exorcist."

26 Xu [許子東], *Xianggang duan pian xiaoshuo chu tan* [香港短篇小說初探 / A study of Hong Kong novellas], 3–18.

27 Yeung and Magramo, "Hong Kong Suffers Biggest Ever Population Drop."

28 See Fran Martin's important work on the memorializing trope of the "backward glance" that characterizes many lesbian representations in films, novels, and media from Hong Kong, Taiwan, and the PRC in her *Backward Glances*, 64–67. Martin's reading of Wong focuses exclusively on the short story "She Is a Woman, I Am Also a Woman" within the broader tradition of "school-girl romance."

29 Wong B. [黃碧雲], *Lienü tu* [烈女圖 / Portraits of martyred women].

30 Wong B. [黃碧雲], *Lienü tu* [烈女圖 / Portraits of martyred women], 74. The use of second-person narration in the novel runs across the three time periods of World War II, 1960s, and the contemporary 1990s, when the novel was written. This nar-

rative technique defamiliarizes the reader from the conventional third-person narration by placing the reader across different temporalities of Hong Kong history through feminist and queer sensibilities.

31 Manning, *The Minor Gesture*, 1.

32 Salaff, *Working Daughters of Hong Kong*, 20.

33 Wong B. [黃碧雲], *Lienü tu* [烈女圖 / Portraits of martyred women], 120.

34 Leung, "Queerscapes in Contemporary Hong Kong Cinema," 434.

35 Freeman, *Time Binds*, 120.

36 Yoneyama, "Toward a Decolonial Genealogy," 471–82.

37 Yoneyama, "Toward a Decolonial Genealogy," 472.

38 Chan, *Diaspora's Homeland*, 13.

39 Derrida, *Archive Fever*, 7.

40 Ma K. F. [馬家輝], *Long tou feng wei* [龍頭鳳尾 / Once upon a time in Hong Kong], 20.

41 Ma K. F. [馬家輝], *Long tou feng wei* [龍頭鳳尾 / Once upon a time in Hong Kong], 22.

42 Similar to mafia gangs, triad societies are traditional Chinese criminal organizations that value heroism and brotherhood among members.

43 Barlow, *The Question of Women in Chinese Feminism*.

44 Stoler, *Along the Archival Grain*, 50.

45 Carroll, *A Concise History of Hong Kong*, 117.

46 Doyle, "Inter-imperiality," 160.

47 Derrida, *Archive Fever*, 7.

48 For a parallel study on the absence and presence of queer sexuality in the colonial archive, see Arondekar, *For the Record*.

2. POSTCOLONIALITY BEYOND CHINA-CENTRISM

A portion of chapter 2 appeared as "Postcoloniality beyond China-Centrism: Queer Sinophone Transnationalism in Hong Kong Cinema," in *Keywords in Queer Sinophone Studies*, ed. Howard Chiang and Alvin K. Wong (New York: Routledge, 2020): 62–79.

1 Chow, "King Kong in Hong Kong," 94.

2 Shih, *Visuality and Identity*, 30.

3 Lionnet and Shih, "Introduction," 8.

4 Leung, *Undercurrents*, 1; Kim and Atanasoski, "Unhappy Desires and Queer Postsocialist Futures."

5 Reynaud, "High Noon in Hong Kong."

6 Rey Chow makes a similar argument by reading the early sex scene as "for sure, a moment of erotic passion, but it is also what we may call a moment of indifferentiation, a condition of perfect unity that was not only (perhaps) chronologically past but also seemingly *before difference and separation*" ("Nostalgia of the New Wave," 34).

7 Kim and Atanasoski, "Unhappy Desires and Queer Postsocialist Futures," 703.

8 Schoonover and Galt, *Queer Cinema in the World*, 25.

9 Eng, *The Feeling of Kinship*, 90.

10 For the most up-to-date study on the effect of CEPA on Hong Kong cinema, see
E. C. M. Yau, "Watchful Partners, Hidden Currents."

11 Szeto, "Sinophone Libidinal Economy," 120–21.

12 Shih, "Introduction," 11.

13 On the gendered geopolitics of China-centrism, see A. K. Wong, "Including
China?," 1105.

14 Duggan, "The New Homonormativity," 190.

15 For a rich body of scholarship that examines the intersection between capitalism,
queer love and romance, and economic sustainability in Hong Kong, see Kong,
Chinese Male Homosexualities; and Tang, *Conditional Spaces*.

16 For a definition of necropolitics, see Mbembe, "Necropolitics."

17 For a critique on homonationalism and the Israeli state's pinkwashing, see Puar,
The Right to Maim, 96.

18 See Gomez-Barris, *The Extractive Zone*.

19 Ong, *Flexible Citizenship*, 6.

20 Abbas, *Hong Kong*, 12, original emphasis.

21 Abbas, *Hong Kong*, 6, original emphasis.

22 For a concise study of land redevelopment regimes in Hong Kong, see Lee and
Tang, "The Hegemony of the Real Estate Industry."

23 On global disjuncture, see Appadurai, *Modernity at Large*; on flexible migration,
see Ong, *Flexible Citizenship*; on center-periphery dynamics, see Wallerstein,
World-Systems Analysis.

24 Hamashita, *China, East Asia, and the Global Economy*; Wang, "The Politics of
Imagining Asia."

25 Duara, "Asia Redux," 981.

26 Chen Xue [陳雪], *Hudie* [蝴蝶 / Butterfly], 78.

27 See Leung, *Undercurrents*, 61; Martin, *Backward Glances*, 159.

28 Leung, *Undercurrents*, 63.

29 Chen Xue [陳雪], *Hudie* [蝴蝶 / Butterfly], 83.

30 Choi, "(Post)coloniality as a Chinese State of Exception," 408.

31 See A. K. Wong, "Including China?"

3. TRANSNATIONALIZING TRANSGENDER

A portion of chapter 3 appeared as "Beyond Queer Liberalism: On Queer Globalities and Regionalism from Postcolonial Hong Kong," in *Sexualities, Transnationalism, and Globalisation: New Perspectives*, ed. Yanqiu Rachel Zhou, Christina
Sinding, and Donald Goellnicht (London: Routledge, 2021): 107–19.

1 The extradition law refers to the Fugitive Offender amendment bill, introduced
by the Hong Kong government in February 2019 as a measure to "close the loop-
hole" in the current legal system and as an immediate measure to extradite a criminal named Chan Tong-kai, who murdered his girlfriend in Taiwan back in 2018.

However, the amendment bill, if passed successfully, could also result in increasing numbers of extraditions and transfers of criminals and fugitives from Hong Kong to mainland China. Voicing opposition against an unclear and not popularly backed amendment, the protestors have come up with Five Demands, including the full withdrawal of the extradition bill, an independent commission of inquiry into alleged police brutality, retracting the classification of protestors as "rioters," amnesty for arrested protestors, and dual universal suffrage (meaning free elections of the Chief Executive and Legislative Council members).

2 Berlinger, "China Interrupts Hong Kong Pop Star during UN Speech."

3 Cheng, "Hong Kong Police Accused of Indecent Assault."

4 Yue and Leung, "Notes Towards the Queer Asian City."

5 Martin et al., *AsiaPacifiQueer*, 17.

6 Altman, "Global Gaze/Global Gays."

7 For queer of color critiques that scrutinize the workings of queer liberalism and the violence of the neoliberal state, see Ferguson, *Aberrations in Black*; Eng, *The Feeling of Kinship*; and Reddy, *Freedom with Violence*. For a theory of homonationalism that unpacks the ways in which queer liberal subjects in the United States are complicit with Islamophobia, see Puar, *Terrorist Assemblages*.

8 Eng with Halberstam and Muñoz, "Introduction," 15.

9 On the excavation of queer liberalism as a concept and political force, see Eng, *The Feeling of Kinship*. For a study that counters the force of queer liberalism through the theorization of queer "illiberal pragmatism," see Yue and Zubillaga-Pow, eds., *Queer Singapore*.

10 Lawrence and Taylor, "UK Government LGBT Action Plan."

11 Halberstam, *In a Queer Time and Place*, 36.

12 Aizura, *Mobile Subjects*, 21.

13 On the "included out" mechanism of cultural citizenship in Hong Kong, see Erni, "Citizenship Management."

14 W v. Registrar of Marriages, HKCFA 39 (2013).

15 Chiang, "Intimate Equality and Transparent Selves," 169.

16 Goodwin v. United Kingdom 35 EHRR 18 at 101 (2002).

17 On the geopolitical fragility of Hong Kong in judicial rule, see Chiang, "Intimate Equality and Transparent Selves."

18 W v. Registrar of Marriages, HKCFA 39 at 2 (2013).

19 Chiang, "Intimate Equality and Transparent Selves," 172.

20 Chiang, "Intimate Equality and Transparent Selves," 172.

21 Leung Chun Kwong v. Secretary for the Civil Service and Commissioner of Inland Revenue, HKCFA 19 (FACV8.2018).

22 Leung Chun Kwong v. Secretary for the Civil Service and Commissioner of Inland Revenue, HKCFA 19 (FACV8.2018).

23 Leung Chun Kwong v. Secretary for the Civil Service and Commissioner of Inland Revenue, HKCFA 19 (FACV8.2018).

24 Leung Chun Kwong v. Secretary for the Civil Service and Commissioner of Inland Revenue, HKCFA 19 (FACV8.2018).

25 Leung Chun Kwong v. Secretary for the Civil Service and Commissioner of Inland Revenue, HKCFA 19 (FACV8.2018).

26 My invocation of queer legal friction is drawn from Tsing's concept in *Friction*.

27 Chiang and Wong, "Queering the Transnational Turn," 1645.

28 Freeman, *Time Binds*, 95–96.

29 For a critique of this myth of trans liberal freedom that reinforces Euro-American modernity, see Aizura, *Mobile Subjects*.

30 For a concise history of Cantonese opera and cross-dressing, see Li, *Cross-Dressing in Chinese Opera*. By traditional Cantonese culture, I do not mean a fossilized and essentialized notion of cultural identity but rather local practices and gendered rituals of Cantonese opera that still exist in modern-day Hong Kong.

31 For a concise history of transgender formation in the Sinophone world, see Chiang, *After Eunuchs*.

32 For a queer critique on this public versus private binary of the hierarchy of sex, see Rubin, "Thinking Sex."

33 For a phenomenological approach to trans studies, see Salamon, *Assuming a Body*.

34 Gopinath, *Unruly Visions*, 5.

35 I would like to thank Mimi Wong, the film producer, for pointing out the significance of this scene to me during our lunch conversation.

36 For a definition of gender performativity as citationality, see Butler, *Bodies That Matter*.

37 Yau, ed., *As Normal as Possible*.

38 Salamon, *Assuming a Body*, 2.

39 Halberstam, *In a Queer Time and Place*, 78.

40 Tang, "Everyday Erotics in Urban Density," 1651.

41 For a discussion of the "gender revelation" moment in representations of trans subjects in popular cinema, see Halberstam, *In a Queer Time and Place*, 76–96.

42 Hong Kong Women Filmmakers, "Wong, Mimi (黃欣琴)."

43 The very idea of "human library" is inspired by an organization in Denmark that tries to overcome prejudice by staging conversations between marginalized individuals and people with whom they might not come into contact in everyday life. See Human Library, accessed June 22, 2024, https://humanlibrary.org/.

44 Shih, "Towards an Ethics of Transnational Encounter," 119.

45 Spivak, *Death of a Discipline*, 36.

46 Shih, "Is Feminism Translatable?," 187.

47 The exhibit was made possible by private donations, financial support from NGOs such as the Association of World Citizens Hong Kong, and the photographer Candy Yeung and her studio.

48 On the Western fetishization of Others, see Clifford, "Museums as Contact Zones"; for readings on the liberatory potential of museum spaces, see Tyburczy, *Sex Museum*; see also Rofel, *Desiring China*, 65–83.

49 Chen, *Asia as Method*, 25.

1   Shih, "Racializing Area Studies, Defetishizing China."
2   On the concept of right to the city, see Harvey, "The Right to the City"; on neoliberalism as exception, see Ong, *Neoliberalism as Exception*; for a summary of the "global care chains" concept, see Yeates, "Global Care Chains."
3   Fu and Desser, "Introduction," 5.
4   E. C. M. Yau, "Introduction," 2.
5   For major works in the existing literature on ethnic minorities in Hong Kong, see Erni and Leung, eds., *Understanding South Asian Minorities in Hong Kong*.
6   Chuh, *The Difference Aesthetics Makes*, xii.
7   Lowe, *Intimacies of Four Continents*, 3.
8   Rangan, *Immediations*, 5.
9   Parreñas, *Servants of Globalization*, 29.
10 For an optimistic account of the competition for "global talent" and "brain gain" in globalizing Asia, see Shin and Choi, *Global Talent*.
11 Patterson, "Queer, Brown, Migrant," 1018.
12 Rangan, *Immediations*, 4.
13 McRuer, *Crip Theory*, 15. Arguing that "compulsory heterosexuality is contingent on compulsory able-bodiedness, and vice versa," Robert McRuer has painstakingly shown how popular culture and cultural politics have made having an able body a prerequisite for embodying heterosexuality; however, he falls short of offering an intersectional analysis of race. In a passing comment on the film *Titanic*'s logic of heterosexual epiphany, he insists that "the problem of the twentieth century, symbolically resolved in its final years by this film, had been heterosexual separation and reunification." Here, McRuer seems to be going against W. E. B. Du Bois's definition of the problem of the twentieth century as "the color line" by emphasizing the analytic of disability over race.
14 Bolton, *Crip Colony*, 8.
15 Heberer, "Sentimental Activism as Queer-Feminist Documentary Practice," 42.
16 Shih, "Introduction," 11.
17 Lan, "Migrant Women's Bodies as Boundary Markers."
18 Lan, "Migrant Women's Bodies as Boundary Markers," 834.
19 See Lan, *Global Cinderellas*.
20 For a study that addresses this blind spot in current transnational feminist scholarship on migrant domestic work and global care chains, see Lai, *Maid to Queer*.
21 For an in-depth analysis of Sinophone words that describe homoeroticism, queerness, and LGBT identity in Sinitic-language communities, see Martin, *Situating Sexualities*, 1–43. See also Lim, "How to Be Queer in Taiwan."
22 *T* is the phrase usually used to describe the butch-looking masculine partner in a lesbian relationship in Taiwan, while *Po* refers to more feminine lesbians. The word *Po* may also refer to the word "wife" in Mandarin. See Ho [何春蕤], *T po de kua xingbie landiao shi* [T婆的跨性別籃調詩 / "T/Po transgender blues"].
23 Tadiar, *Remaindered Life*, 14.
24 Heberer, *Asians on Demand*, 103.

25 Manalansan, "Messy Mismeasures."

26 Manalansan, "Messy Mismeasures," 496.

27 Vallejos v. Commission of Registration (2013), para. 16, as quoted in Erni, "Citizenship Management," 335.

28 Erni, "Citizenship Management," 330.

29 Gopinath, *Impossible Desires*, 177.

30 Lai, "Sexuality at Imagined Home," 910.

31 Tadiar, *Remaindered Life*, 179.

32 Manalansan, "Queering the Chain of Care Paradigm."

33 Filguys Association Hong Kong, *4th Anniversary Booklet*.

5. TRESPASSING THE SINOPHONE BORDER

A large portion of chapter 5 appeared as "Queering the Cinematic Border of the PRC and Hong Kong: On Fruit Chan's Prostitute Trilogy," *Journal of Chinese Cinemas* 17, no. 1 (2023): 37–51.

1 For a study on the US state construction of racial, classed, gendered, and sexual deviance within its disciplinary regime of immigration and border security control, see Luibhéid, *Entry Denied*.

2 Anzaldúa, *Borderlands/La Frontera*, 3.

3 Anzaldúa, *Borderlands/La Frontera*, 82.

4 For transnational feminist work that insists on the necessity of accounting for differences across race, gender, class, and sexuality as well as for the possibility of feminist solidarity across borders, see Mohanty, *Feminism without Borders*. For a feminist cultural studies work that explores the multiple hegemonic discourses on gender violence and the possibility of transnational activism across the US-Mexico border, see Fregoso, *meXicana Encounters*.

5 L. Wong, *Transpacific Attachments*.

6 See Cheah, "Global Dreams and Nightmares," 198.

7 Shih, *Visuality and Identity*, 164.

8 Berry, "What Is Transnational Chinese Cinema Today?," 195.

9 L. Wong, *Transpacific Attachments*, 6.

10 Lowe, *Immigrant Acts*, 11.

11 Chow, *Primitive Passions*.

12 Chow, "'Woman,' Fetish, Particularism," 210.

13 See Smallwood, *Saltwater Slavery*.

14 Chow, "'Woman,' Fetish, Particularism," 211.

15 Gan, *Fruit Chan's "Durian Durian,"* 49.

16 See also Yue, "Mobile Intimacies."

17 Shih, "Gender and a New Geopolitics of Desire," 305.

18 Cheah, "Global Dreams and Nightmares," 198.

19 See Shih, "Gender and a New Geopolitics of Desire."

20 A. K. Wong, "Including China?," 1114.

21 Cheah, "Global Dreams and Nightmares," 203.

22 This myth and the first mention of Lo Ting trace back to the Tang Dynasty (618–907) in *Records of the Unusualness in Lingnan* [嶺表異錄 / *Lingbiao Yilu*]. See Sala, "Lo Ting."

23 See also Shih's analysis of the cultural obsession with the mythological figure of Lo Ting before and after the 1997 handover in *Visuality and Identity*, 158–64.

24 Livingston and Puar, "Interspecies," 3–4.

25 For an excellent study of hypersexuality and queer racialized femininity, see Shimizu, *The Hypersexuality of Race*.

26 For an analysis of queerness as disorientation, see Ahmed, *Queer Phenomenology*.

27 A. K. Wong, "Where Jameson Meets Queer Theory," 135.

EPILOGUE

1 For an approach of transnational queer sociology, see Kong, *Sexuality and the Rise of China*. For a minor transnational study of lesbian desire and mobility that places Hong Kong in meaningful comparison with Taiwan and Singapore, see D. T.-S. Tang, "Of Long and Waiting."

2 My use of the term queer undercommons is inspired by Fred Moten and Stefano Harney's open-ended theory of the Undercommons. They write, "In the face of these conditions one can only sneak into the university and steal what one can. To abuse its hospitality, to spite its mission, to join its refugee colony, its gypsy encampment, to be in but not of—this is the path of the subversive intellectual in the modern university." Moten and Harney, "The University and the Undercommons," 101.

3 De Certeau, *The Practice of Everyday Life*, 37.

4 Butler and Athanasiou, *Dispossession*, 102.

5 Yip, "Fricatives," ll. 1–2. Hereafter I cite lines parenthetically.

6 Eng, *Racial Castration*.

Filmography

Bowers, Joanna, dir. *The Helper*. Hong Kong, 2017.

Cai Chusheng [蔡楚生], dir. *Xin nuxing* [新女性 / *New Women*]. China, 1935.

Chan, Fruit [陳果], dir. *Liu lian piao piao* [榴槤飄飄 / *Durian Durian*]. Hong Kong, 2000.

Chan, Fruit [陳果], dir. *San fu* [三夫 / *Three Husbands*]. Hong Kong, 2018.

Chan, Fruit [陳果], dir. *Xianggang you ge he li huo* [香港有個荷里活 / *Hollywood Hong Kong*]. Hong Kong, 2001.

Chan, Fruit [陳果], dir. *Xianggang zhizao* [香港製造 / *Made in Hong Kong*]. Hong Kong, 1997.

Chan, Fruit [陳果], dir. *Xi lu xiang* [細路祥 / *Little Cheung*]. Hong Kong, 1999.

Chan, Oliver Siu Kuen [陳小娟], dir. *Lun luo ren* [淪落人 / *Still Human*]. Hong Kong, 2018.

Chan, Peter [陳可辛], dir. *Tian mi mi* [甜蜜蜜 / *Comrades: Almost a Love Story*]. Hong Kong, 1996.

Chen Huai Ai [陈怀皑], and Cui Wei [崔嵬], dirs. *Qingchun zhi ge* [青春之歌 / *Song of Youth*]. China, 1959.

Chen, Susan [陳素香], dir. *Caihong ba le* [彩虹芭樂 / *Rainbow Popcorn*]. Taiwan, 2012.

Chen, Susan [陳素香], dir. *T po gong chang* [T婆工廠 / *Lesbian Factory*]. Taiwan, 2010.

Cheung, Alfred [張堅庭], dir. *Biaojie ni haoye* [表姐, 你好嘢! / *Her Fatal Ways*]. Hong Kong, 1990.

Cheung, Chi Leung Jacob [張之亮], dir. *Zi shu* [自梳 / *Intimates*]. Hong Kong, 1997.

Kwan, Stanley [關錦鵬], dir. *Yanzhi kou* [胭脂扣 / *Rouge*]. Hong Kong, 1987.

Li, Jun [李駿碩], dir. *Cui si* [翠絲 / *Tracey*]. Hong Kong, 2018.

Li, Jun [李駿碩], dir. *Zhuo shui piaoliu* [濁水漂流 / *Drifting*]. Hong Kong, 2021.

Mak, Johnny Mak Tong-hung [麥當雄], dir. *Sheng gang qi bing* [省港旗兵 / *Long Arm of the Law*]. Hong Kong, 1984.

Mak Yan Yan [麥婉欣], dir. *Hudie* [蝴蝶 / *Butterfly*]. Hong Kong, 2004.

Scud [雲翔], dir. *An fei ta ming* [安非他命 / *Amphetamine*]. Hong Kong, 2010.

Scud [雲翔], dir. *Yongjiu juliu* [永久居留 / *Permanent Residence*]. Hong Kong, 2009.

Suen, Maisy Goosy [孫明希], dir. *Nuren jiushi nuren* [女人就是女人 / *A Woman Is a Woman*]. Hong Kong, 2018.

Villarama, Baby Ruth, dir. *Sunday Beauty Queen*. Hong Kong, 2016.

Wong Kar-wai [王家衛], dir. *Chun guang zha xie* [春光乍洩 / *Happy Together*]. Hong Kong, 1997.

Wong Kar-wai [王家衛], dir. *Zhongqing senlin* [重慶森林 / *Chungking Express*]. Hong Kong, 1994.

Wu Yonggang [吳永剛], dir. *Shennu* [神女 / *The Goddess*]. China, 1934.

Yuan Muzhi [袁牧之], dir. *Malu tianshi* [馬路天使 / *Street Angel*]. China, 1937.

Abbas, Ackbar. *Hong Kong: Culture and the Politics of Disappearance*. Minneapolis: University of Minnesota Press, 1997.

Ahmed, Sara. *Queer Phenomenology: Orientations, Objects, Others*. Durham, NC: Duke University Press, 2006.

Aizura, Aren Z. *Mobile Subjects: Transnational Imaginaries of Gender Reassignment*. Durham, NC: Duke University Press, 2018.

Allen, Jafari S. "Black/Queer/Diaspora at the Current Conjuncture." *GLQ* 18, nos. 2–3 (2012): 211–48.

Altman, Dennis. "Global Gaze/Global Gays." *GLQ* 3, no. 4 (1997): 417–36.

Apter, Emily. *The Translation Zone: A New Comparative Literature*. Princeton, NJ: Princeton University Press, 2006.

Ang, Ien. *On Not Speaking Chinese: Living between Asia and the West*. London: Routledge, 2001.

Anzaldúa, Gloria. *Borderlands/La Frontera: The New Mestiza*. San Francisco: Aunt Lute Books, 1987.

Appadurai, Arjun. *Modernity at Large: Cultural Dimensions of Globalization*. Minneapolis: University of Minnesota Press, 1996.

Arondekar, Anjali. *For the Record: On Sexuality and the Colonial Archive in India*. Durham, NC: Duke University Press, 2009.

Arondekar, Anjali, and Geeta Patel. "Area Impossible: Notes toward an Introduction." *GLQ* 22, no. 2 (2016): 151–71.

Bardoloi, Yashvardhan. "An Ecosystem of Incentives and Policies: Economic Lessons We Can Learn from the Four Asian Tigers." *South China Morning Post*, November 2, 2017. https://www.scmp.com/yp/discover/yourvoice/opinion/article/3067155/ecosystem-incentives-and-policies-economic-lessons.

Barlow, Tani E. *The Question of Women in Chinese Feminism*. Durham, NC: Duke University Press, 2004.

Berlinger, Joshua. "China Interrupts Hong Kong Pop Star during UN Speech." CNN, July 9, 2019. https://edition.cnn.com/2019/07/08/asia/denise-ho-un-intl-hnk/index.html.

Bernards, Brian. *Writing the South Seas: Imagining the Nanyang in Chinese and Southeast Asian Postcolonial Literature*. Seattle: University of Washington Press, 2015.

Berry, Chris. "What Is Transnational Chinese Cinema Today? Or, Welcome to the Sinosphere." *Transnational Screens* 12, no. 3 (2021): 183–98.

Blackwood, Evelyn. "Transnational Sexualities in One Place: Indonesian Readings." *Gender and Society* 19, no. 2 (April 2005): 221–42.

Bolton, Sony Coráñez. *Crip Colony: Mestizaje, US Imperialism, and the Queer Politics of Disability in the Philippines*. Durham, NC: Duke University Press, 2023.

Boutaghou, Maya, and Emmanuel Bruno Jean-Francois. "Introduction: The Minor in Question." *Cultural Dynamics* 32, nos. 1–2 (2020): 3–13.

Butler, Judith. *Bodies That Matter: On the Discursive Limit of Sex*. New York: Routledge, 1993.

Butler, Judith, and Athena Athanasiou. *Dispossession: The Performative in the Political*. Malden, MA: Polity, 2013.

Carroll, John M. *A Concise History of Hong Kong*. Lanham, MD: Rowman and Littlefield, 2007.

Chan, Ho-him. "Hong Kong Protests: Student Reporter Alleges Police Officer Made Reference to Sexual Assault in Threats during Arrest." *South China Morning Post*, November 5, 2019. https://www.scmp.com/news/hong-kong/law-and-crime/article/3036468/hong-kong-protests-student-reporter-alleges-police.

Chan, Shelly. *Diaspora's Homeland: Modern China in the Age of Global Migration*. Durham, NC: Duke University Press, 2018.

Cheah, Pheng. "Global Dreams and Nightmares: The Underside of Hong Kong as a Global City in Fruit Chan's *Hollywood, Hong Kong*." In *Hong Kong Culture: Word and Image*, edited by Kam Louie, 193–212. Hong Kong: Hong Kong University Press, 2010.

Cheah, Pheng. *What Is a World? On Postcolonial Literature as World Literature*. Durham, NC: Duke University Press, 2016.

Chen Guanzhong [陳冠中], and Li Oufan [李歐梵]. "Xianggang zuowei fangfa" [香港作為方法 / Hong Kong as method]. In *Xianggang yanjiu zuowei fangfa* [香港研究作為方法 / Hong Kong studies as method], edited by Zhu Yao-wei [朱耀偉], 128–44. Hong Kong: Zhonghua Book Company, 2016.

Chen, Kuan-Hsing. *Asia as Method: Toward Deimperialization*. Durham, NC: Duke University Press, 2010.

Chen Xue [陳雪]. *Hudie* [蝴蝶 / *Butterfly*]. Taipei: INK Publishing, 2007.

Cheng, Kris. "Hong Kong Police Accused of Indecent Assault after Protester Strip Searched Days after Arrest." *Hong Kong Free Press*, August 23, 2019. https://www.hongkongfp.com/2019/08/23/hong-kong-police-accused-metoo-assault-protester-strip-searched-days-arrest/.

Chiang, Howard. *After Eunuchs: Science, Medicine, and the Transformation of Sex in Modern China*. New York: Columbia University Press, 2018.

Chiang, Howard. "(De)Provincializing China: Queer Historicism and Sinophone Postcolonial Critique." In *Queer Sinophone Cultures*, edited by Howard Chiang and Ari Larissa Heinrich, 19–51. London: Routledge, 2013.

Chiang, Howard. "Intimate Equality and Transparent Selves: Legalising Transgender Marriage in Hong Kong." *Culture, Theory and Critique* 58, no. 2 (2017): 166–81.

Chiang, Howard. *Transtopia in the Sinophone Pacific*. New York: Columbia University Press, 2021.

Chiang, Howard, and Ari Larissa Heinrich, eds. *Queer Sinophone Cultures*. London: Routledge, 2013.

Chiang, Howard, and Alvin K. Wong, eds. *Keywords in Queer Sinophone Studies.* London: Routledge, 2020.

Chiang, Howard, and Alvin K. Wong. "Queering the Transnational Turn: Regionalism and Queer Asias." *Gender, Place and Culture* 23, no. 11 (2016): 1643–56.

Choi, Wai Kit. "(Post)coloniality as a Chinese State of Exception." *Postcolonial Studies* 10, no. 4 (2007): 391–411.

Chow, Rey. *The Age of the World Target: Self-Referentiality in War, Theory, and Comparative Work.* Durham, NC: Duke University Press, 2006.

Chow, Rey. "Introduction: On Chineseness as a Theoretical Problem." *boundary 2* 25, no. 3 (1998): 1–24.

Chow, Rey. "King Kong in Hong Kong: Watching the 'Handover' from the U.S.A." *Social Text* 55 (1998): 93–108.

Chow, Rey. "Nostalgia of the New Wave: Structure in Wong Kar-wai's *Happy Together*." *Camera Obscura* 14, no. 3 (1999): 30–49.

Chow, Rey. *Primitive Passions: Visuality, Sexuality, Ethnography, and Contemporary Chinese Cinema.* New York: Columbia University Press, 1995.

Chow, Rey. "'Woman,' Fetish, Particularism: Articulating Chinese Cinema with a Cross-Cultural Problematic." *Journal of Chinese Cinemas* 1, no. 3 (2007): 209–21.

Chu, Yiu-Wai. *Lost in Transition: Hong Kong Culture in the Age of China.* Albany: State University of New York Press, 2013.

Chuh, Kandice. *The Difference Aesthetics Makes: On the Humanities "After Man."* Durham, NC: Duke University Press, 2019.

Clifford, James. "Museums as Contact Zones." In *Routes: Travel and Translation in the Late Twentieth Century.* Cambridge, MA: Harvard University Press, 1997.

Crossley, Pamela Kyle. *A Translucent Mirror: History and Identity in Qing Imperial Ideology.* Berkeley: University of California Press, 1999.

de Certeau, Michel. *The Practice of Everyday Life.* Translated by Steven Rendall. Berkeley: University of California Press, 1984.

Derrida, Jacques. *Archive Fever: A Freudian Impression.* Translated by Eric Prenowitz. Chicago: University of Chicago Press, 1996.

Dimock, Wai Chee. *Through Other Continents: American Literature across Deep Time.* Princeton, NJ: Princeton University Press, 2006.

Doyle, Laura. "Inter-imperiality: Dialectics in a Postcolonial World History." *Interventions* 16, no. 2 (2014): 159–96.

Doyle, Laura. *Inter-imperiality: Vying Empires, Gendered Labor, and the Literary Arts of Alliance.* Durham, NC: Duke University Press, 2020.

Duara, Prasenjit. "Asia Redux: Conceptualizing a Region for Our Times." *Journal of Asian Studies* 69, no. 4 (2010): 963–83.

Duggan, Lisa. "The New Homonormativity: The Sexual Politics of Neoliberalism." In *Materializing Democracy: Toward a Revitalized Cultural Politics*, edited by Russ Castronovo and Dana D. Nelson, 175–94. Durham, NC: Duke University Press, 2002.

Elliott, Mark C. *The Manchu Way: The Eight Banners and Ethnic Identity in Late Imperial China.* Stanford, CA: Stanford University Press, 2001.

Eng, David L. *The Feeling of Kinship: Queer Liberalism and the Racialization of Intimacy*. Durham, NC: Duke University Press, 2010.

Eng, David L. *Racial Castration: Managing Masculinity in Asian America*. Durham, NC: Duke University Press, 2001.

Eng, David L., with Judith Halberstam and José Esteban Muñoz. "Introduction: What's Queer about Queer Studies Now?" *Social Text* 23, nos. 3–4 (Winter 2005): 1–17.

Erni, John Nguyet. "Citizenship Management: On the Politics of Being Included-Out." *International Journal of Cultural Studies* 19, no. 3 (2016): 323–40.

Erni, John Nguyet. "Like a Postcolonial Culture: Hong Kong Re-imagined." *Cultural Studies* 15, nos. 3–4 (2001): 389–418.

Erni, John Nguyet, and Lisa Yuk-ming Leung, eds. *Understanding South Asian Minorities in Hong Kong*. Hong Kong: Hong Kong University Press, 2014.

Ferguson, Roderick A. *Aberrations in Black: Toward a Queer of Color Critique*. Minneapolis: University of Minnesota Press, 2003.

Filguys Association Hong Kong. *4th Anniversary Booklet*. December 26, 2010.

Freeman, Elizabeth. *Time Binds: Queer Temporalities, Queer Histories*. Durham, NC: Duke University Press, 2010.

Fregoso, Rosa Linda. *meXicana Encounters: The Making of Social Identities on the Borderlands*. Berkeley: University of California Press, 2003.

Fu, Poshek, and David Desser. "Introduction." In *The Cinema of Hong Kong: History, Arts, Identity*, edited by Poshek Fu and David Desser, 1–11. Cambridge: Cambridge University Press, 2000.

Gan, Wendy. *Fruit Chan's "Durian Durian."* Hong Kong: Hong Kong University Press, 2005.

Ghaziani, Amin, and Matt Brim. "Queer Methods: Four Provocations for an Emerging Field." In *Imagining Queer Methods*, edited by Amin Ghaziani and Matt Brim, 3–27. New York: New York University Press, 2019.

Gomez-Barris, Macarena. *The Extractive Zone: Social Ecologies and Decolonial Perspectives*. Durham, NC: Duke University Press, 2017.

Goodwin v. United Kingdom. 35 EHRR 18 at 101 (2002).

Gopinath, Gayatri. *Impossible Desires: Queer Diasporas and South Asian Public Cultures*. Durham, NC: Duke University Press, 2005.

Gopinath, Gayatri. *Unruly Visions: The Aesthetic Practices of Queer Diaspora*. Durham, NC: Duke University Press, 2018.

Halberstam, Jack. *Female Masculinity*. Durham, NC: Duke University Press, 1998.

Halberstam, Jack. *In a Queer Time and Place: Transgender Bodies, Subcultural Lives*. New York: New York University Press, 2005.

Hamashita, Takeshi. *China, East Asia, and the Global Economy: Regional and Historical Perspectives*. New York: Routledge, 2008.

Harvey, David. "The Right to the City." *New Left Review* 53 (2008): 23–40.

Heberer, Feng-Mei. *Asians on Demand: Mediating Race in Video Art and Activism*. Minneapolis: University of Minnesota Press, 2023.

Heberer, Feng-Mei. "Sentimental Activism as Queer-Feminist Documentary Practice;

or, How to Make Love in a Room Full of People." *Camera Obscura* 34, no. 2 (2019): 41–69.

Ho, Josephine [何春蕤]. *T po de kua xingbie landiao shi* [T婆的跨性別籃調詩 / T/Po transgender blues]. In *Kua xingbie* [跨性別 / Trans-gender], edited by Josephine Ho, 377–84. Zhongli, Taiwan: Center for the Study of Sexualities, National Central University, 2003.

Hong, Grace Kyungwon, and Roderick A. Ferguson. "Introduction." In *Strange Affinities: The Gender and Sexual Politics of Comparative Racialization*, edited by Grace Kyungwon Hong and Roderick A. Ferguson, 1–22. Durham, NC: Duke University Press, 2011.

Hong Kong Women Filmmakers. "Wong, Mimi (黃欣琴)." Accessed August 28, 2023. https://hkwomenfilmmakers.wordpress.com/wong-mimi/.

Hoskins, Janet, and Viet Thanh Nguyen. "Introduction: Transpacific Studies; Critical Perspectives on an Emerging Field." In *Transpacific Studies: Framing an Emerging Field*, edited by Janet Hoskins and Viet Thanh Nguyen, 1–38. Honolulu: University of Hawai'i Press, 2014.

Hung, Ho-fung. *City on the Edge: Hong Kong under Chinese Rule*. Cambridge: Cambridge University Press, 2022.

Jackson, Peter A. "Capitalism and Global Queering: National Markets, Parallels among Sexual Cultures, and Multiple Queer Modernities." *GLQ* 15, no. 3 (2009): 357–95.

Kim, Jinah, and Neda Atanasoski. "Unhappy Desires and Queer Postsocialist Futures: Hong Kong and Buenos Aires in Wong Kar-wai's *Happy Together*." *American Quarterly* 69, no. 3 (2017): 697–718.

Kincaid, Jamaica. *A Small Place*. New York: Farrar, Straus and Giroux, 1988.

Kong, Travis S. K. *Chinese Male Homosexualities: Memba, Tongzhi, and Golden Boy*. London: Routledge, 2011.

Kong, Travis S. K. *Sexuality and the Rise of China: The Post-1990s Gay Generation in Hong Kong, Taiwan, and Mainland China*. Durham, NC: Duke University Press, 2023.

Lai, Francisca Yuenki. *Maid to Queer: Asian Labor Migration and Female Same-Sex Desires*. Hong Kong: Hong Kong University Press, 2020.

Lai, Francisca Yuenki. "Sexuality at Imagined Home: Same-Sex Desires among Indonesian Migrant Domestic Workers in Hong Kong." *Sexualities* 21, nos. 5–6 (2018): 899–913.

Lan, Pei-Chia. "Migrant Women's Bodies as Boundary Markers: Reproductive Crisis and Sexual Control in the Ethnic Frontiers of Taiwan." *Signs* 33, no. 4 (2008): 833–61.

Lan, Pei-Chia. *Global Cinderellas: Migrant Domestics and Newly Rich Employers in Taiwan*. Durham, NC: Duke University Press, 2006.

Lau, Joseph. "The 'Little Woman' as Exorcist: Notes on the Fiction of Huang Biyun." *Journal of Modern Literature in Chinese* 2, no. 2 (January 1999): 149–63.

Lawrence, Matson, and Yvette Taylor. "The UK Government LGBT Action Plan: Discourses of Progress, Enduring Stasis, and LGBTQI+ Lives 'Getting Better.'" *Critical Social Policy* 40, no. 4 (2020): 586–607.

Lee, Joanna Wai Ying, and Wing-Shing Tang. "The Hegemony of the Real Estate Industry: Redevelopment of 'Government/Institution or Community' (G/IC) Land in
Hong Kong." *Urban Studies* 54, no. 15 (2017): 3403–22.

Leung Chun Kwong v. Secretary for the Civil Service and Commissioner of Inland Revenue. [2017] 2 HKLRD 1132 (HCAL258/2015).

Leung Chun Kwong v. Secretary for the Civil Service and Commissioner of Inland Revenue. [2019] HKCFA 19 (FACV8.2018).

Leung, Helen Hok-Sze. "Queerscapes in Contemporary Hong Kong Cinema." *positions*
9, no. 2 (2001): 423–47.

Leung, Helen Hok-Sze. *Undercurrents: Queer Culture and Postcolonial Hong Kong.*
Vancouver: University of British Columbia Press, 2009.

Li, Siu Leung. *Cross-Dressing in Chinese Opera.* Hong Kong: Hong Kong University
Press, 2003.

Lim, Song Hwee. "How to Be Queer in Taiwan: Translation, Appropriation, and the
Construction of a Queer Identity in Taiwan." In *AsiaPacifiQueer: Rethinking Genders
and Sexualities*, edited by Fran Martin, Peter A. Jackson, Mark McLelland, and Audrey Yue, 235–50. Urbana: University of Illinois Press, 2008.

Lionnet, Françoise, and Shu-mei Shih. "Introduction: Thinking through the Minor,
Transnationally." In *Minor Transnationalism*, edited by Françoise Lionnet and Shu-
mei Shih, 1–26. Durham, NC: Duke University Press, 2005.

Lionnet, Françoise, and Shu-mei Shih, eds. *Minor Transnationalism.* Durham, NC:
Duke University Press, 2005.

Liu, Petrus. *Queer Marxism in Two Chinas.* Durham, NC: Duke University Press,
2015.

Liu, Petrus. *The Specter of Materialism: Queer Theory and Marxism in the Age of the
Beijing Consensus.* Durham, NC: Duke University Press, 2023.

Livingston, Julie, and Jasbir K. Puar. "Interspecies." *Social Text* 29, no. 1 (2011): 3–14.

Love, Heather. "Close Reading and Thin Description." *Public Culture* 25, no. 3 (2013):
401–34.

Lowe, Lisa. *Immigrant Acts: On Asian American Cultural Politics.* Durham, NC: Duke
University Press, 1996.

Lowe, Lisa. *The Intimacies of Four Continents.* Durham, NC: Duke University Press,
2015.

Lowe, Lisa, and Kris Manjapra. "Comparative Global Humanities after Man: Alternatives to the Coloniality of Knowledge." *Theory, Culture and Society* 36, no. 5 (2019):
23–48.

Luibheid, Eithne. *Entry Denied: Controlling Sexuality at the Border.* Minneapolis: University of Minnesota Press, 2002.

Ma Ka Fai [馬家輝]. *Long tou feng wei* [龍頭鳳尾 / Once upon a time in Hong Kong].
Taipei: ThinKingDom Publisher, 2016.

Manalansan, Martin F., IV. *Global Divas: Filipino Gay Men in the Diaspora.* Durham,
NC: Duke University Press, 2003.

Manalansan, Martin F., IV. "Messy Mismeasures: Exploring the Wilderness of Queer
Migrant Lives." *South Atlantic Quarterly* 117, no. 3 (2018): 491–506.

Manalansan, Martin F., IV. "Queering the Chain of Care Paradigm." *s&f Online* 6, no. 3 (Summer 2008). https://sfonline.barnard.edu/immigration/print_manalansan.htm.

Manning, Erin. *The Minor Gesture.* Durham, NC: Duke University Press, 2016.

Marchetti, Gina. "Hong Kong as Feminist Method." In *Hong Kong Culture and Society in the New Millennium: Hong Kong as Method,* edited by Yiu-Wai Chu, 59–76. Singapore: Springer, 2017.

Martin, Fran. *Backward Glances: Contemporary Chinese Cultures and the Female Homoerotic Imaginary.* Durham, NC: Duke University Press, 2010.

Martin, Fran. *Situating Sexualities: Queer Representation in Taiwanese Fiction, Film and Public Culture.* Hong Kong: Hong Kong University Press, 2003.

Martin, Fran, Peter A. Jackson, Mark McLelland, and Audrey Yue, eds. *AsiaPacifiQueer: Rethinking Genders and Sexualities.* Urbana: University of Illinois Press, 2008.

Mbembe, Achille. "Necropolitics." *Public Culture* 15, no. 1 (2003): 11–40.

McRuer, Robert. *Crip Theory: Cultural Signs of Queerness and Disability.* New York: New York University Press, 2006.

Melas, Natalie. *All the Difference in the World: Postcoloniality and the Ends of Comparison.* Stanford, CA: Stanford University Press, 2007.

Metzger, Sean. *The Chinese Atlantic: Seascapes and the Theatricality of Globalization.* Bloomington: Indiana University Press, 2020.

Meyer, David R. *Hong Kong as a Global Metropolis.* Cambridge: Cambridge University Press, 2000.

Mirzoeff, Nicholas. *The Right to Look: A Counterhistory of Visuality.* Durham, NC: Duke University Press, 2011.

Mohanty, Chandra Talpade. *Feminism without Borders: Decolonizing Theory, Practicing Solidarity.* Durham, NC: Duke University Press, 2003.

Moten, Fred, and Stefano Harney. "The University and the Undercommons: Seven Theses." *Social Text* 22, no. 2 (2004): 101–15.

Mullaney, Thomas S., James Leibold, Stephane Gros, and Eric Vanden Bussche, eds. *Critical Han Studies.* Berkeley: University of California Press, 2012.

Muñoz, José Esteban. *Cruising Utopia: The Then and There of Queer Futurity.* New York: New York University Press, 2009.

Muñoz, José Esteban. *Disidentifications: Queers of Color and the Performance of Politics.* Minneapolis: University of Minnesota Press, 1999.

Ong, Aihwa. *Flexible Citizenship: The Cultural Logics of Transnationality.* Durham, NC: Duke University Press, 1999.

Ong, Aihwa. *Neoliberalism as Exception: Mutations in Citizenship and Sovereignty.* Durham, NC: Duke University Press, 2006.

Parreñas, Rhacel Salazar. *Servants of Globalization: Women, Migration, and Domestic Work.* Stanford, CA: Stanford University Press, 2001.

Patterson, Christopher. "Queer, Brown, Migrant: Documenting the Hong Kong 'Helper.'" *Cultural Studies* 33, no. 6 (2019): 1008–28.

Perdue, Peter C. *China Marches West: The Qing Conquest of Central Eurasia.* Cambridge, MA: Harvard University Press, 2005.

Ponce, Martin Joseph. *Beyond the Nation: Diasporic Filipino Literature and Queer Reading*. New York: New York University Press, 2012.

Puar, Jasbir K. *The Right to Maim: Debility, Capacity, Disability*. Durham, NC: Duke University Press, 2017.

Puar, Jasbir K. *Terrorist Assemblages: Homonationalism in Queer Times*. Durham, NC: Duke University Press, 2007.

Rangan, Pooja. *Immediations: The Humanitarian Impulse in Documentary*. Durham, NC: Duke University Press, 2017.

Reddy, Chandan. *Freedom with Violence: Race, Sexuality, and the US State*. Durham, NC: Duke University Press, 2011.

Reynaud, Bernice. "High Noon in Hong Kong." *Film Comment* 33, no. 4 (1997): 20–24.

Rofel, Lisa. *Desiring China: Experiments in Neoliberalism, Sexuality, and Public Culture*. Durham, NC: Duke University Press, 2007.

Rubin, Gayle S. "Thinking Sex: Notes for a Radical Theory of the Politics of Sexuality." In *Pleasure and Danger: Exploring Female Sexuality*, edited by Carole S. Vance, 275–301. Boston: Routledge and Kegan Paul, 1984.

Sala, Ilaria Maria. "Lo Ting: The Legend of Hong Kong's Rebellious Human-Fish Hybrid." *Zolima City Mag*, July 28, 2021. https://zolimacitymag.com/lo-ting-the -legend-of-hong-kongs-rebellious-human-fish-hybrid/.

Salaff, Janet W. *Working Daughters of Hong Kong: Filial Piety or Power in the Family?* New York: Columbia University Press, 1995.

Salamon, Gayle. *Assuming a Body: Transgender and Rhetorics of Materiality*. New York: Columbia University Press, 2010.

Schoonover, Karl, and Rosalind Galt. *Queer Cinema in the World*. Durham, NC: Duke University Press, 2016.

Sharpe, Christina. *In the Wake: On Blackness and Being*. Durham, NC: Duke University Press, 2016.

Shih, Shu-mei. "Comparison as Relation." In *Comparison: Theories, Approaches, Uses*, edited by Rita Felski and Susan Stanford Friedman, 79–98. Baltimore, MD: Johns Hopkins University Press, 2013.

Shih, Shu-mei. "Gender and a New Geopolitics of Desire: The Seduction of Mainland Women in Taiwan and Hong Kong Media." *Signs* 23, no. 2 (1998): 287–319.

Shih, Shu-mei. "Introduction: What Is Sinophone Studies?" In *Sinophone Studies: A Critical Reader*, edited by Shu-mei Shih, Chien-hsin Tsai, and Brian Bernards, 1–16. New York: Columbia University Press, 2013.

Shih, Shu-mei. "Is Feminism Translatable? Spivak, Taiwan, A-Wu." In *Comparatizing Taiwan*, edited by Shu-mei Shih and Ping-hui Liao, 169–89. London: Routledge, 2015.

Shih, Shu-mei. "Race and Relation: The Global Sixties in the South of the South." *Comparative Literature* 68, no. 2 (2016): 141–54.

Shih, Shu-mei. "Racializing Area Studies, Defetishizing China." *positions* 27, no. 1 (2019): 33–65.

Shih, Shu-mei. "Towards an Ethics of Transnational Encounter, or 'When' Does a 'Chinese' Woman Become a 'Feminist'?" *differences* 13, no. 2 (2002): 90–126.

Shih, Shu-mei. *Visuality and Identity: Sinophone Articulations across the Pacific*. Berkeley: University of California Press, 2007.

Shimizu, Celine Parreñas. *The Hypersexuality of Race: Performing Asian/American Women on Screen and Scene*. Durham, NC: Duke University Press, 2007.

Shin, Gi-Wook, and Joon Nak Choi. *Global Talent: Skilled Labor as Social Capital in Korea*. Stanford, CA: Stanford University Press, 2015.

Smallwood, Stephanie E. *Saltwater Slavery: A Middle Passage from Africa to American Diaspora*. Cambridge, MA: Harvard University Press, 2007.

Spivak, Gayatri Chakravorty. *A Critique of Postcolonial Reason: Toward a History of the Vanishing Present*. Cambridge, MA: Harvard University Press, 1999.

Spivak, Gayatri Chakravorty. *Death of a Discipline*. New York: Columbia University Press, 2003.

Standing Committee of the National People's Congress. "The Law of the People's Republic of China on Safeguarding National Security in the Hong Kong Special Administrative Region." June 20, 2020. Accessed December 17, 2023. https://www.elegislation.gov.hk/fwddoc/hk/a406/eng_translation_(a406)_en.pdf.

Stockard, Janice. *Daughters of the Canton Delta: Marriage Patterns and Economic Strategies in South China, 1860–1930*. Stanford, CA: Stanford University Press, 1989.

Stoler, Ann Laura. *Along the Archival Grain: Epistemic Anxieties and Colonial Common Sense*. Princeton, NJ: Princeton University Press, 2009.

Szeto, Mirana M. "Sinophone Libidinal Economy in the Age of Neoliberalization and Mainlandization: Masculinities in Hong Kong SAR New Wave Cinema." In *Sinophone Cinemas*, edited by Audrey Yue and Olivia Khoo, 120–46. New York: Palgrave Macmillan, 2014.

Tadiar, Neferti X. M. *Remaindered Life*. Durham, NC: Duke University Press, 2022.

Tan, E. K. *Rethinking Chineseness: Translational Sinophone Identities in the Nanyang Literary World*. Amherst, NY: Cambria Press, 2013.

Tan, E. K. "Parasite: Conceptualizing a Sinophone Approach and Ethics." In *Sinophone Studies across Disciplines*, edited by Howard Chiang and Shu-mei Shih, 176–92. New York: Columbia University Press, 2024.

Tang, Denise Tse-Shang. *Conditional Spaces: Hong Kong Lesbian Desires and Everyday Life*. Hong Kong: Hong Kong University Press, 2011.

Tang, Denise Tse-Shang. "Everyday Erotics in Urban Density: An Ethnography of Older Lesbian and Bisexual Women in Hong Kong." *Gender, Place and Culture* 28, no. 11 (2020): 1649–68.

Tang, Denise Tse-Shang. "Of Longing and Waiting: An Inter-Asia Approach to Love and Intimacy among Older Lesbians and Bisexual Women." *Sexualities* 25, no. 4 (2022): 365–80.

Tang, Nelson Chak-man. "Where Are You Going? Where Have You Been?" In *Unruly Visions Exhibition Catalog*. Hong Kong, WMA Space, 2021.

Tsing, Anna Lowenhaupt. *Friction: An Ethnography of Global Connection*. Princeton, NJ: Princeton University Press, 2004.

Tsu, Jing. *Sound and Script in Chinese Diaspora*. Cambridge, MA: Harvard University Press, 2010.

Tyburczy, Jennifer. *Sex Museum: The Politics and Performance of Display*. Chicago: University of Chicago Press, 2015.

W v. Registrar of Marriages. HKCFA 39 (2013).

Walcott, Rinaldo. *Queer Returns: Essays on Multiculturalism, Diaspora, and Black Studies*. Ontario: Insomniac Press, 2016.

Wallerstein, Immanuel. *World-Systems Analysis: An Introduction*. Durham, NC: Duke University Press, 2004.

Wang, Hui. "The Politics of Imagining Asia: A Genealogical Analysis." *Inter-Asia Cultural Studies* 8, no. 1 (2007): 1–33.

Williams, Raymond. *Marxism and Literature*. New York: Oxford University Press, 1977.

Wilson, Ara. "Queering Asia." *Intersections* 14, no. 3 (November 2006): 25. http://intersections.anu.edu.au/issue14/wilson.html.

Wong, Alvin K. "Including China? Postcolonial Hong Kong, Sinophone Studies, and the Gendered Geopolitics of China-centrism." *Interventions* 20, no. 8 (2018): 1101–20.

Wong, Alvin K. "Where Jameson Meets Queer Theory: Queer Cognitive Mapping in 1990s Sinophone Cinema." In *Fredric Jameson and Film Theory: Marxism, Allegory, and Geopolitics in World Cinema*, edited by Keith B. Wagner, Jeremi Szaniawski, and Michael Cramer, 131–45. New Brunswick, NJ: Rutgers University Press, 2022.

Wong Bik-wan [黃碧雲]. *Lienü tu* [烈女圖 / Portraits of martyred women]. Hong Kong: Cosmos Books, 2004.

Wong Bik-wan [黃碧雲]. *Ta shi nüzi, wo ye shi nüzi* [她是女子，我也是女子 / She is a woman, I am also a woman]. Taipei: Maitian, 1994.

Wong Bik-wan [黃碧雲]. *Wenrou yu baolie* [溫柔與暴烈 / Tenderness and violence]. Hong Kong: Cosmos Books, 1994.

Wong, Lily. *Transpacific Attachments: Sex Work, Media Networks, and Affective Histories of Chineseness*. New York: Columbia University Press, 2018.

Wong Nim Yan [黃念欣]. *Wanqi fengge: Xianggang nu zuojia san lun* [晚期風格:香港女作家三論 / Late style: Three essays on Hong Kong women writers]. Hong Kong: Cosmos Books, 2007.

Xu Zidong [許子東]. *Xianggang duan pian xiaoshuo chu tan* [香港短篇小說初探 / A study of Hong Kong novellas]. Hong Kong: Cosmos Books, 2005.

Yau, Ching, ed. *As Normal as Possible: Negotiating Sexuality and Gender in Mainland China and Hong Kong*. Hong Kong: Hong Kong University Press, 2010.

Yau, Esther C. M. "Introduction: Hong Kong Cinema in a Borderless World." In *At Full Speed: Hong Kong Cinema in a Borderless World*, edited by Esther C. M. Yau, 1–28. Minneapolis: University of Minnesota Press, 2001.

Yau, Esther C. M. "Watchful Partners, Hidden Currents: Hong Kong Cinema Moving into the Mainland of China." In *A Companion to Hong Kong Cinema*, edited by Esther M. K. Cheung, Gina Marchetti, and Esther C. M. Yau, 17–50. Malden, MA: Wiley Blackwell, 2015.

Ye, Ziling. "*Zishu nü* (自梳女): Dutiful Daughters of the Guangdong Delta." *Intersections: Gender and Sexuality in Asia and the Pacific* 17 (July 2008). http://intersections.anu.edu.au/issue17/ye.htm.

Yeates, Nicola. "Global Care Chains." *International Feminist Journal of Politics* 6, no. 3 (2004): 369–91.

Yeung, Jessie, and Kathleen Magramo. "Hong Kong Suffers Biggest Ever Population Drop as Exodus Accelerates." CNN, August 12, 2022. https://edition.cnn.com/2022 /08/12/asia/hong-kong-population-record-fall-covid-intl-hnk/index.html.

Yip, Eric. "Fricatives." *The Poetry Society*. Accessed August 18, 2023. https://poems .poetrysociety.org.uk/poems/fricatives/.

Yoneyama, Lisa. "Toward a Decolonial Genealogy of the Transpacific." *American Quarterly* 69, no. 3 (2017): 471–82.

Yue, Audrey. "Mobile Intimacies in the Queer Sinophone Films of Cui Zi'en." *Journal of Chinese Cinemas* 6, no. 1 (2012): 95–108.

Yue, Audrey, and Helen Hok-Sze Leung. "Notes Towards the Queer Asian City: Singapore and Hong Kong." *Urban Studies* 54, no. 3 (2017): 747–64.

Yue, Audrey, and Jun Zubillaga-Pow, eds. *Queer Singapore: Illiberal Citizenship and Mediated Cultures*. Hong Kong: Hong Kong University Press, 2012.

Zhu Yao-wei [朱耀偉], ed. *Xianggang yanjiu zuowei fangfa* [香港研究作為方法 / Hong Kong studies as method]. Hong Kong: Zhonghua Book Company, 2016.

Index

Italicized page numbers refer to figures.

feminism: and borders, 116; and migrant domestic workers, 88, 94–95, 102; and Hong Kong, 1, 3, 16, 24, 26, 39, 118, 148n13; intersectional, 11; in *Intimates*, 33; in *Once Upon a Time in Hong Kong*, 36; in *Portraits of Martyred Women*, 18, 27–29; transnational, 82, 124; woman of color, 2

Ferguson, Roderick A., 12

fetishization, 8, 14, 83, 89, 99, 120–23, 132

Filguys Association Hong Kong, 89, 106, 111–13, *112*

Filipino people, 89–94, 96, 98, 100–112

film (Hong Kong). *See individual titles*

Freeman, Elizabeth, 32, 71

free trade, 5, 24–25, 34, 91

Fregoso, Rosa Linda, 154n4

Freud, Sigmund, 121

Friedman, Milton, 24

Fu, Poshek, 88

Galt, Rosalind, 45

Gan, Wendy, 122

gay men: in *Amphetamine*, 51–55; in film, 9, 24, 56; in *Happy Together*, 43–46; in Hong Kong, 136; in *Once Upon a Time in Hong Kong*, 35–39; in *Permanent Residence*, 11, 46–50; in *Tracey*, 64, 69, 73. *See also* marriage rights

gentrification, 106, 127, 131, 137–38

Ghaziani, Amin, 23

Glissant, Édouard, 11

globalization, 88–90, 94, 106, 125

Goddess, The (1934), 121

Gopinath, Gayatri, 5, 12, 20, 75, 109–10

governmentality, 3, 9, 50, 103, 106, 120

Guattari, Félix, 30

Halberstam, Jack, 20, 63, 65, 77–78

Han-centrism, 99, 113, 136, 146n37

handover (of Hong Kong to PRC), 1–4, 25, 28, 31, 41, 44–46, 89, 117

Happy Together (1997), 16, 42–46

Harney, Stefano, 155n2

Heberer, Feng-Mei, 100, 106

Helper, The (2017), 88–89, 91–95, 99

Her Fatal Ways (1990–94), 124

heteronormativity: and borders, 115–16; in *But-*

terfly, 43, 59; of Hong Kong, 4, 17, 27, 30, 75, 113; and migrant domestic workers, 19, 89, 100, 102, 104, 107, 110; and sex workers, 120, 122, 124; in *Three Husbands*, 131; in *Tracey*, 64, 71–74; and the transgender gaze, 77; in *A Woman Is a Woman*, 76, 78, 85

historical materialism, 12, 27

Ho, Denise, 3, 61–62

Hollywood Hong Kong (2001), 20, 118, 124–29, 132

homelessness, 20, 136–40, 142

homonationalism, 12, 63

homonormativity, 5, 16, 45, 48–49, 63

Hong Kong (queer). *See* queer Hong Kong (as method)

Hong Kong (special administrative region): Kowloon, 83, 90, 106, 121, 125, 127–28, 137–38; Kowloon City, 79; Mongkok, 90, 120–21, 125; Sheung Wan, 7

Hong Kong as method, 16–17, 25

Hong Kong New Wave, 54

Hong Kong Riots (1967), 27, 30

Hong Kong SAR New Wave cinema, 47

Hong Kong studies, 4, 26

Hoskins, Janet, 17

Hudie. See Butterfly (2004)

humanism: illiberal, 10; liberal, 10, 88–89, 91–92, 94–97, 99–102, 106, 110–13, 138

human libraries, 80–83, 152n43

Hung, Ho-fung, 3

included-outness, 107

incommensurability: definition of, 2; in *Drifting*, 142; Hong Kong as site of, 2, 5, 9, 17, 50, 65; queer, 16, 82–83, 85, 89, 135–36; and Sinophone geographies, 11, 31, 43, 71; and unruly comparison, 10, 20, 26–27, 139, 145n19

Indonesia, 70, 74, 95, 102, 109–10

interimperiality, 11, 37

interracial intimacy, 16, 26, 92, 137, 142, 147n7; queer, 36, 39, 71, 99

intersectionality, 2–3, 11–12, 20–21, 50, 63, 77, 97, 142, 153n13

interspecies (concept of), 130

Intimates (1997), 18, 27, 31–35, *33*, 39

Israel, 18, 49–51, *51*, 136